THE EFFECTIVE USE OF ADVERTISING MEDIA
a practical handbook

THE EFFECTIVE USE OF ADVERTISING MEDIA

a practical guide

by Martyn P. Davis,
FCAM, FIPR, FInstM, DipFEd, BSc(Econ)

*Head of Department of Marketing and Advertising Studies,
College for the Distributive Trades, London*

Published in association with
The Institute of Marketing
and the CAM Foundation

BUSINESS BOOKS

London   Melbourne   Sydney   Auckland   Johannesburg

Business Books Ltd

An imprint of the Hutchinson Publishing Group

17–21 Conway Street, London W1P 5HL

Hutchinson Group (Australia) Pty Ltd
30-32 Cremorne Street, Richmond South, Victoria 3121
PO Box 151, Broadway, New South Wales 2007

Hutchinson Group (NZ) Ltd
32-34 View Road, PO Box 40-086, Glenfield, Auckland 10

Hutchinson Group (SA) (Pty) Ltd
PO Box 337, Bergvlei 2012, South Africa

First published 1981
Reprinted 1982

© Martyn P. Davis 1981

Set in 11 on 12pt IBM Theme

Printed in Great Britain by The Anchor Press Ltd
and bound by Wm Brendon & Son Ltd,
both of Tiptree, Essex

British Library Cataloguing in Publication Data
Davis, Martyn
    The effective use of advertising media.
    1. Advertising media planning
    I. Title
    659.13   HF5826.5

ISBN 0 09 142970 6 (Cased)
        0 09 142971 4 (Paper)

Contents

Part 2   THE ORGANISATION OF MEDIA

Ltd — Parker Research Ltd — Pritchard Brown
& Taylor Ltd — Retail Audits Ltd — Research
Services Ltd — Research Surveys of Great
Britain Ltd — Gordon Simmons Research Ltd —
Social Surveys (Gallup Poll) Ltd — Stats (MR)
Ltd — Television Advertising Bureau (Surveys)
Ltd — Taylor Nelson & Associates Ltd —
Television Companies' Research and Marketing
Facilities — Telmar Communications Ltd —
Tempo Computer Services Ltd — Trade Studies
Ltd

Part 3   THE EFFECTIVE USE OF ADVERTISING MEDIA

Foreword

by JOHN W. HOBSON, CBE, FIPA, FRSA
Honorary President of Ted Bates Ltd
Former President of the Institute of Practitioners in Advertising
Chairman of the Advertising Association
President of the European Association of Advertising Agencies
Author of 'The Selection of Advertising Media'

It is a puzzling fact that, while so much attention and so many books are devoted to the creative and marketing sides of advertising, the media side is so thinly documented. The explanation lies, no doubt, in the glamour element in creative work, and in the commercial interest in effective marketing. Yet the choice of media, the correct analysis of each medium's value, the use of each for its proper purpose, the combination of various media into a powerful orchestration, are not only the governing factors in the wise spending of millions of pounds, but are in themselves a fascinating study and science.

It is, therefore, with particular pleasure that I welcome a new, up-to-date and comprehensive book on this important subject; and I would think that no one is better qualified to write it than Mr Martyn Davis.

In particular I have been impressed by the pains he has taken to assemble the views of advertisers, agencies and media-owners and by the response his enquiry form received from busy top executives in all three fields. Actual quotations from their replies are featured and give practical weight to the substance of his text.

I believe I am right in saying that the first analytical study of the subject was my own book *The Selection of Advertising Media* and to many students of advertising it was their first introduction to this side of the business. But the changes in media are so fast-moving that it was out-of-date in detail (though not in its principles) almost from the time of publication. In particular, it was written when television was only a gleam in someone's eye. It was consecutively updated by myself and others, but this could be no more than a process of tinkering.

Mr Martyn Davis' earlier book * was written particularly from the viewpoint of educating the advertisement departments in the techniques of selling media, and it is now high time to have a new

*Handbook for Media Representatives.

coverage of the subject as a whole — seeing it from the advertiser, the agency and the media angles.

It is a sobering thought, but one that needs to be constantly impressed, that with a budget of say £1 million, unsound media selection can waste £100,000 or £200,000 — sums that an advertiser would never think of wasting in some other context. The causes are many, and complex. They start with the failure to study the up-to-date figures of readership or viewing, and their value relationship to the target audience for the product. They go on with disregard of the basic 'Concentration — Domination — Repetition' pattern of good media selection. They derive from a slap-happy repetition of some traditional schedule or even from some concession to what the client Chairman's wife likes to see his advertising in. The truth is that scientific media selection can now be based on such a wealth of information about readership, attention values, size and frequency values and so on (not to mention the subjective elements of atmosphere and the company you keep) that it is a very challenging and complex operation to get the answer right.

Equally, in selling space in media, it is not easy to get away from the wishful thinking that expects one's own medium to be acceptable in all cases, and to limit one's own selling operation to those contexts where the statistics show it is an appropriate choice.

For the selfish financial values alone, the knowledge of media selection that this book promotes is essential. But also for the general reputation of advertising, and to avoid the impression of reckless spending in inappropriate contexts, the subject is of importance.

I hope that the book will be well received and well studied, and I wish it all success.

JOHN W. HOBSON

Preface

The media world and advertising practice have both become increasingly sophisticated in recent years, but people in all branches of advertising — advertisers, agencies and media-owners — often seem hindered rather than helped by the wealth of media data and techniques at their disposal. Immense energy is devoted to gathering information and great skill applied to devising new techniques, but unfortunately all this effort is often undermined by failure to build on a sound base. There appear to be more than a few 'blind spots': some matters are so fundamental they are taken for granted, and therefore receive insufficient attention. The chart overleaf shows the six fundamentals — the media themselves, the criteria by which they can be compared, the principles of media planning, and the three groups of organisations involved: advertisers, agencies and media-owners. Not only must all six operate efficiently in their own right, they must also interact effectively before optimum use can be made of advertising media.

My view is that any book on the use of media must necessarily at the same time be a book on advertising administration. This will no doubt present problems to librarians and booksellers — having ordered it, where should it go on the shelves? Should it go under *Media, Media Planning* or under *Advertising Administration*? Under *Advertisers, Agency Practice* or *Media-owners*? I leave this decision to the booksellers and librarians. If they opt for the safest course and buy more copies than they would otherwise have done, I would prefer, in the interests of modesty and good taste, that the suggestion should not come from me!

The book is really three books in one:

The first part, 'The World of Media', outlines the range of media available to communicate your advertising message, reviews the data known about them, and discusses the criteria by which you can compare one with another.

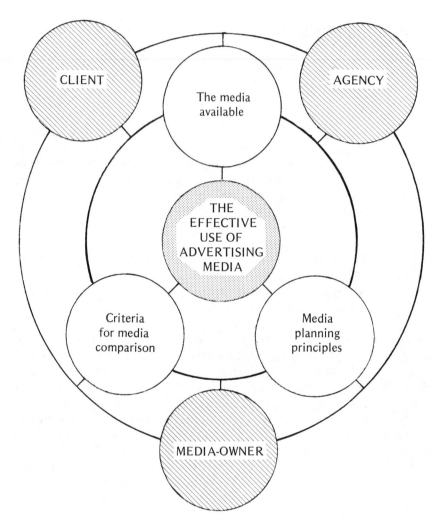

THE SIX FUNDAMENTALS

The second part on 'The Organisation of Media' covers the firms and the individuals concerned with these media: the media-owners, the advertisers and their agencies.

The third part, optimistically titled 'The *Effective* Use of Advertising Media' devotes itself to how the individuals and organisations discussed in the second part can best ensure that the media described in the first part are used to maximum effect.

To attempt to produce a comprehensive media manual incorporating all the facts and figures needed for effective media planning would be an impossible, unnecessary and pointless task. Impossible in that any volume incorporating all these facts would be vast beyond proportion; unnecessary in that the facts and figures are readily available elsewhere in the sources listed in this book, and pointless in that, should any statistics be included, they would soon be out of date. This book, therefore, concentrates on principles, and you will find statistics conspicuous by their absence.

In seeking to make the book a practical one, I immediately acknowledged my own blind spots and hence, rather than approach this vital matter in an abstract manner, sought the comments of those currently working full-time in the industry. My line of investigation was simple:

● *there are generally accepted principles of media planning*

● *applied by a variety of individuals*

● *working in a range of different organisations*

but, in practice, the principles, the individuals and the organisations all have strengths and weaknesses. This is perhaps a self-evident statement, but it is one that has not been investigated: hence my invitation to various advertising practitioners to complete a simple form letting me have their views on the paths to be followed and the pitfalls to be avoided.

As was made clear to my respondents, my investigations did not involve a formal market research questionnaire, nor was this distributed to a structured sample, nor have results been quantified: it was never my intention to gather a statistical base for asserting, for example, that 'A' category advertisers adopt approach 'B' in their relationship with 'C' type agencies when buying from the owners of media 'D'.

I approached experts who could make meaningful comments, and my criteria for selection were that all comments must be based on practical experience, and should cover as wide a range as possible — hence the list on pages xix-xxii includes advertisers, agencies and media-owners as well as certain specialists organisations and services: it covers firms large and small, long established and newly formed, producers and service organisations, industrial and consumer markets, fast-moving and durable products; and the individuals range from very senior executives to those more recently appointed. The common factor is that all comments are based on practical experience.

The list of respondents is impressive but, however wide I cast my net, there must inevitably be gaps. There are no doubt many individuals who would willingly have let me have valuable comments had I approached them: to these individuals I express my regrets. Equally, not all those I approached returned their forms (nor did I 'chase' them with reminders, on the premise that most people with something to say will want to say it, and one volunteer is worth ten pressed men). This in no way diminishes the validity of the comments received, every one of which is of practical value.

What I sought were the fundamental points which came immediately to mind, rather than the outcome of profound deliberations or extensive consultations with colleagues — although these too were welcome. Indeed, many accepted this secondary invitation and let me have most detailed comments. I invited help in the practical development of media planning, whether confirming or challenging existing practices, by letting me have frank views. If respondents wished to criticise advertisers, agencies or media-owners, they were asked to be as constructive as possible, on the understanding that their views would not be attributed to them as individuals. All quotations contained in this book are, nevertheless, authentic.

The quotations are worded as received, and have not been altered or paraphrased in any way. The only 'editing' was that forced on me, in that clearly it was impossible for me to include *all* the comments made. My contribution has been to insert them in relevant places in the text to reinforce the points being made. Where appropriate, I have grouped comments together, when these have been illustrative of the same point. If I am at fault in these groupings, or in inserting comments in particular places in the text, responsibility for error rests with me and not my respondents, to whom must go all credit for the practical value of the book.

In discussing the paths to be followed and the pitfalls to be avoided, many of the points are necessarily the mirror-image of each other, whilst others are complementary. A simple example is the time needed to do a proper job — quoted by many as a key requirement for effective planning at the same time as lack of it was cited by many others as a common error militating against effective use of media. Equally many respondents, in making recommendations for good advertiser/agency/media-owner working relationships, urged that sufficient time be given, whilst other respondents, commenting on mistakes to avoid, mentioned giving insufficient time. To avoid exessive repetition of the same point I have, therefore, consolidated as much as possible: the points are, nevertheless, fundamental to all these different aspects and reinforce my view that you cannot separate principles from the people applying them or the organisations in which they work.

The quotations come into four main categories. Many of the points made are those unanimous views you would expect, but it is of great value to have them confirmed by current practitioners.

In the second category are those matters where opinions are divided, but it is no surprise that there is more than one approach to media planning. I have tried to select quotations that illustrate all major approaches.

A third category relates to points which, like the time needed to do the job, are perhaps blind spots — never thought of, but admitted as soon as mentioned.

The comments in the fourth category, also perhaps unexpected, may not be so welcome. These quotations draw attention to some home truths, but ones which were always raised with a constructive rather than negative purpose: unless you are made aware of weaknesses, how can you correct them? Where criticisms are clearly sectional, e.g. advertisers commenting adversely on agencies or media-owners, or *vice versa*, the direction from which the criticism comes stated. In many instances there are counter-criticisms — and there is thus clearly a difference of views between sections of the industry: such differences are again clearly identified.

If there are weaknesses (or, equally important, if people *think* there are) then they should be brought into the open — even if these weaknesses are justified and the realities of life make them unavoidable. All parties should be made aware of the views of the others, so that they can act accordingly. What we must not do is ignore any flaws in current advertising practice: the other alternative, as in mediaeval times, is to behead instantly the herald of bad news who is, in this case . . .

MARTYN P. DAVIS

Acknowledgements

I wish to express my sincere thanks to many individuals and organisations for the co-operation and encouragement I received when writing this book:

- to Vivien James of Business Books for her guidance at all stages of publication.

- to Frank Monkman, Brian Scudder and the CAM Publications Committee, for their helpful comments on the synopsis.

- to Ray Morgan and David Peck for their constructive criticism of my research form.

- to John Hobson for writing the Foreword.

- to the library staff at the College for the Distributive Trades for their patience in locating numerous reference sources.

- to McGraw-Hill International Publications and the Institute of Practitioners in Advertising for permission to include certain quotations.

- to Rachel Woodhouse, for so carefully checking the draft manuscript.

- to Joyce Brooks for her help in typing the manuscript.

- to Ray Cowen and Alastair Paterson, who were kind enough to read and comment on the manuscript, and to Nigel Moss for his help with proofs.

- to the following organisations, for their co-operation in providing information of great value to me in writing the book:

Agridata, Association of Independent Radio Contractors,

Attwood Statistics, Audit Bureau of Circulations, Auditplan, Audits of Great Britain, British Rate & Data, British Market Research Bureau, Communication Research, Evening Newspaper Advertising Bureau, The Economist, Financial Times, Holborn Research Services, Independent Broadcasting Authority, Independent Television Companies Association, IMS (Interactive Market Systems) UK, IPC Magazines, Carrick James Market Research, JICNARS, JICPAS, JICRAR, JICTAR, London Association of Regional Press, MEAL, Media Audits, A.C. Nielsen Company, NOP Market Research, Parker Research, Poster Audit Bureau, Radio Luxembourg (UK), Research Services, Research Surveys of Great Britain, Retail Audits, Screen Advertising Association, Gordon Simmons Research, Social Surveys (Gallup Poll), Stats (MR), Target Group Index, Taylor Nelson & Associates, Television Advertising Bureau (Surveys), Telmar Communications, Tempo Computer Services, and the Weekly Newspaper Advertising Bureau.

Finally, I give particular thanks to those practitioners listed on pages xix—xxii who gave this book its practical value by providing the quotations featured in the text. This book has got off to an excellent start, in that at least one person has learned a great deal from it even before publication — the author, who readily acknowledges his debt to those whose brains he has picked, with or without their knowledge.

Quotations key and sources

The book features the practical views of those individuals listed below, and these were expressed on the understanding that comments would not be attributed to individuals. It is important, however, to know the viewpoint represented and this is indicated by one of the following symbols appearing after each quotation in the text:

(ad)   = Advertiser
(ag)   = Advertising agency
(m-o)   = Media-owner
(other) = Some other category

The quotations themselves are set in italic and preceded by a ●.

Job mobility in advertising is high and the list below shows the post held at the time views were expressed: there may have been subsequent job changes.

James Adams, Chief Executive, J.R. Adams & Associates
Brian Allt, Head of Market Research, Mirror Group Newspapers
John Alway, Product Manager, Nicholas Laboratories
Don Bailey, Joint Managing Director, Brickman Advertising
Nicholas Balmforth, Managing Director, Zetland Advertising
Leonard R. Barkey, Deputy Managing Director, Saatchi & Saatchi Garland-Compton
Christopher John Barnes, Group Media Research Manager, Mills & Allen International
Don Beckett, Director, The Media Business
L.A.A. Berrington, Advertising & Sales Promotion Manager, Monsanto (Europe)
Douglas Bird, Group Sales Manager, Eastern Counties Newspapers

Edwin Blackwell, Managing Director, AIR Group

Joyce Blake, Media Executive, City Marketing

Roger Bowes, Advertisement Sales Director, Mirror Group Newspapers

Tim Bradshaw, Sales Director, Radio Luxembourg (London)

Brian Braithwaite, Publisher (Cosmopolitan) and Director, National Magazine Co.

Roderick Braithwaite, Chief Executive, Charles Barker Recruitment

Simon Broadbent, Research Director, Leo Burnett

Philip Byford, International Media Controller, Dorland Advertising

Vivian Burchill, Marketing Co-ordinator, Ess-Food (UK)

Michael Chapman, Media Director, Ogilvy, Benson & Mather

Bryan J.M. Connon, Manager, Advertising and Publicity Department, National Westminster Bank

Peter Clifford, Group Market Research Manager, Westminster Press

Phil Collinge, Media Manager, Mars

Freddy Cooper, Publicity Executive, Vent-Axia

David Coulson, Marketing Director, Earls Court & Olympia

Derek Davies, Ad Marketing Controller, IPC Magazines

E.W. Davies, Marketing Director, Blue Sky Holidays

Robert Davies, Managing Director, Sterling Advertising

Ronald Davis, Product Group Manager & Media Co-ordinator, Nabisco

Kenneth Deadman, Media Executive, Collett Dickenson Pearce

Graham Dimond, Director of Advertising, Diners Club International

Eric Dore, Head of Advertising, Newspaper Society

David S. Dunbar, Associate Director, J. Walter Thompson

Jon Dutfield, Marketing Services Manager, Westward Television

Donald Earl, Managing Director, Don Earl Publicity

Frank Farmer, Advertisement Director, IPC Women's Magazines

Michael W. Forrest, Publicity Manager, Moore Paragon UK

Graeme R. Forsyth, Brand Group Manager, The Nestle Company

John French, Account Director, Saatchi & Saatchi Garland-Compton

Jeffrey Galvin Wright, Associate Director, Reader's Digest

Roger Hugh Gentry, Managing Director/Media Director, Multimedia Advertising Services

Roy Gibbs, Advertisement Controller, Daily Express

Michael Goldman, Joint Managing Director, Kraushar & Eassie

Jack W. Gray, Sales Director, Yorkshire Post Newspapers

Martyn D. Griffiths, Managing Director, Severn Advertising

Mike Hardwick, Advertisement Director, Time Out

Chris Hargraves, Marketing Manager, Thomson Yellow Pages

Geoff C. Harper, Publicity Manager, Thorn Lighting

Clifford Harris, Advertising Manager, Marks & Spencer

Cliff Harrison, Head of Research and Information, Evening Newspaper Advertising Bureau
Tom Hartshorne, Chairman, Hartshorne Joyce Lloyd Lyons
Dick Hawkes, Media Group Manager, McCann-Erickson Advertising
Brian Henry, Marketing and Sales Director, Southern Television
Hugh Henry, Managing Director, Scottish Television & Grampian Sales
Geoffrey Hilton, Marketing Manager, Baxter Fell Northfleet
Brian E. Holland, Managing Director, Brian Holland & Partners
Roger Holland, Chief Executive, Weekly Newspaper Advertising Bureau
Kenneth Hook, Media Director, Royds London
Reg Howes, Advertisement Sales Manager, Country Life Group, IPC Magazines
James Irvine, Head of Media Planning, Lintas
Brian Jacobs, Media Research Manager, Davidson Pearce Berry & Spottiswoode
Ron Jephcote, Advertisement Manager, Coventry Evening Telegraph
Jennifer Kearl, Sales Promotion Assistant, BICC
Adrian Kennedy, General Sales Manager, Granada Television
Gladys Knock, Publicity Manager, Electronic Instruments
Roy Langridge, Media Director, J. Walter Thompson
Richard Ashleigh Lee, Advertising Manager, Ford Motor Co.
Richard Lewis, Senior Product Group Manager, H.P. Bulmer
Bruno Lloyd Lyons, Managing Director, Hartshorne Joyce Lloyd Lyons
Douglas Lowndes, Director, Newspaper Society
Peter McCarthy, P.W. McCarthy
Bill MacDonald, Managing Director, Radio Hallam
Eric McGregor, Marketing Director, International Chemical Company
David Marsh, Senior Campaign Manager, Central Office of Information
Mike Marshall, Managing Director, Everetts
John Mallows, Deputy Media Director, Young & Rubicam
Ray Morgan, Media Director, Benton & Bowles
Phill Mottram Brown, Head of Sales/Sales Director, Channel Television/Channel Promotions
Charles Meyerstein, Group Brand Manager, Nabisco
Frank Monkman, Deputy Chairman, Media Buying Services
Bob Murphy, London Manager, West Country Publications
John Mutimer, London Advertisement Manager, Coventry Evening Telegraph
Michael Nieman, Chairman, Richmond Towers
Kevin O'Sullivan, Director, Dorey, Walton, Sharland Advertising
Leslie Joe Parsons, Advertising Manager, UK, Monsanto

Alastair Paterson, Media Planning Consultant

John Perriss, Assistant Media Director, Sattchi & Saatchi Garland-Compton

Alan Phillips, Chairman/Managing Director, Frost Phillips Russell, (Media Centre & Marketstudy)

Terry Prue, Account Planner, J. Walter Thompson

William Rail, Deputy Advertisement Director, Manchester Evening News

Tom Redgrove, Advertising Manager, British Gypsum

Alec Reynolds, Director of Information, Portsmouth & Sunderland Newspapers

M.A. Richardson, Publicity Manager, ITT Consumer Products (UK)

Brian Roberts, Media Manager, Boase Massimi Pollitt Univas

David Roscoe, Director, Group Public Relations, Rolls Royce Motors

Brian Scudder, Freelance Media Consultant

Kenneth Shard, Marketing Director, Daily Telegraph

Digby Shuttleworth, Ad Controller, New Scientist

Dale Sklar, Commercial Director, Capital Wine & Travers

Brian Smith, Deputy Media Director, Everetts

Alan Smith, Head of Marketing Research, IPC Magazines

Victor John Smith, London Manager, The Birmingham Post & Mail

Anthony Sonvico, Deputy Media Director, Ted Bates

Eric Starkey, Marketing Director, Radio Rentals

John A. Stayt, Sales & Marketing Group Head (Marketing Manager), PIRA

Derek Stevenson, General Sales & Marketing Manager, Thames Television

Susanne Stoessl, Head of Research & Management Services, London Weekend Television

Edward Michael Tarling, Publicity and Information Services Manager, ICI Mond Division

Arthur J. Thompson, Media Director, Cogent Elliott

Rob Van Pooss, Sales Development Manager, London Weekend Television

Peter Varlow, Publicity & Promotions Manager, Brighton Borough Council

Philip Walker, Product Manager (Feudor Lighters), J. John Masters & Company

Colin David Watts, Managing Director, Media Campaign Services

Stephen White, Media Director, Wight Collins Rutherford & Scott

David Williams, Chairman, Ketchum International

Ray Willsmer, Managing Director, Cunningham Willsmer & Cook

John Winkler, Group Managing Director, Winkler Marketing

James Woods, Advertisement Manager, Bradford & District Newspapers

John E. Wright, Managing Director, Almaco
Peter Yate, Head of Marketing Communications, Mullard
Christopher Yates, Managing Director, Radio 210

Terminology

Throughout this book general terms such as 'advertiser', 'product' and 'customer' are used for reasons of simplicity: 'advertiser' may mean a manufacturer, retailer, service organisation or a non-profit government department; 'product' covers services as well as goods; and 'customer' must be taken to mean not only the man or woman in the street — in many cases, the buyer may be a large industrial group or some official department.

Other general terms are used when referring to media, again for simplicity. Any mention of advertisement 'size' should be taken to include all variations of the concept and thus covers the length of a television or radio or cinema commercial just as much as press or poster media. Similarly, 'insertions' should be taken to include transmission of commercials, or any other form of appearance of an advertisement. References to copy cover the spoken just as much as the printed word, and design includes moving as well as conventional illustrations. Unless specifically stated, media terms should be interpreted as broadly as possible.

Generally, the reader is addressed as 'You' to avoid reference to any specific job title in any particular type of organisation. Whether your concern is selling advertising space or time, or buying it on behalf of a manufacturer's advertising department or advertising agency, the underlying fundamentals remain the same: you simply approach them from a different standpoint. Where specific posts are mentioned, jobs are described in terms of their being held by men: this is, again, for simplicity, rather than any male chauvinism.

Part 1
THE WORLD OF MEDIA

1
THE MEDIA
AVAILABLE

To use anything to best advantage, it is essential that you know precisely what you are using. This first chapter in 'The World of Media' reviews the range of media available to transmit your advertising messages, the second chapter in this part then examines what we know about them, whilst a third chapter discusses the criteria by which you can compare one advertising medium with another.

There are many ways in which your advertising messages can be communicated to potential purchasers. Statistics would soon be out-of-date, so this review of media is necessarily limited to broad generalisations about the different categories. These media categories are by no means watertight compartments: some media can be considered under more than one heading, or even shift from one category to another. Some publications, for example, are really magazines in newspaper format, while others originated as newspapers and became magazines, and colour supplements can be considered under the twin headings of newspapers and magazines.

The media available to you will be considered in alphabetical order.

Cinema

Since the mid-1960s, the UK cinema industry has undergone a major moderisation programme. The less attractive and less profitable cinemas have closed and many single-auditorium cinemas been converted into modernised multi-unit complexes with greater appeal to the cinema-goer. Provision of modern facilities has not been restricted to existing locations, however, and there have been completely new cinema developments. In many provincial cities throughout the country these take the form of three- or four-unit cinemas within new entertainment complexes which include discotheque, restaurant, bar and other facilities.

Cinema advertising offers you the advantages of colour, sound and movement, giving creative scope to demonstrate your product in full colour and with high technical quality on the large screen, to show people enjoying its use, and with music and the human voice heightening the effect. Other creative approaches such as animation are also possible. In addition, your message is screened to what is descriptively termed a 'captive' audience, sitting facing the screen in a darkened auditorium. The cinema audience is a distinct one, composed largely of young adults with freely disposable purchasing power, at a point in their lives when they make many important decisions, thus providing a market of considerable attraction to many advertisers.

In some cases, additional advantages stem from the fact that cinema advertising can be localised: you control the area of coverage and can localise your campaign to a town, an area, a region, or alternatively mount a nationwide campaign. The benefit of this to the local trader is obvious — he can appeal to his local audience and attract enquiries by featuring his name and address on the cinema screen. Other advertisers with broader distribution can follow the same principle by building a schedule based on cinemas that match their particular geographical requirements and, after demonstrating their product in the opening part of the film, conclude with the name and address of the local dealer, perhaps on a shared-cost basis.

For advertisers whose needs are more general, the major cinema contractors offer a number of special packages, which ease adminis-tration and often include bonuses or discounts. Operation varies slightly between different contractors, but the principles on which these packages are based remains the same. It is, therefore, relatively simple to match comparable packages available from different contractors, and thus build a total cinema schedule.

A number of packages relate to one or more of a combination of defined marketing areas — ITV areas, conurbation areas, London (West End), all seaside or holiday towns, and all university towns. Within any one of these defined marketing areas, two alternative schemes qualify for discounts — area coverage plans (which use all cinemas in the area) and run of cinema plans (which do not specify the actual cinemas to be used, but allow the contractors to spend a specified sum within a given time period).

Other facilities also available include new product discounts (for products new to the cinema) and X-film packages (your commercial can be screened exclusively in X-certificate programmes, subject to payment of a handling surcharge). Alternatively, on payment of a similar surcharge, you may buy into non-X (U, A or AA) programmes, or children's packages (matinees, Disney films and U- and A-certificate films) to enable you to reach the under-15 market. Other facilities may be offered from time to time, including opportunities to buy packages of advertising built around particular feature films. These facilities are popular with advertisers who wish to capitalise on the large audiences of outstanding films, to ensure that their films are shown in an environment that is helpful for the product, or to take advantage of the audience patterns created by films with different film certificates.

Cinema advertising commercials are shown within one reel which is screened at all performances (except children's matinees) after the interval, with the house lights down, prior to the main feature film. You can buy screen time in this reel on the basis of standard time-lengths, of 15, 30, 45 and 60 seconds. Longer timelengths can usually be accommodated, subject to negotiation.

The basic booking unit is one week's advertising in one cinema, but most campaigns cover a number of cinemas over a period of several weeks or months. In planning such a campaign, you may find it advantageous to adopt a one-week-in/one-week-out pattern, for reasons of economy. This is known as an alternate-week campaign, and calls for only one print of your commercial for each cinema. Should you require a consecutive week campaign, two prints will be needed. In both cases you should make an allowance of 10 per cent for additional prints to cover breakages and other contingencies.

Direct mail

Among the advantages of using postal services to deliver advertising messages is selectivity, since your mailing can be directed to a selected list of individuals. Further advantages are complete coverage of your market and the absence of wastage, since the mailing covers and is restricted to those within the defined market. All depends, of course, on the accuracy of your mailing list. This can be obtained in a number of ways, and in some cases you can build up a mailing list from your own records. Where internal records are not suitable, external sources can be consulted. Published reference books can provide much information, but this source suffers from two drawbacks. One is that frequently there is more than one reference book and the task of cross-checking one against the others is unavoidable, for clearly there is no point in mailing the same individual more than once. Removal of duplicate names, though laborious, is straightforward in comparison with the problem raised when two sources show different names for the holder of one given job. Only one can be correct, and the discrepancy no doubt stems from the fact that one reference source went to press later than the other and staff changes took place in the meantime.

Such changes highlight the second drawback of using published sources — the problem of keeping any list up-to-date. This involves carefully checking relevant publications regularly for news of staff changes, and this is no small task. For these reasons many firms turn to direct mail houses or list brokers, relying on them to provide mailing lists that are both comprehensive and up-to-date.

Use of direct mail as a medium brings other advantages, such as personalisation. Direct mail letters can be run off in bulk, but with the name and address of each recipient 'matched in' at the head of each letter to give the appearance of individual typing, and your signature realistically reproduced to give the effect of a personal letter. Indeed, some direct mail letters are individually typed on automatic machines and personally signed for greater authenticity.

Further benefits come from direct mail's flexibility and ease of control, which allow you to send different messages to different groups of people. Timing is another advantage of direct mail, since you can select the most suitable dates and frequency for delivery of your advertising message and need not be restricted by any media-owner's publication dates.

Yet another advantage of direct mail is that inclusion of reply-paid postcards or envelopes can stimulate replies. Certainly you can include reply-paid folders or freepost coupons in press advertise-ments, but this takes up costly space and is often unattractive. With such press advertisements you cannot be so selective and your prospective customer must still write in his name and address, while with direct mail you can enter the recipient's particulars on the card beforehand, so that all he need do is post it. Such direct response makes evaluation of results and control of your campaign that much easier.

Direct mail shots can also include leaflets, booklets, or even samples. In short, there is no limit to the information you can include. Some direct mail shots in fact amount to reference books and are kept by recipients as useful sources of information.

The attention factor of direct mail is somewhat controversial. Many claim that some people receive so much direct mail that they pay no attention to mailings, but throw them straight into the waste-paper basket. No doubt some people do receive a large number of mailings, but this is perhaps a creative rather than a media problem. If a direct mail letter is thrown away, this is proof that the mailing *did* receive attention — if only to detect that it was a direct mail shot. Attention *was* given and the problem is thus a creative one, of devising a mailing shot to retain that attention.

Direct mail houses can help here, and their services can be considered under three broad headings: provision of mailing lists, physical handling of the mailing, and creative advice on the type of direct mail campaign to be mounted.

The main drawback to direct mail is its cost. Though often low in total outlay, direct mail can be very expensive when considered on a cost per contact basis, though a well-planned campaign often gives a low ratio of cost per enquiry, or even cost per sale. The advantages, however, are many, and as always your task is to assess the benefits against cost.

Exhibitions

Exhibitions, one of the oldest advertising media, originated with the mediaeval trade fairs. Exhibitions range from those of general public interest to those appealing to special interest groups, with many intermediate categories. Some exhibitions may be considered in more than one category, as when entrance is restricted to the trade for the first few days, after which the exhibition opens to the public. In the course of time, exhibitions may perhaps shift their position in the scale, as when a special interest exhibition arouses such general interest that public attendance gradually outnumbers special interest visitors. Cutting across this scale of special interest and general exhibitions are geographical variations, since exhibitions may be local, national or even international in their coverage.

With some special interest exhibitions you have the benefit of a selected audience, implied by the exhibition's subject matter. A drawback that the medium shares with the special interest or trade press is that frequently all you know about the exhibition's coverage is what you can deduce by commonsense from its title. Often there is little or no information about where visitors come from, the type of firm they represent, their position in the organisation, and so on. The Audit Bureau of Circulations, described in the next chapter, has an Exhibitions Data Division and so the position is improving, but in too many cases there is still a serious lack of information.

The advantages this medium offers really speak for themselves. Exhibitions afford you the double benefit of demonstration combined with personal contact. You can demonstrate your product (a tremendous advantage when it is too bulky to take around) and can do so under ideal conditions, in settings specially designed for the purpose. Prospective buyers can see and handle your product, try it for themselves and ask questions. As an exhibitor you can for your part answer their queries, distribute samples or literature, obtain names and addresses to follow up for subsequent action, or take orders on the spot.

7

An additional benefit with many special interest exhibitions is that they represent the one opportunity in the year when you can contact virtually all your prospective customers, since the opportunity to view all the current models ensures a consistently high attendance. Exhibitions can also provide opportunity to express appreciation of support given during the year, with your company's sales director and other senior staff using the stand as a basis for dispensing hospitality and greeting those they cannot call on regularly themselves. Admittedly, this is sometimes abused, with exhibits being reduced to the role of free bars and buyers making the rounds of the stands. Accordingly, the main advantages of exhibitions — demonstration and personal contact — should always be kept to the fore.

A further benefit of exhibitions arises from the descriptive entry you receive in the catalogue, which visitors frequently keep for reference. In addition, there is always the possibility, for a fortunate few, of valuable editorial publicity: most exhibitions merit considerable comment in the press and other media, and those with revolutionary products or striking stands may be the subject of many editorial features.

Other than the lack of audience statistics already mentioned, the main drawback to exhibitions is their high cost. They are often very much more expensive than would appear at first sight, for the cost of designing and constructing your stand can far outweigh the site costs, particularly where advertisers compete for visitors' attention by the lavishness of their exhibits. In addition, there are many running costs: electricity, telephone, literature and samples, direct mail shots inviting people to your stand, advertisements in the catalogue, hospitality, insurance and staff. On top of the expense of hired demonstrators are the hidden costs of your own staff, who must be present to deal with those questions temporary staff cannot answer: there may also be hotel and other expenses. Frequently, too, exhibitions occupy far more top management time, before and during the exhibition, than is customary with other media. The attention paid by management shows, however, that although exhibitions may be costly, the benefits clearly outweigh the drawbacks, where personal contact and demonstration are of major importance.

Other forms of demonstration   Formal exhibitions are not the only medium to offer you facilities for demonstration and personal contact. Some advertisers mount their own exhibitions, either on their own premises or by using a portable display which they erect in premises hired for the occasion. This type of exhibition can often be combined with an invited audience film show. Some advertisers, in preference to portable exhibition stands, construct mobile exhibitions in special trailers or railway carriages which they then send round the country.

The very extreme of personal contact and demonstration is, of course, salesmanship. Rather than use conventional advertising media, your company's representatives may demonstrate the product. Even here, however, the range of media includes activities which can assist you in your marketing operation. Demonstrators can be hired to promote your product in retail outlets and distribute samples; demonstration can also be achieved by distributing samples from door to door. Sales aids such as display cases and back-projection film units that assist representatives in their selling task, are further examples which show that personal selling by representatives and indirect selling through advertising are not separate activities but overlap considerably. There is also overlap with another marketing area: merchandising and sales promotion.

Merchandising and sales promotion

There are no watertight compartments between media, and there is no fast line where advertising ends and merchandising or sales promotion begins. They must, however, interlock.

Merchandising can include use of advertising in the form of trade press advertisements, sales letters and co-operative advertising schemes as well as 'marketing' activities such as display competitions and dealer conferences — all with the common aim of making stockists eager to display your product with the confidence that it will sell.

The term 'merchandising' is sometimes extended to include coupon schemes, premiums, or '10p off' offers, but within this book it is restricted to those activities linked with advertising, rather than sales promotions linked more directly with product aspects of the marketing mix. Accordingly, important though sales promotion is, it is inappropriate to cover it within the scope of this book.*

Outdoor advertising

Facilities exist for poster displays in most urban areas in Great Britain. Availability naturally fluctuates but the current situation can always be obtained either from British Posters or from Independent Poster Sales or from the individual contractors, i.e. site-owners,

*Those with particular interest in this matter are recommended to read Christian Petersen's *Sales Promotion in Action* published by Associated Business Press.

concerned, most of whom use a common system of site classification. Advertising rates vary according to site but are subject to discounts for six-month or twelve-month orders. Sites can be bought individually, by preselected campaigns, or by selected packages.

The standard poster sizes are: Double Crown (30" x 20"), Quad Crown (30" x 40"), 4-sheet (60" x 40"), 12-sheet (60" x 120"), 16-sheet (10' x 6'8") and 48-sheet (10' x 20').

Double Crowns and Quad Crowns are known as Public Information Panels and are mostly used for entertainment advertising, estate agents and local authority notices. The larger sizes usually feature advertising for consumer goods and services. In many of the new and re-development areas — including the vast majority of shopping precincts and parades — the size available nowadays is the 4-sheet, which is also available on a large and growing number of bus shelters and motorway service areas. In addition to the sizes quoted there are larger structures known as Supersites or Bulletin Boards. These are normally on main roads and can be hand-painted, with cut-outs if required.

There is also a wide variety of transport sites on buses, and trains and stations.

Posters, whether on hoardings or transport sites, offer you the full benefit of colour. This can be of particular advantage since printing the posters rests within your own control and high quality can be assured. With other media you must accept the colour quality uniformly available to all, but with posters you can if you wish achieve a quality unobtainable in press media, simply by printing in more than the standard four colours.

The poster medium offers many additional advantages. You control the area of coverage and — subject to availability — can localise your campaign to a street, a town, an area, a region or alternatively mount a nationwide campaign. You can, in fact, book sites in exactly those areas where you most need advertising support. A further advantage is that you achieve almost complete coverage of the active population within the selected area, together with a very high repetition factor (depending on the number of sites booked) for nearly everybody goes out and does so frequently, and therefore has opportunity to see posters. The greater the number of sites booked, the faster will 100 per cent coverage of the population of the area be achieved, and the greater will be the repetition factor.

For these reasons, posters are regarded by many as the ideal reminder medium. This view is reinforced by the fact that posters are usually read at a glance, and are thus well suited to a brief message. When the factors of high coverage and repetition, colour and reminder close to the point of sale in selected areas are considered together, it becomes clear why a large number of manufacturers, selling fast-moving consumer goods purchased on impulse, place great faith in poster advertising.

Poster advertising need not always be restricted to a brief message: on a number of occasions, particularly where the audience is captive as in railways and buses, there is an excellent opportunity for you to convey a more detailed message.

The many advantages of the poster medium are almost self-evident but there are, of course, drawbacks. One of these is the danger of defacement. Another is the problem of deciding just how many sites to use to achieve a given coverage and repetition level. An additional problem lies in making bookings, for here you may encounter a shortage of sites, all the best being already booked on a semi-permanent basis. Furthermore, there is no central reference source (such as readership or viewing reports discussed in the next chapter) in which to look up the relative merits of individual sites. Various poster agencies have for many years maintained their own records, however, and make their services available to advertisers and agencies and there is an industry-recognised poster site classification system, the use of which is recommended by the Councils of the British Poster Advertising Association and the Solus Outdoor Advertising Association.

Point-of-sale material

Display material can serve as a vital reminder at the very point of purchase, delivering your advertising message at the time and place most likely to result in sales. The range of display material is too wide to cover fully here, and extends from showcards of various shapes and sizes, through window stickers and crowners and other display pieces to dispenser units which both sell and display your product.

Adequate display at the place of purchase can make or mar the success of your marketing campaign, and point-of-sale material is therefore of great importance. As a medium, however, it differs markedly from others. It has been said, with some justification, that 90 per cent of all display material is wasted. Usually, the reason is failure to realise why point-of-sale is a unique medium. With other media, you pay the media-owner and have the assurance that he will deliver your advertising message: with display material, however, this depends entirely on the retailer who selects, from the vast amount of material available to him, the few display units he will use. The high wastage of display material arises usually from one or both of two basic faults — production of poor material, and failure to merchandise this material. And in this context poor material means not only that which is inferior in quality but also high-quality material that does not suit the retailer's needs. Much display material is alas based on what the advertiser would like, and ignores the hard fact that only the material that the retailer wants is put on display. And even when you have produced exactly the right display material, you must still devise a complete selling programme to ensure its effective use at point of sale. Sending out a showcard with your merchandise, to be unpacked in the warehouse and thrown away, its existence unknown to the display manager, illustrates lack of attention to this point. There are many ways of ensuring the dealer's co-operation in display (see Merchandising and Sales Promotion above and also Part 3); all have the common aim of making the dealer confident your product will sell, and eager to use your display material to promote it to best advantage.

Press

This overall category covers several distinct types of printed advertising media.

Newspapers

As a group, newspapers permit you to deliver a detailed message on a given day, and at short notice, to a media audience whose size and composition are usually known, as circulation and readership figures are generally available. Space is usually sold by the single-column centimetre (S.C.C.), and in multiples thereof. A wide variety of special positions is usually available, as is classified or semi-display advertising.

National newspapers   In addition to the advantages just mentioned, the benefits of national newspapers can be summarised by considering the two parts of the name — 'national' and 'news' papers. There is a sense of urgency and immediacy about the advertising message which is distributed on a national basis (allowing, of course, for area variations in penetration). Although 'national', it is nevertheless sometimes possible to advertise on a regional edition basis. There are different papers to cover different markets — ABC1/C2DE. Colour is sometimes available either as separate supplements or, to a limited extent, in the normal run of printing.

Sunday newspapers have the additional advantage of being read in a more leisurely atmosphere, and present you with opportunity to appeal to husband and wife or the entire family together. The fact that Sunday is a non-shopping day is rarely a hindrance, for consumer durables are seldom purchased on impulse and Sunday is ideal for writing for further information. In addition, some Sunday newspapers have a longer life, being kept and re-read later in the week, or even retained for reference, which is rarely the case with daily newspapers.

In a category of their own — not truly national but too large to be considered 'local' — are the two London evenings. In that readership figures are included in the National Readership Surveys, however, they are best considered under that heading — or at least as semi-national.

Local newspapers   This media group is frequently the mainstay of local retailers' advertising. It is also used by national advertisers to give area boosts, to benefit from essentially local interest, and to tie-in with local stockists. As before, your advertising message can be quickly spread on a selected day, and detailed information included. Colour is frequently available. Circulation figures are usually published, but readership information is not as universally available as with the nationals. This, to some extent, inhibits advertisers and their agencies from using some local media, which they cannot evaluate so precisely as they can the nationals.

The local morning papers usually have a serious-minded approach and thus a higher-level coverage, with circulations spreading some way outside the publishing centre. Local evening papers, on the other hand, generally have more of a mass appeal and consequently larger circulations than the morning papers. This larger circulation is usually more concentrated on those who live and work near the publication centre. Local Sunday newspapers are few in number, and combine the benefits of local interest with the advantages of Sunday publication described above. Finally, there are the local weeklies with small circulations (where quoted, which is by no means always the case) but with comparatively wide geographical coverage frequently extending into outlying rural areas. Local weeklies usually have a longer life, being kept a full week for reference.

Series and groups, and bureaux   A factor that sometimes prevents media planners from using local media is the sheer physical labour of sending individual orders and advertising material and subsequently correcting proofs and paying individual invoices, which becomes the more burdensome the more local papers are used. The combination of individual papers into series or groups, through which you can cover a number of publications with a single order, advertisement, proof and invoice, makes it far easier from the administrative point of view to justify the use of local media. The services of ENAB and

WNAB, the Evening and Weekly Newspaper Advertising Bureaux described in the next chapter, are also relevant in this context as is RNAB, the Regional Newspaper Advertising Bureau.

Freesheets   Some newspapers — and magazines — are issued free of charge, either distributed door-to-door or given out at important central points (such as stations) where they are handed to people on their way to work. This type of free publication must be distinguished from the controlled-circulation journals described below, which are distributed through the post.

Magazines

Magazines, as newspapers, afford you an opportunity to deliver a detailed message. The exact manner of delivery can vary widely for there is great variety in magazine format, in size, number of pages, printing quality, colour availability, and advertising facilities. Space is usually sold by the page and in fractions thereof and a variety of special positions, e.g. inside front cover or facing matter may be available.

One of the main reasons which leads advertisers to select magazines is mood — the reader's state of mind when your advertising message is delivered. This aspect of magazine media is frequently linked with another point in their favour, in that a finer degree of audience selection is often possible, since readership is usually in more clearly defined groups than the broad coverage of newspapers. These two points together give you considerable advertising advantages, since you reach a clearly defined group of prospects when they are likely to be receptive to your message.

A point which may count against magazines on the other hand is that of timing, since magazines are not precision instruments capable of delivering your message on a selected day, as can newspapers. The physical life of magazines is far longer, and your advertising message may be delivered at any time during this period. Indeed, cases are known where advertisers have received replies to magazine advertisements years after the cover date. Another aspect of timing is long copy dates, which may count against use of magazines by advertisers seeking to make swift announcements, or whose advertising content is subject to sudden and unexpected changes. Marketing considerations will determine which of the two contrasting points is more important to you: lack of precise timing, or the far longer life of magazine advertisements (see page 64).

This preamble has, of course, contained generalisations and it would be unrealistic to group all magazines together and view them as one homogenous media group. They can be sub-divided into many further categories — general interest magazines; special interest or technical publications appealing to groups having in common a certain occupation, hobby, sport or other special interest; the trade press; and controlled-circulation journals.

General interest magazines   These appeal to the broad mass of men or women or both, but even here there is usually scope for a finer degree of audience selection, as readers tend to have more clearly defined characteristics than for newspapers. Advertisers know these audience characteristics, because most general magazines are included in the National Readership Surveys described in the next chapter. Accordingly, total readership can be sub-divided into the various categories of age, sex and socio-economic group, or by specific characteristics such as ownership of appliances, and this makes precise audience selection much easier. This finer degree of selectivity is coupled with the other media factor of a receptive audience. With some general interest magazines, split-run and test-town facilities are available as well as advertising on a national basis.

Special interest magazines   These, as the name implies, appeal to groups having a special interest in common, but can be sub-divided into different categories according to the nature of that interest, which may be an occupation (industrial, commercial or professional) or a hobby, sport or other specialist activity. When considering publications where the special interest is a technical/occupational one, you should bear in mind the difference between 'vertical' and 'horizontal' media. The former cover a single trade or occupation at all management levels from top to bottom, whereas the circulation of horizontal media implies coverage of readers occupying similar positions but spread across a wide range of industries. (See also 'Points in Common' below.)

Retail trade journals   These are, in fact, also special interest publications, but are singled out for separate attention since advertisers use them in a particular way. In using general or special interest magazines, you try to persuade readers to buy in their own right, as consumers of your merchandise. Only a few advertisers, selling such things as shop fittings, use the trade press to promote their merchandise direct. Most advertisers use the trade press to contact retailers in their vital role as intermediaries between the manufacturer and the public. Accordingly, trade press advertising messages usually urge 'Be ready for the demand that public advertising will stimulate — stock up, display and make a profit!' rather than 'Buy for your own use'. Trade press advertisements, therefore, tend to feature incentives such as details of coming consumer advertising, display material available, and profit to be gained.

Special interest and trade press: points in common   Despite the major differences in the way in which the two media groups are used, special interest and retail publications have certain characteristics in common, relating to the number and type of readers. With general magazines, you usually have circulation and readership figures to evaluate, but with special interest journals and the trade press it is often impossible for you to form a considered opinion in the same way. Circulation figures may be available, but not always. Furthermore, where circulation is known, this frequently reveals that the publication does not fully cover the group in question. A counter argument to incomplete market coverage is that the proportion reached are the enthusiasts and 'trend setters', and that those who do not read the publication cannot have the same degree of interest as those who do. This, however, only highlights another point often made against these magazines: that more often than not, all you know about coverage is what is implied by the magazine's title. When considering a trade or special interest magazine, you need to know where the readers are located within the country, whether they are large or small buyers, traditional or modern in outlook, and so on. In some cases a Media Data Form (see page 30) may be available, but in others, however, no readership information is available, and you are left to deduce what you can by commonsense, from the name and contents of the magazine.

In short, the special interest and trade press may reach only a proportion of your total market, and you know little or nothing about the characteristics of the proportion you do reach. This is perhaps a harsh statement, but it accurately summarises the problem you often face when attempting to evaluate these media.

Controlled-circulation publications   The incomplete market coverage and lack of readership information just mentioned have led to an interesting development, namely controlled-circulation publications sent to individuals in certain defined categories. The magazine is not sold but distributed free of charge, through the post, in the same way as subscription copies. Conventional publishers have argued that readers are unlikely to value anything they do not pay for, but the counter-argument is that the cost of many special interest publications is borne by employers: the actual readers are unaware of the source of the copy that arrives on their desks, and value it according to the subject matter.

The benefits of a controlled-circulation publication depend on its distribution, which overcomes the two main drawbacks to conventional publications: incomplete coverage and lack of readership information. Controlled-circulation journals cover the market completely, by definition, and readership information is automatically available simply through analysis of the mailing list to which the journal is sent. Thus, in theory, the medium is near perfect. Any medium has its drawbacks, however, and those of controlled circulation arise from defining and compiling the journal's mailing list.

Controlled circulation gives you full coverage of the market only if your market matches precisely the publication's market. Should the controlled-circulation journal's definition be wider or narrower than yours, this must mean either waste circulation or incomplete coverage. Further, there is the vital question of how the mailing list was compiled. Giving a definition is one thing, but obtaining a list of all those coming within this definition is another. This problem is further complicated by the normal difficulty of keeping any mailing list up-to-date. The Audit Bureau of Circulations described in the next chapter provides data on controlled-circulation journals, but some media planners undertake additional 'spot checks' on reader attitudes and mailing-list accuracy, by telephoning a dozen or so individuals who should be on the mailing list to ask if they receive copies, and their opinion of them.

Radio

Radio as an advertising medium is available on a local and national basis through the various independent local radio stations (ILR), and through Manx Radio and Radio Luxembourg.

Independent local radio differs from the advertising media so far discussed in that it is under the official control of the Independent Broadcasting Authority (IBA) which has the responsibility for administering the ILR system. The frequency, amount and nature of the advertisements must be in accordance with the IBA Act and the extensive rules and principles laid down under it by the Authority. Advertising is limited to a maximum of nine minutes in each hour. No programmes are sponsored by advertisers, and the Authority's rules require that advertising must be clearly separated from programmes and obvious for what it is. As with other media, advertising that is created for radio should be compatible with the medium that carries it, and there is evidence of growing awareness of the special needs of radio: the Authority's copy controls have not inhibited advertisers from creating entertaining, informative and interesting commercials which make a special contribution to the sound of Independent Local Radio.

One of the great advantages of radio as an advertising medium is its ability to communicate your advertising message to the listening consumer at very short notice. A commercial can be scripted, cleared in relation to the IBA Code of Advertising Standards, recorded and transmitted in a matter of hours.

Advertising time on ILR is sold in standard units of 15, 30, 45 or 60 second commercials. On Radio Luxembourg and Manx Radio, as well as 'spot' advertisements, a limited number of sponsored programmes are available, subject to individual negotiation. Advertisers wishing to sponsor programmes normally undertake a sponsorship of not less than 13 weeks.

As well as being flexible by time and day, radio is also flexible by area.

The Independent Local Radio Network   At the time of writing, the Independent Local Radio companies in operation are:

Belfast	Downtown Radio
Birmingham	BRMB Radio
Bournemouth	Two Counties Radio
Bradford	Pennine Radio
Cardiff	Cardiff Broadcasting
Coventry	Mercia Sound
Edinburgh	Radio Forth
Glasgow	Radio Clyde
Ipswich	Radio Orwell
Liverpool	Radio City
London	LBC Radio and Capital Radio
Manchester	Piccadilly Radio
Nottingham	Radio Trent
Peterborough	Hereward Radio
Plymouth	Plymouth Sound
Portsmouth	Radio Victory
Reading	Radio 210
Sheffield and Rotherham	Radio Hallam
Swansea	Swansea Sound
Teeside	Radio Tees
Tyne/Wear	Metro Radio
Wolverhampton/Black Country	Beacon Radio

Airtime can be booked direct for local advertisers or through three national sales offices responsible for maintaining contact with national advertisers and advertising agencies:

Air Services   Representing:
48 Leicester Square   BRMB Radio
London WC2H 7PF   Cardiff Broadcasting
                                Mercia Sound   Pennine Radio

18

Piccadilly Radio   Plymouth Sound
Radio Orwell
Radio Tees
Radio 210
Severn Sound — see below
Two Counties Radio

Broadcasting Marketing Services   Representing:
7 Duke of York Street   Downtown Radio
London SW1Y 61A   Hereward Radio
                                   Radio City
                                   Radio Clyde
                                   Radio Forth
                                   Radio Tay — see below
                                   Metro Radio
                                   Swansea Sound
                                   Radio Trent

Radio Sales and Marketing   Representing:
94/97 Fetter Lane   Beacon Radio
London EC4A 1DE   Devonair Radio — see below
                                   LBC Radio
                                   Radio Hallam
                                   Radio Victory   Manx Radio

Capital Radio sells its own advertising, direct from the London office at 356 Euston Road, London NW1, and radio advertising is also available on Radio Luxembourg at 34-35 Dean Street, London W1.

Other Independent Local Radio Companies have been appointed but, at time of writing, are not yet on the air:

Aberdeen   North of Scotland Radio
Bristol   Radio Avonside
Coventry   Midland Community Radio
Dundee/Perth   Radio Tay
Exeter/Torbay   Devonair Radio
Gloucester & Cheltenham Gloucestershire Broadcasting
                        Company (Severn Sound)
Inverness   Moray Firth Community Radio

These names are not necessarily the station names by which the companies will come to be generally known.

The Independent Broadcasting Authority has also invited applications for contracts to provide independent local radio services for Ayr, Leeds (West Yorkshire Broadcasting), Leicester (Centre Radio), Luton/Bedford (Chiltern Radio) and Southend/Chelmsford (Radio Eastway).

19

Government authorisation of more local radio stations was announced in November 1979: the new stations are to be sited at Barnsley, Bury St Edmunds, Guildford, Londonderry, Newport (Gwent), Preston/Blackpool, Swindon, Worcester/Hereford and Wrexham/Deeside. Further consideration is being given to the proposal for an ILR station in East Kent.

Radio, one of the most recent media, is frequently a 'companion' to its listeners, and so your advertising message is received in an intimate and personal atmosphere. Successful advertising requires an appreciation of radio's one-to-one relationship between listener and broadcaster. The medium is a transient one and your message is received through one sense only: that of hearing. Messages on the whole should usually be brief, and clearly it is necessary for you to make maximum effective choice of words. Their actual delivery and the supporting sound effects or music are equally important.

People listen to the radio in the car, on the beach, in parks, in the kitchen at home and in the factory at work. It thus reaches people at different times and in different moods from other media's.

As ILR is a local medium, many broadcasters speak with an intimate knowledge of their local community, so establishing a link with their audience. It can serve the needs of local firms and equally give area boosts where necessary for national advertisers.

The composition of the radio audience varies with different periods of the day, and selective timing can communicate your advertising message to various important groups, e.g. housewives, teenagers, young adults.

The pattern of listening to the ILR network naturally differs, according to each station's programme pattern. Contrast this with Radio Luxembourg which itself declares that it 'is unashamedly a night-time entertainment medium with a much higher proportion of casual listeners'. A direct comparison of the weekly audiences to ILR and Radio Luxembourg is, however, not valid because ILR is often on the air 24 hours per day, whereas Radio Luxembourg is only available for 8 hours per evening.

Because of operational flexibility, radio executives can accept and transmit your advertising message at short notice and therefore meet urgent and specific needs for swift transmissions when marketing conditions call for this. Frequency of market stimulus is also possible, simply through repeat transmissions.

A further advantage is that radio is relatively inexpensive to use, and commercials are normally cheap to make. And although there are many radio production companies available to you, all the ILR stations and Radio Luxembourg can make your commercials. For advertisers seeking a low cost medium, radio advertising is thus often extremely attractive.

Television

Like ILR, television differs from other media in that it is under the official control of the Independent Broadcasting Authority, which has the central responsibility for administering the ITV system. The frequency, amount and nature of the advertisements must be in accordance with the IBA Act and the extensive rules and principles laid down under it by the Authority. As with ILR, no programmes are sponsored by advertisers and there must be a total distinction between programmes and advertisements. Television advertising is limited to six minutes an hour, averaged over the day's programmes, with normally a maximum of seven minutes in any 'clock-hour', e.g. 6—7 pm, 7—8 pm. The IBA Act provides for the insertions of these advertisements not only at the beginning or end of a programme but 'in the natural breaks therein'.

The ITV network   Independent television is a regional system of broadcasting in which fifteen individual companies appointed by the IBA provide the programme service in fourteen separate areas of the country (London is served by two companies on a split-week basis). These companies are:

Anglia Television	East of England
ATV Network	Midlands
Border Television	The Borders and Isle of Man
Channel Television	Channel Islands (1)
Grampian Television	North-East Scotland (2)
Granada Television	Lancashire
HTV	Wales and West of England
London Weekend Television	London (weekends)
Scottish Television	Central Scotland (2)
Southern Television	South of England
Thames Television	London (weekdays)
Tyne Tees Television	North-East England (3)
Ulster Television	Northern Ireland
Westward Television	South-West England
Yorkshire Television	Yorkshire (3)

(1)   Sold by Westward Television.
(2)   These two sell jointly as STAGS (Scottish Television and Grampian Sales).
(3)   These two sell jointly as Trident Management.

The ITV areas seem to present convenient regional advertising facilities but transmitters do not recognise lines on a map and, although television coverage is almost at saturation level, there are still households within areas which cannot receive signals, and other households which are in overlap areas.

The great impact of television comes from its ability to demonstrate your product's benefits, actually in the home, to a family audience in a relaxed atmosphere, with precise control of timing and the additional benefits of sound and special effects and also, to an increasing extent, colour. Other creative approaches, such as animation, are also possible.

The programme contractors' areas tend to be larger than those served by essentially local media. For this reason many advertisers regard television as a regional medium rather than a local one. This had led a number of manufacturers, who place great reliance on television, to revise their sales areas to correspond with the TV transmission areas, thus reversing the original practice of seeking a medium whose coverage coincided with the advertiser's sales area.

Television, though regional in structure, gives you the benefit of an impact on the media audience equivalent to that of a national medium. Viewers think of television as a medium of national importance, and many advertisers value it for this reason.

Television as a medium is flexible by time and day as well as area: advertising time is sold in standard units of 7, 15, 30, 45 and 60 seconds duration, booked into different time segments with advertising rates appropriate to the size and composition of the audience you are likely to reach. So-called decimal or metric-length commercials of 5, 10, 20, 40 and 50 seconds duration are also being introduced by some contractors. Subject to availability, longer spots may also be booked.

Costs may vary with the degree of certainty with which your advertising is likely to appear. Spots booked at a relatively inexpensive 'broad spot advertisement rate' may be pre-empted (or omitted) without notice by spots sold to other advertisers at a higher cost, such as bookings made at a first-level 'pre-emptible fixed spot' rate. These fixed spots may, however, be pre-empted without notice by spots sold at a higher-level pre-empt rate. These higher-rate pre-empt spots may in their turn be pre-empted without notice by spots sold to other advertisers at the highest rate — that for non-pre-emptible fixed spots, which are the only ones certain to appear. This is a straightforward matter of supply and demand for the media-owner, but for the advertiser and his agency it makes more complex the already difficult problem of planning and buying a television campaign.

Television rate cards thus call for detailed study and television schedules — under such circumstances — demand constant attention, review and adjustment. The volatile nature of television can be contrasted with other media where advertising is a 'once-off' operation in which you plan and book your schedule and then wait for your advertisements to appear. With television advertising, on the other hand, schedule adjustment is virtually more important than the original basic plan.

Television programme contractors' rate cards are frequently more complex than those for other media and, in addition to the different categories of spot rates already mentioned, may include a wide range of other facilities — support spots which you can book on a 'run-of-day', 'run-of-week', 'run-of-campaign' or 'seasonal' basis — all of which may have separate rates for peak and off-peak screenings. Rate cards are also likely to include a wide variety of different discount rates as well as other advertising packages (such as the GHI's, or Guaranteed Home Impressions, described in the next chapter), by which the television programme contractors attempt to balance supply and demand for television advertising time.

As well as transmitting your advertising message, many television contractors also offer a range of services to advertisers, including production of commercials and a wide range of merchandising facilities.

The regular flow of research information about the size and composition of the television audience (described in the next chapter) enables you to gauge the audience you are likely to reach. To some, particularly the less experienced in television advertising, this wealth of information causes some embarrassment, especially when taking into account additional research information provided by some programme contractors. In passing, this view highlights the two ends of the complaints scale about research: some complaints are based on lack of information, and others on the fact that there is too much!

Television — the future

The fast-changing nature of television advertising has already been stressed, but certain current events may make it even more complex in the future. Three possible changes must be mentioned:

1   The present contractors   The contracts of the present ITV Contractors expire in December 1981, and may or may not be renewed. The widespread assumption is that most will be renewed, but perhaps with some reshuffling, as happened the last time this situation arose in 1967.

2   A fourth channel   The Government has announced its intention to authorise the introduction of a second commercial channel, controlled by the Independent Broadcasting Authority, to commence transmission in 1982/3. Two major questions arise. The first is whether this second channel will be entrusted to the present companies currently running ITV, or whether it should be placed in the hands of a different network of companies (or even one company). The other controversy is whether it will be run so as to complement ITV 1 or in competition, i.e. will it run its most popular shows at the same time as the least popular or most popular shows on the existing channel. Either way, advertisers on present channels are likely to get lower ratings and higher costs-per-thousand. For mass consumer products, time buying and planning will become more difficult but, looking on the brighter side, the greater the fragmentation of TV audiences then the greater in theory is the possibility of selectivity. Further selectivity may be possible through hours to provide 'breakfast TV'. Any further comment under this heading will be overtaken by events by the time of publication and so, other than alerting you to this vital development, this brief reference must suffice.

3   Video developments   Other current developments are likely to affect future television audiences, including ITV's Oracle, the BBC's Ceefax and the Post Office's Prestel. All three represent a danger to the TV advertiser in that they offer viewers the facility to switch from the commercials, to seek information offered by these other services, and then back to the programme. Prestel differs from the other two in being a combination of TV set, telephone and computer. Through a small keypad, rather like a pocket calculator, a specially adapted TV set puts the viewer in direct contact with a Post Office computer. Prestel's interactive qualities are thus likely to affect marketing activities as well as advertising — viewers will be able to answer advertisements there and then, leave their names and addresses and instructions for action and, eventually, not only buy goods and services but also pay for them by keying their credit card number into the computer.

Other developments are video-cassette recorders and long players. Far simpler, but equally a danger to TV advertisers, are the various games (such as squash or tennis) which viewers can play on their own screens, through facilities which now sell at relatively low cost. Since they offer another alternative to the current ITV programme material they may have a dramatic effect on viewing levels.

Other advertising media

The range of advertising media is considerable, and within this chapter it has been possible to review only a limited number of them. Printed material has deliberately been omitted, for though print plays a vital role in marketing, it is best regarded as a sales tool rather than an advertising medium, since booklets and leaflets only gather dust if they are not distributed by advertising or personal selling: hence the omission. The chapter could be extended to include a whole range of miscellaneous publications, gifts and premiums, juke box commercials, book matches, promotion of special events, and many others. If you are concerned with evaluating media, the basic questions are the same and apply equally to those media not specifically discussed here. The fundamental questions you should ask in selecting the media best suited to your marketing objective will be discussed in Chapter 3.

2
MEDIA RESEARCH AND SERVICES

Having reviewed in general terms the media you can use to communicate your advertising message, the next step is to examine what we know about them: the quantitative or qualitative data available which permit you to evaluate properly the various media and make comparisons. To quote current facts would be of very limited value as such information goes out-of-date all too quickly: for example, any statistics about circulation, readership or viewing habits would be invalid by the time this book was published. In any event, some figures are already 6–12 months old before new data is published. This chapter therefore reviews the data sources available, rather than giving actual figures. Mention is also made of various services that may facilitate your effective use of advertising media.

Since various sources cover more than one medium, they will be reviewed by title rather than by media. The following brief cross-reference will, however, facilitate your locating those data sources relevant to the media that interest you:

All media	BRAD
Cinema	JICNARS, SAA, TGI
Exhibitions	ABC
Press	ABC, ENAB, JICMARS, JICNARS, MEAL, RNAB, TGI, WNAB
Outdoor	JICPAS, PAB, TGI
Radio	AIRC, JICNARS, JICRAR, MEAL, TGI
Television	JICNARS, JICTAR, MEAL, TGI

These various sources are discussed in more detail below, in alphabetical order. This chapter necessarily has a 'list' format, and it is suggested that initially you read through it rapidly to acquaint yourself with the range of information available, and then return to the chapter for more detailed study later, *together with actual copies of the data sources mentioned.*

ABC (Audit Bureau of Circulations)
(13 Wimpole Street, London W1M 7AB)

ABC is a non-profit company, limited by guarantee, which has a tripartite membership of advertisers, advertising agencies and publishers.

ABC's primary function is the certification of circulation and exhibition data by independent professional auditors using standard audit procedures for each category of publication and exhibition. Thus ABC protects advertisers and agencies from false claims, at the same time furnishing publishers and exhibition organisers with a certifying document which is accepted as authentic by all who purchase space in member publications and exhibitions.

It is estimated that well over 90 per cent of the total advertising placed in the UK press goes into publications that have ABC-certified circulation figures.

To ensure that audits are conducted on a uniform basis, the Bureau sends each publisher member, in advance of the particular audit period, forms for completion and return to the Bureau by an approved independent auditor. In general the independent auditors are also the financial auditors to the publishing company and ABC welcomes this as most ABC audits involve the financial records and audit programmes and these are best administered by one firm of accountants. Where the circulation auditors are not the financial auditors, the publisher must grant the circulation auditors full access to the financial records necessary to validate the circulation figures.

When the completed *Publisher's Return Form* is received, the Bureau checks it and, subject to it being correct, issues an *ABC Certificate* covering the period audited and publishes the results.

The Bureau operates a random inspection of publishers' records throughout the year. This is conducted by a chartered accountant from the Bureau's staff, and the main purpose is to ensure that the circulation audit is being carried out in the proper way. Such visits are also useful in clearing any operational queries and providing a cross flow of information between the Bureau, publisher members and their auditors.

Circulation audits

The Audit Bureau has various circulation audit categories and audit periods. Before reviewing these, some general points must be considered, as certain copies cannot be included in any ABC figures. These are:

1   Returned, unsold or undelivered copies.
2   Copies sold in bulk and then distributed free.
3   Copies sent to advertising agencies, contributors and employees.
4   Copies not carrying all advertising.
5   Back issues dated more than 12 months prior to the date of actual distribution.
6   Bound volumes of back issues.
7   Copies given away at exhibitions, conferences, etc.

There is also provision for certain issues to be excluded at the request of the publisher . When an industrial dispute, a mechanical failure or any other cause beyond the publisher's control results in a material loss of distribution of a publication, the publisher can apply to the Bureau for the issues so affected to be excluded from the audit period.

Unless there are exceptional circumstances all audit periods are continuous. Reviewed in terms of the media to which they relate, the Audit categories and periods are:

Newspapers and consumer magazines   For national newspapers and consumer magazines there are four overlapping six-month audit periods, and the Bureau publishes six-month rolling averages. Regional newspapers have two audit periods per year.

Net sales are the only audit category: these are *bona fide* copies bought by individual readers either from the retail point or by direct subscription, and represent the audited primary paid readership of a newspaper or magazine. Where the full cover price or the full subscription rate has not been paid, or discounts to wholesale or retail distributors have been increased on a temporary basis, the copies so sold must be shown separately on the audit form.

Business and professional journals, and consumer specialised journals
Consumer specialised journals and business and professional journals
can have either two six-month audits or an annual audit.

Whereas general consumer magazines report on average net sales,
these types of publication are issued with an *ABC Certificate of
Average Net Circulation,* i.e. in addition to net sales they may
include certain categories of auditable free circulation.

The primary rule for free distribution is that each copy must be
auditable down to the individual recipient. In the main, therefore,
only normal postal distribution can be included. In all cases, each
copy must be separately wrapped and addressed. There are three
main types of free circulation recognised by the ABC:

1   Controlled circulation   This category (not applicable to consumer specialised journals) consists solely of single copies sent free
and post-free to *individuals* who precisely fit the 'Term of Control',
which must be published in each issue of the journal. This Term
of Control must define the industrial, commercial or professional
classification covered by the journal together with the job qualification the reader must have in order to qualify for receipt of the
journal. Controlled circulation is further sub-divided into three
categories:

a   Individually requested   Each copy in this category must be
backed by a signed Request Card dated no more than three
years before the date on which the copy is despatched. The
recipient must receive every issue addressed to him by name.

b   Company requested   This term is used when the request
document is signed by a senior official of a qualifying company,
designating specific executives who are to receive the journal.
Again each recipient must individually receive every issue
and the request document signature must be within the three-
year limit.

c   Non-requested   This term covers all other controlled-circulation
copies, i.e. where no valid requesting document is on file.
Recipients need not receive every issue nor is it necessary to
address each copy to an individual by name. However, the
address must bear the job function of the recipient where
the individual name is not known. Non-requested copies also
include copies previously shown under the two headings above
but where the request document has gone out of date.

2   Society/association free circulation   The second main type of
free circulation recognised by ABC relates to societies or associations.
As with controlled-circulation journals, this type of free circulation

is again sub-divided into three categories:

a   *Non-optional circulation* is where the journal is sent to the whole membership of the society or association without additional cost to the normal annual subscription.

b   *Unpaid optional circulation* is where, without extra cost, a section only of the membership receives the journal.

c   *Paid optional circulation* is where members pay a sum additional to their normal subscription in order to receive the journal.

Society/association journals sent to non-members must not appear in this section of ABC returns but can be included as Net Sales or within the Controlled or Other Unpaid sections depending on circumstances.

3   Other unpaid circulations   The third main type of free circulation recognised by the ABC consists of free copies of value to an advertiser which do not fit the rules for controlled circulation. Such copies must be capable of audit and adequate records of despatch are therefore necessary.

Qualitative information

Publishers' statements   All *Publisher's Return Forms* have provision for a *Publisher's Statement* in which the publisher can include a brief note which may be to his advantage in explaining to advertisers and agencies other information not given on the *Certificate*. This statement is automatically transferred to the *ABC Certificate*, but is not subject to audit and the Bureau accepts no responsibility for its content.

Media data forms   For business and professional journals and consumer specialist journals the ABC operates an additional service. Certificates of net circulation give a *quantitative* analysis of average net distribution over a defined period. To show the *quality* of this circulation a publisher may, after his annual certification has been granted, complete a *Media Data Form*. Entry to the scheme is voluntary. The contents are not independently audited but are subject to ABC inspection and verification. The completed MDF is checked by the Bureau and given the stamp of approval prior to its reproduction. An MDF is constructed in four parts:

Part I contains details of the publishing company, its staff, its advertisement rates, the market served by the journal and brief details of any research carried out.

Part II is a reproduction of the latest *ABC Certificate of Net Circulation*.

Part III gives a geographical breakdown of a normal issue included in the ABC average together with brief details of the analyses available.

Part IV reports on editorial policy, analyses an issue within the audit period and contains optional statements by the publisher giving any information which may assist the buyer of space.

Although the *Media Data Form* is issued in blank as a four-page document, publishers may extend any or all sections at will. Eight-, ten- and twelve-page MDFs are frequently produced and have proved most successful.

Possible future press services

Free sheets   Plans are near fruition to launch a system for verifying the distribution of local free distributed publications, in a new division under the control of the Audit Bureau of Circulations.

Regional weekly newspapers   MDFs for regional weekly newspapers are an area of growth for which the ABC is trying hard to reach agreement and develop.

Exhibitions

For this medium, the Audit Bureau of Circulation administers through its Exhibition Data Division a system to audit attendances at exhibitions both as to quantity and quality. The ABC-verified document issued is named the *Exhibition Data Form:* the form and content of the EDF, audit rules, fees and charges are all considered by a Joint Industry Committee having equal representation of organisers and exhibitors.

Like the MDF described above, the EDF is constructed in four parts:

Part I contains general information about the exhibition, the organisers and sponsors, what items were exhibited and the target audience. Last, the certified attendance both paid (registered and unregistered) and free (registered only).

31

Part II is devoted to analyses of the registered attendance. It is mandatory to analyse geographically, by job function/qualification and by industrial, commercial or professional classification. Other analyses are at the discretion of organisers but must be based on a full count of all visitor registration cards.

Part III gives details of the stand space sold and of the exhibitors together with research information.

Part IV contains optional statements by the organiser and details of any conference or symposium held in conjunction with the exhibition.

Any part of the EDF can be extended to allow fuller information to be given.

The audience, stand space and exhibitor statistics must be certified to the Bureau by a nominated independent auditor, normally the financial auditor to the organiser. All information contained in the EDF is further subject to ABC inspection and verification.

AIRC (Association of Independent Radio Contractors)
(8 Great James Street, London WC1N 3DA)

This Association was established by the contracting companies to act as their trade association and to represent them in their national affairs.

Among its many activities, the Association provides information to advertisers and agencies on developments in the radio industry and on the progress of the broadcasting companies. In particular, monthly figures are released for radio broadcasting revenue, and the Association publishes a guide entitled *Independent Local Radio – The Facts.* Included in these facts is information about

1   ILR audience size and growth.
2   Share of total radio listening market.
3   Brand share by radio station.
4   Reach by demographics — average week.
5   Comparison of profiles (sex, age, class).
6   Average half-hour audiences (weekdays, Saturdays, Sundays).
7   Population and listener statistics for each ILR station.

BRAD (British Rate & Data)
(76 Oxford Street, London WIN OHN)

This company provides various services which can assist you in making the most effective use of advertising media.

BRAD National Guide to Media Selection

This comprehensive reference book is perhaps the company's main service, containing full details of all media which carry advertising. Many concerned with the use of media find it more convenient to refer to BRAD than attempt to keep an up-to-date rate-card filing system. Published every month, it contains updated information on rates, mechanical requirements, circulations, personnel, etc. All circulation figures quoted in entries must be substantiated: the ABC just described maintains close liaison with BRAD's editor to ensure that ABC information in BRAD is as accurate as possible. The latest ABC figure for each audit period is automatically passed to BRAD for inclusion in the publication's entry.

To keep its entries up-to-date, BRAD issues every month a form to which is attached the medium's listing as it currently appears. The media-owner then marks on the form corrections for the following month's issue.

The topicality of BRAD is demonstrated by the fact that each issue contains between 1200 and 2200 amended listings.

BRAD Directories and Annuals

Published once a year, with the January issue of BRAD, this publication does for annuals what BRAD does for the rest of the media market. It is a comprehensive, classified directory of all annual publications and directories in Great Britain, both consumer and trade, technical and professional.

BRAD Advertiser & Agency Listing

This reference book, published four times a year (January, April, July and October), provides up-to-date information on national advertisers, brand names, publishing groups, market research and direct mail companies. It gives full information about advertising agencies and lists their clients and the appropriate executive for each, wherever possible.

In conclusion, it is worth mentioning that BRAD not only provides an information service but is also an advertising medium in its own right, used by those whose target market is those personnel whose judgment affects media decisions. Reference is made below to research information provided by media-owners rather than the central sources listed here, and BRAD itself has undertaken two such surveys — one on 'Advertising Agencies' Usership of Advertising and Marketing Publications' and another on 'National Consumer, Trade & Industrial Advertisers' Usership of British Rate & Data'.

ENAB (Evening Newspaper Advertising Bureau)
(Victoria House, Vernon Place, Southampton Row, London WC1B 4DS)

ENAB was formed in 1962 to co-ordinate information and present a corporate case for the regional evening press. It was re-formed in 1972 as a promotions spearhead with a view to projecting regional evenings as advertising media. ENAB is a co-operative and draws its revenue from membership subscriptions. It is divided operationally into various sections:

Research and information   ENAB administers the inclusion, collectively and individually, of evening newspapers in the National Readership Survey. It analyses information from the Target Group Index (TGI), Media Expenditure Analysis (MEAL) — both described below — and the Office of Population Census and Statistics. It mounts its own surveys into attitudes towards the regional evenings, e.g. *Attitudes to Advertising — a major study in media research*, and provides a regular breakdown of member newspaper circulations by local government area, publishing the results in *Where?*. The Bureau also maintains a regularly up-dated historical record of the progress of all regional evening newspapers in terms of circulation, rates, household coverage and cover prices.

Central billing   ENAB enables national advertisers and their agencies to book space in all, or any selection of, member newspapers on a one-order, one invoice basis. It negotiates on the availability of sizes, positions and dates of insertion with member newspapers on the advertiser's behalf.

National Classified Advertising Service (NCAS)   ENAB runs the NCAS on behalf of all regional evening newspapers, to facilitate the placing of linage classifieds in all or any regional selection of evenings. Copy is distributed centrally to all the newspapers concerned and the advertiser receives one invoice charged at a national or regional rate per word.

Co-partnership   ENAB enables national advertisers to support local stockists through its co-partnership service. Manufacturers are kept aware of the advantages of supporting their stockists with advertising funds to be spent locally, usually on a shared basis and, ideally, with allowances geared to the purchase of goods or services by the retailer. Each member newspaper employs a trained co-partnership co-ordinator to explain manufacturers' offers to retailers. The Bureau also informs member newspapers — through a Dealer Aid Index — of shared advertising opportunities for retailers.

Colour co-ordination   ENAB maintains records on the availability of full-registered pre-printed full colour in member newspapers. It assists the colour advertiser with information on the mechanics involved in mounting colour campaigns.

Other ENAB services   ENAB also mounts a regular planned programme of presentations to national and regional advertisers and their agencies either collectively or individually. It further promotes the medium through press advertising campaigns and regular direct mail shots, and its quarterly tabloid newspaper — *Evening Extra* — provides a vehicle for communication with the advertising industry. ENAB also undertakes press and public relations work, as part of its overall promotional programme.
Note: see separate entry for RNAB, below, regarding ENAB's merger with WNAB, the Weekly Newspaper Advertising Bureau.

ITCA (Independent Television Companies Association)
(Knighton House, 52-66 Mortimer Street, London W1N 8AN)

Incorporated as a company limited by guarantee, ITCA is the trade association of the programme companies appointed by the Independent Broadcasting Authority. A voluntary non-profit-making organisation, it provides a channel for joint action on matters of concern to the programme companies. Several committees deal with the detailed work of the Association: these include Network Programme, Finance, Management, Labour Relations, Marketing, Rights and Technical.

Among its many activities, ITCA provides information about the television medium: it publishes its own marketing journal, *Viewpoint,* and also an annual guide entitled *ITV Facts and Figures.* Included in these facts and figures is information about

1   ITV coverage.
2   Profiles of ITV population.
3   Viewing levels.
4   Media penetration.
5   Expenditure information (various categories).

JICMARS (Joint Industry Committee for Medical Advertising Readership Surveys): *see Chapter 8*

JICNARS (Joint Industry Committee for National Readership Surveys)
(44 Belgrave Square, London SW1X 8QS)

The Committee represents the Newspaper and Periodical Contributors Committee, the Institute of Practitioners in Advertising and the Incorporated Society of British Advertisers. JICNARS was formed in 1968 when it took over responsibility for the National Readership Surveys from the IPA, which had in its turn taken over from the Hulton Readership Surveys in 1956.

Currently the NRS publishes the results of 30,000 interviews a year. Over 100 publications, national and Sunday newspapers and a number of national magazines, are included. The two main criteria for regular inclusion are 100,000 circulation or 2 per cent readership but from time to time certain specialist magazines are included and special questions asked on relevant topics. The research is currently undertaken on behalf of JICNARS by Research Services Ltd.

Since the NRS series began in 1956 there has been a consistent procedure for the classification of informants into grades A,B,C1, C2,D and E. This system of social grading (explained in Chapter 3) has been widely adopted throughout the advertising industry. In addition to readership data, the NRS provides information on other matters, as detailed below.

Subscribers to the National Readership Survey receive the following:

Volume 1   This is based on fieldwork for the period July to the following June, and contains information on the following:
1   Average issue readership of all major publications analysed by sex, age, six social grades, survey region and ITV region.
2   Profile tables showing the composition of all adults, men, women and housewife readership of each publication in terms of sex, age, social grade and region, and weight of ITV viewing.
3   Tables showing ITV viewing, ILR listening and cinema-going, analysed by sex, age, social grade and ITV region.

4   Readership of each publication by weight of ITV viewing and radio listening.
5   Readership of each publication among special interest groups such as housewives with children, members of car-owning households, by terminal education age, possession of consumer durables, etc. There are also sections on readership by male heads of household/chief wage earner and heads of household/ housewives.
6   Group readership figures.
7   Frequency of reading each publication plus the group probabilities for informants claiming each reading frequency. Cumulative readership tables are included.

Volume 2   This further report has the same contents as Volume 1, but is based on the calendar year's fieldwork January to December.

Volume 3   Contains duplication tables showing the extent to which readers of one publication also read other individual publications.

NRS Bulletins   Subscribers to the NRS also receive various bulletins, including:
1   Bulletins giving total readership figures in advance of the main reports.
2   Bulletins giving additional information about the surveys including interim figures for publications that have undergone major change or relaunch.
3   A regular quarterly bulletin giving results for the four quarters ending with the latest period, and for the four previous twelve months' moving averages.

Additional services

Although the published reports contain several hundred tabulations, the amount of data stored on punched cards and tapes is very much larger, and facilities are provided for the extraction of such additional information as may be required by subscribers.

Tapes   Subscribers can purchase tapes relating to each quarter's or half-year's fieldwork period.

Post-survey information service   A post-survey information service to provide tabulations not contained in the reports is available to subscribers through the Secretary of JICNARS. In addition, a number of companies have been authorised to provide a post survey information service. The services offered by these companies are extensive in terms of individual methods of schedule analysis and schedule construction services, apart from the production of simple additional tabulations. The authorisation of a company is not a reflection of JICNARS' approval or disapproval of any particular model or system, but is based on the belief that the company can offer a competent and efficient service, and on the agreement by the company to pay a royalty to the Joint Industry Committee to assist financing the survey. The costs of extra analysis by authorised companies are a matter for individual negotiation.

The future

JICNARS is undertaking development work which could lead to a change of interviewing method and possibly other changes such as an increased media list, but this is not likely to happen for some time. Following discussion of short-term media problems, JICNARS has mounted a feasibility study to examine the viability of producing monthly data in certain special circumstances, such as the introduction of a new publication or the aftermath of a strike.

JICRAR (Joint Industry Committee for Radio Audience Research)
(44 Belgrave Square, London SW1X 8QS)

JICRAR is formed of representatives of three organisations: the Institute of Practitioners in Advertising, the Incorporated Society of British Advertisers and the Association of Independent Radio Contractors (AIRC).

The Committee was formed to agree a specification for commercial audience research, following the start of independent local radio in October 1973. Since 1974 ILR stations have commissioned and published surveys of their audiences constructed to the specification laid down. Since 1977 there has been an annual survey covering all ILR stations. This has allowed the provision of network audience information, as well as for each individual area. Unlike JICNARS and JICTAR (see below) the research contractor is appointed by AIRC which currently funds all the costs of surveys initially. About 10 per cent of the cost is recouped by sale of copies. In 1980 there will be two surveys and from 1980 three surveys annually.

The main features of the methodology are random samples of individuals in each ILR station area; personal placement and collection of a seven-day diary; diary recording on a quarter-hour basis; the appropriate ILR station, Radio Luxembourg and BBC stations are shown in the diary, together with an 'Any Other Station' category. Diary completion is spread over four weeks by allocating sample points to different start dates. The Survey, conducted by Research Surveys of Great Britain, comprises two volumes, one of which contains the following tables for each station and area:

1   Cumulative weekly audience (reach), total and average hours — ILR station and all stations.
2   Average half-hour audience — Monday-Friday (averaged) — ILR station.
3   Average half-hour audience — Saturday — ILR station.
4   Average half-hour audience — Sunday — ILR station.
5   Cumulative weekly audience (reach), total and average hours — other stations.

The second volume contains the following tables for each station and area:

1   Average audience by rate card segments.
2   Cumulative audience by rate card segments.
3   Reach and frequency for six standard packages.
4   Frequency distribution for total audience packages.
5   Frequency distribution for daytime packages.

In both volumes analysis is provided in terms of age, social class and housewives — the complexity of the sub-divisions depends on the sample size selected.

JICRAR continues to monitor the research carried out, to consider amendments and improvements to the service and the best methods of publishing the data.

The future

Certain changes are possible as regards JICRAR's activity: the main changes likely are revised methods of funding and the possibility of revising the specification, but all depends on discussions within the constituent organisations.

Other radio research

Information on radio audiences is also available from other sources, such as JICNARS and TGI which are discussed elsewhere in this chapter. Further information on radio audiences is also contained in other documents which do not, however, receive detailed discussion other than the following brief descriptive mentions:

Gallup Viewing and Listening Survey (November 1978)   Commissioned by Radio Luxembourg. National information on Radio Luxembourg, ILR and BBC. Half-hour ratings and cumulative audience data on Radio Luxembourg. Current listenership data for Radio Luxembourg and ILR. Another survey is to be published in 1980.

NOP Young Report (September 1978)   A national survey of young people aged 15-21. The survey covered social attitudes, media exposure and purchasing habits. Information on Radio Luxembourg, BBC and the 19 individual ILR stations.

JICPAS (Joint Industry Committee for Poster Audience Surveys)
(44 Belgrave Square, London SW1X 8QS)

JICPAS is formed by representatives of the poster organisations, the Institute of Practitioners in Advertising and the Incorporated Society of British Advertisers. Unlike the other main Joint Industry Committees, JICPAS does not undertake continuous research: its purpose it to determine the terms and conditions under which tripartite poster audience surveys should be undertaken.

JICPAS was formed in 1967 and in 1969 the Newport Survey technical document was published. This was a survey carried out in 1966 by Research Services Ltd in Newport, Monmouthshire. The survey dealt with the demographic composition of the poster audience. It investigated the primary media audiences provided by campaigns comprising different types of poster sites; there is a theoretical explanation for one of the fundamental relationships of poster exposure; and it discusses the implications of the research and derives a 12 towns formula.

On the poster audience front relatively little has happened recently and, in fact, this particular Committee has not met for some years.

JICTAR (Joint Industry Committee for Television Audience Research)
(44 Belgrave Square, London SW1X 8QS)

The three organisations represented on the Committee are the Independent Television Companies Association, the Institute of Practitioners in Advertising and the Incorporated Society of British Advertisers.

Unlike JICNARS which uses a large number of personal interviews, JICTAR uses a system of automatic electronic meters attached to television sets in a representative sample of homes throughout the

UK. A sufficient reserve of homes is maintained on the panel to enable the research company to report weekly on a net panel of 2580 households (7000+ individuals) balanced so as to be represent-ative of the ITV network as a whole. Within this total there are net balanced panels in each ITV area, each representative of its own area.

In every panel home a SETmeter is attached to the television set (one to each set in homes with more than one television set). These meters record on a minute-by-minute basis whether the receiver is switched on and, if so, to which station it is tuned. In addition diaries are completed within each household showing for each quarter-hour period the details of age, sex and other characteristics of those who are viewing. The information allows a statistically accurate estimate to be made of the size and composition of the audience to every programme in every area. Reports are published weekly.

The basic breakdown of the standard JICTAR Report is as follows:
1   Population estimate and panel composition.
Then, in order of TV area and by day:
2   Chronological list of commercials.
3   Minute-by-minute TVR (television ratings).
4   Analysis of commercial slots and segments.
5   Holiday statistics.
6   Weekly schedule of commercials, by brand.
7   Network report.

Weekly reports are based on a viewing week running from Monday morning to Sunday night. Detailed audience composition reports are issued three times per year and an establishment survey issued annually.

The JICTAR contract for the measurement of television audiences is held by AGB (Audits of Great Britain Ltd).

The future

Following the Annan Committee Report and the Government White Paper on Broadcasting, talks have been in progress for some time between ITCA and the BBC, with a view to establishing a joint audience measurement service. The new Broadcasters' Audience Research Board will be responsible for commissioning audience research, both quantitative (audience measurement) and qualitative (audience reaction).

MEAL (Media Expenditure Analysis Ltd)
(110 St Martin's Lane, London WC2B 4BH)

This company provides continuous trend information about the advertising expenditure (based on rate card costs) of individual brands, as an aid to the marketing management of manufacturers, media-owners and advertising agencies.

The monitoring service is based on comprehensive coverage of display advertising in the national press, magazines and television. It also includes national advertising in a complete list of regional newspapers. In each case the details are validated and checked before they are added to the latest month's data.

MEAL publishes regularly *Selected Product Group Reports* and also *Special Reports,* relating to 350 product groups which, in turn, are classified by 22 categories:

A   Agricultural and horticultural
B   Charity, educational and societies
C   Drink
D   Entertainment
E   Financial
F   Food
G   Government, development corporations and service recruitment
H   Holidays travel and transport
J   Household appliances
K   Household equipment
L   Household stores
M   Institutional and industrial
N   Leisure equipment
P   Motors
Q   Office equipment
R   Pharmaceutical
S   Publishing
T   Retail and mail order
U   Tobacco
V   Toiletries and cosmetics
W   Wearing apparel
X   Local advertisers

There are various regular services relating to these product groups and categories:

1   Advertisement analysis   This detailed description of advertising in a product group is a record of each advertisement placed in the media covered during the month. Every advertisement is listed in detail by date within medium within product. The details given for each advertisement are:
1   Date.
2   Duration or size.
3   Station or publication.
4   Rate card cost.

5   Whether it is a range advertisement (in which case the cost is divided equally between the products in the range).
6   Whether it is a co-operative advertisement (in which case the total cost is given to the prime advertiser, but the secondary advertiser is listed).
7   Whether it is a dealer advertisement.
In addition, the total expenditure and the sub-total for press and television are shown for each brand.

2   Brand advertising by media group (press)   The purpose of this report is to show the allocation of a brand's expenditure over the various media groups when the main interest is in the press. The report shows the distribution of a brand's expenditure on television and across the major press media groups:
1   Popular dailies
2   Popular Sundays
3   Quality dailies
4   Quality Sundays
5   London evenings
6   Weekend magazines
7   Provincial mornings and Sundays
8   General weeklies
9   Women's weeklies
10   Women's monthlies
11   General monthlies
12   Juvenile and special interest magazines
   For each brand in the product group the expenditure is shown in £'000s. In addition, the total expenditure is shown in two profile forms: first, total expenditure between television and total press and, secondly, expenditure in each of the press media groups as a percentage of total press expenditure.

3   Brand advertising by media group (television)   This report gives a detailed analysis of expenditure in television and total expenditure in the press. For each brand, information is given on:
1   Expenditure in total for both press and television for the previous month and the last twelve months.
2   Expenditure with each TV contractor.
3   The percentage profile, where expenditure on each station is percentaged on the total television expenditure.

4   Brand advertising by selected titles   MEAL also provides a flexible tabulation service to meet individual requirements. There are the following options when specifying an analysis:
1   Up to 17 columns may be specified and each of these may

be an individual publication or television contractor, e.g. Southern TV, London *Evening Standard*, Bournemouth *Evening Echo*, or a combination of media, e.g. large TV contractors, colour supplements, popular daily newspapers. The specified media may be taken from any of those which are regularly monitored.

2   The expenditure information shown for each brand may be either monthly or quarterly together with either year to date or moving annual total.

3   The percentage profiling of expenditure across the specified media is completely flexible, and may be produced with sub-totals profiled on the grand total; individual media profiled on the sub-total or the grand total, etc.

5   Brand advertising by area   This report shows the allocation of brand expenditure by area for television and press together with total expenditure. This provides marketing management with the amount of advertising pressure being applied in each area.

The areas are defined by TV regions and the allocation of press expenditure is according to the JICNARS readership profiles. In the case of publications not covered by JICNARS, the expenditure is allocated in line with the population.

The report shows the profile for television, press and total, both for the latest month and the last twelve months.

6   Microfilmed advertisement service   Copies of advertisements cut from a selection of publications are coded into the MEAL product groups and microfilmed. For the product group selected by the client, reproductions of the advertisements are sent each month (supplied on A4 paper in a loose-leaf folder) thus providing a continuous flow of information on the advertising strategy of competitive brands. The microfilm library has been maintained since 1969 and can also meet *ad hoc* requests for complete product groups or individual brands.

7   Other reports   MEAL also publishes a quarterly digest showing the advertising expenditure of individual brands in total for the latest quarter, each month in the quarter and the last twelve months. All brands spending at least £1500 per month on average, during the last twelve months, are included. If a brand's expenditure is below this threshold it is reported as part of the expenditure of 'Other Brands'.

London Link

This service, added fairly recently, is a monitor of advertising in the main London media for the period September, October, November. MEAL regularly monitors brand expenditures for some of the media that cover the ITV area such as the evening papers and television contractors. In addition, London Link includes brand expenditure results for the two commercial radio stations, a sample of 40 weekly papers, regional magazines and increased coverage of the five regional daily papers. The media included are:

London Weekend Television and Thames Television
Evening News and *Evening Standard*
Capital Radio and London Broadcasting Company
Southern editions of the national daily papers
Southern editions of the national Sunday papers
London editions of the programme weeklies and the *Observer Magazine*
Five regional daily papers
A sample of 40 weekly papers
Selected regional magazines

London Link provides results for brands, product groups, categories and in total for all 350 MEAL product groups. Reports are available to give expenditure in individual months or in total for the period. There are two main types of report:

The Brand Expenditure by Selected London Media Report gives summaries of spending in the month across the main media groups and titles in the area. The purpose of the report is to show the allocation of a brand's expenditure across various London media. Brand information is shown in £'000s for expenditure during the month and the previous twelve months for the media that are regularly monitored. Total expenditure is given for the main media with sub-totals for each media group. Spending in each medium or title is shown as a percentage of the total in the area. The *Brand Expenditure by Selected London Media Report* is available for individual product groups or categories. The complete report for all 350 MEAL product groups is available as a printed volume.

The Advertisement Analysis is a detailed description of advertising of individual brands in each product group. It is a record of each advertisement placed in the media covered during the month. Every advertisement is listed by date within medium and product group. The analysis shows the date of appearance, duration or size, station or publication and the rate card cost of the advertisement. In addition to total expenditure, the sub-totals for press and broadcast media are shown for each brand. The *Advertisement Analysis* is available for individual product groups or categories. The complete report for all 350 MEAL product groups is available on microfiche.

Other summary analyses by product group and categories are also available in various forms.

Special reports

In addition to its regular services, MEAL also produces major special reports on, for example, ten-year trends in product group expenditure information in total, in the press and on television for each of ten consecutive years, summarised with all information shown in £'000s. Another special report covers top spenders and shows the main results of brands spending £250,000 or more and the top agencies, giving all brands spending more than £750,000 in rank order based on total expenditure, the split between television and press for each of these brands, a rank order for the top 500 compared with previous years, the top 50 agencies based on total expenditure, the split between television and press for each of these agencies and the top 50 MEAL product groups based on total expenditure with a press and television split.

PAB (Poster Audit Bureau)
(Tower House, Southampton Street, London WC2E 7HN)

PAB was established 'to bring the poster medium into line with other media by making itself accountable to advertisers in terms of demonstrating that the poster is in the *right place* at the *right time* and in *good condition'*. Accordingly, it audits the posting of campaigns and monitors the poster panels for condition.

PAB was launched in November 1976 and responsibility for policy decisions is taken by the Users' Council, which represents the Incorporated Society of British Advertisers, the Institute of Practitioners in Advertising and the poster contractors. This arrangement is not dissimilar to the other media with Joint Industry Committees. PAB differs from the other industry committees, however, in that its information is of value retrospectively, ensuring that you have received full value for money, rather than providing audience research data on which to base your future planning.

The poster sites included in PAB's inspection are owned by members of either the Solus Outdoor Advertising Association or the British Poster Advertising Association. Campaigns of up to four months are automatically included in the inspection service, which is also available to advertisers with campaigns of more than four months and TC (till countermanded) contracts.

The details required by PAB are the campaign in-charge dates, the advertiser and brand description, and a description of the copy. Normally there are two inspections per month and approximately one third of the campaigns will be inspected on each occasion.

PAB maintains a master file of poster sites, on which addresses are automatically clustered in contiguous groups of an average of 50 addresses, for economical and efficient inspection. PAB audits one third of all qualifying sites on each audit. When PAB was launched, it was anticipated that about 5 per cent of sites (rural ones) would be excluded from auditing, for reasons of efficiency and economy. In practice, of the addresses on the master file, less than 0.25 per cent are excluded.

The administration of PAB is the sole responsibility of NOP Market Research Ltd. PAB results show the date of check, the number of units checked, whether these were the correct design and whether they were 'acceptable' (posted with the correct design and in good condition) or 'routine damage' (which can be repaired in the normal course of business procedures) or 'urgent damage' (which requires immediate attention). The definition of damaged used by PAB auditors is 'any damage which spoils the pack, the brand name, or any part of the wording means that the poster is unacceptable'.

RNAB (Regional Newspaper Advertising Bureau)

The decision to form a Regional Newspaper Advertising Bureau by merging the two existing bureaux, ENAB and WNAB (see separate entries) was taken in December 1979, when the members gave both boards an overwhelming majority to go ahead. One argument in favour of such a merger is that many publishers own evening newspapers as well as weeklies, and therefore belonged to both ENAB and WNAB. Long-term plans envisage that morning and Sunday newspapers outside London, not currently catered for by the two existing bureaux, will be invited to join.

The aims of the Regional Newspaper Advertising Bureau can be summed up as to capitalise on the opportunities to promote the regional press as an entity, and in individual markets, to national clients and advertising agencies, and thus secure a larger slice of national advertising business than at present.

From 1 April 1980 RNAB has operated temporarily from the ENAB address (see above), pending location of new premises.

SAA (Screen Advertising Association)
(127 Wardour Street, London W1V 4AD)

The SAA is the trade association of cinema advertising contractors in the UK and as such is devoted to developing and maintaining high standards of practice and presentation within the medium.

Its role is partly that of watchdog, acting to ensure that professional standards are maintained by the cinema advertising industry. One aspect of this work is that it is responsible for conducting regular checks to ensure that cinema advertising bookings are screened as scheduled, and under optimum conditions, i.e. prior to the main feature film, and with the house lights down. Another aspect of its watchdog role is vetting all commercials prior to screening — a matter discussed in more detail in Chapter 14.

The other major purpose of the SAA — hence its inclusion in this chapter — is to educate and inform, and in this role it aims to provide advertisers and agencies with up-to-date information about the cinema medium and the advertising advantages it has to offer.

Cinema admission statistics are collected and published by the Department of Industry, and information about cinema admissions is available from SAA under various headings: UK total admissions, admissions by cinema seating capacity, and admissions by Registrar General's Standard Regions. The SAA also provides information, based on JICNARS sources, regarding the cinema audience: audience composition, audience penetration, and cinema coverage — the coverage and frequency obtained by typical cinema campaigns. Also available, based on TGI sources (see below) are index figures of product usage by cinema-going frequency. The index figures, available for a range of product groups, give a quantitative measure of the value of the cinema audience for the product group or service in question. For example, an index of 130 means that cinema-goers are 1.30 times as likely to use a product than is the average person. Five index figures are available for each product group: all cinema-goers (those who ever go to the cinema), heavy cinema-goers (go more than once a month), medium cinema-goers (go once a month or every two or three months), light cinema-goers (go less than once in three months) and non cinema-goers (those who never go to the cinema).

TGI (Target Group Index)
(Saunders House, 53 The Mall, Ealing, London W5 3TE)

The Target Group Index is a national product and media survey produced by the BMRB (British Market Research Bureau) and available on subscription to advertisers, agencies and media-owners. The TGI is entirely owned by BMRB and, unlike the usual industry media surveys, e.g. the various JICs described above, there is no guaranteed long-term contract or indeed guaranteed income.

Some while ago a Subscribers' Committee was established consisting of top marketing and media practitioners, to provide advice in all planning areas and to recommend new product categories and brands to be featured in the TGI. One of their more recent innovations was the publication of a *Mid-Term Marketing Report* which gives more up-to-date information on the faster-moving product fields in the middle of a current TGI year. More recently, the main Committee appointed a small Technical Working Party to discuss the more technical aspects of the TGI; this meets approximately six times a year.

TGI findings are based on 24,000 postal questionnaires received from informants who have been previously contacted by random location methods in 200 constituencies in Great Britain. TGI provides an up-to-date data base directly relating media and product usage.

TGI identifies heavy, medium and light users as well as non-users in a vast range of product categories and sub-categories. A full range of demographics and media usage is reported for these groups. TGI tables can explain who these people are, what they are like and what media vehicles are best to reach them.

The TGI product group information provides the foundation for assessing individual markets' major or potential users and their characteristics and media habits. It similarly provides information about brand usage, listing solus users (users of the product group who use a brand exclusively), major users (those who prefer it to another brand also used) and minor users (those who are more casual in their use). These definitions establish some element of brand loyalty and the degree of involvement that users have with a given brand.

TGI reports the users of thousands of brands. As with heavy to light users of product categories, demographics and media usage are reported for brand users. By using TGI, you know who your users are and what they read, watch and listen to. You also have the same information for your competitors.

For the appliance and durables category, TGI provides a further measurement — that of the decision-maker — which establishes who made the decision and if the decision was made alone or with someone else.

The TGI measures the following product and media habits of the population:

Products   Heavy-to-light usage for over 2500 brands in more than 200 fast-moving consumer product fields. Additionally, usage of over 150 other 'brands' are covered in the field of banking, building societies, airlines, holidays, cars, grocery and other retail outlets, etc. Brands with more than a million claimed users are broken down demographically and by media.

Media   Audiences to 128 newspapers and magazines, weight of ITV viewing and hourly viewing behaviour for television, weight of listening to commercial radio and exposure to outdoor media and the cinema. The TGI is designed to be complementary to JICNARS, the industry's readership survey. The levels of readership are, wherever possible, weighted to equal the NRS readership figures for the calendar year prior to publication. Depending upon the relative importance of men or women in the readership, TGI readership levels may be weighted so as to reconcile with the NRS for men only, for women only, or for both.

Characteristics   The full range of standard demographics including social grades, household income, together with special breakdowns such as terminal education age, working status, home ownership, length of tenure in homes, size of household and marital status.

Another special breakdown recently added to the TGI range is ACORN (A Classification of Residential Neighbourhoods) which is increasingly used in special analysis. This classification of the types of neighbourhood in which people live can add a more meaningful dimension for marketing analysis and planning than the conventional socio-economic classification alone, since it provides a discriminator between life-styles, different patterns of expenditure and different levels of exposure to advertising media. To the marketing man and advertisers its importance lies in its ability to show clear life-style differences between neighbourhoods leading to many differences in consumer behaviour. Being area-based, ACORN leads to a more scientific answer to the marketing question *'Where* should I . . . ?'

The TGI reports

There are 34 separate TGI volumes summarising a vast amount of data. In outline, these cover:

Volumes	1–2	Demographics
	3–10	Food (virtually all packaged lines)

11–14	Household goods
15–16	Pharmaceuticals and chemist products
17–20	Toiletries and cosmetics
21–23	Drink (alcoholic and soft drinks)
24–25	Confectionary
26	Tobacco
27	Motoring (cars and accessories)
28–29	Clothing and shopping
30	Leisure
31	Holidays and travel
32	Financial services
33–34	Consumer durables and appliances

Whilst media-owners who are featured in the TGI buy the entire set of volumes, it is possible for advertisers and advertising agencies to buy individual volumes or even to buy separate product fields.

TGI is a 'single source' measurement and all elements of the survey can be cross-referenced, e.g. media usage relating to product usage, brand usage relating to audience or demographics. BMRB has its own computer terminal facilities for conducting any special analyses on behalf of TGI subscribers. Alternatively, should you require direct contact with a computer bureau, there are four companies which offer post-survey analysis on the TGI. Understandably, access to the tapes is only permitted to those who have purchased the relevant TGI volumes.

WNAB (Weekly Newspaper Advertising Bureau)
(Suite 401, Steinway Hall, 1 & 2 St. George Street, London W1R 9DG)

WNAB was formed in 1966 to provide a central promotional function for the regional weekly press. The Bureau is their national voice and has grown steadily and now has the majority of weekly newspaper publishers as members. It provides services not only for its members but also for advertisers and agencies.

The Bureau collects and disseminates all available information on the weekly press. Data is available both from published sources and surveys issued by its member newspapers. As a subscriber to the Target Group Index just discussed, the Bureau can provide advertisers with analyses of weekly newspaper coverage of consumers in particular areas cross-referenced by their purchasing habits over an exhaustive range of branded goods and services. Computer runs of TGI can also be commissioned: the basic volumes are available for study by any member, and computer analysis can be undertaken to assist members in their approaches to specific national advertisers. The Bureau also prepares Data Books based on the Standard Regions, giving basic information and detailed household coverage figures of local government areas by its member newspapers.

As regards the actual use of weekly newspapers, the Bureau enables the national advertiser to isolate specific weekly newspapers covering areas served by individual outlets. Any combination of outlets throughout Great Britain can be matched against appropriate newspapers. With inter-media planning, the Bureau assists advertisers and their agencies in weighing up national and regional campaigns in other media by the addition of weeklies.

The Bureau provides further services, one of which relates to dealer aid and which would thus be of interest to any whose campaigns feature co-operative advertising.

In conjunction with the Evening Newspaper Advertising Bureau, this dealer aid service gives members sales leads from national advertisers: many of these leads are unknown to local retailers. The Bureau's member newspapers are regularly informed of advertising support schemes mounted by national and regional advertisers, thus helping to ensure that retailers are kept aware of the advertiser's plans by the newspapers.

The Bureau also offers advertisers and agencies assistance in drawing up schedules of weekly newspapers against a marketing brief, to provide coverage of particular areas, of towns with particular characteristics, or to match particular sales patterns. The Bureau also offers its members a planned advertising system of helping retailers set their budgets and plan their advertising to maximise results.

Note: see separate entry for RNAB above, regarding WNAB's merger with the Evening Newspaper Advertising Bureau.

Other sources

There are other useful sources of media information, in addition to those already mentioned. Some are covered later in Chapter 8, which is devoted to the specialist services available, and necessarily overlaps with this chapter since various of the organisations just described make available services additional to the basic ones mentioned. Other data sources belong more rightly in this chapter.

Media-owners' research information

As a means of making valuable information available to potential advertisers and also to assist current advertisers in producing more effective media schedules, many media-owners subscribe to various research and other services (see Chapter 8).

Some media-owners also commission their own research: examples are Mirror Group Newspapers *Household Readership, Income and Consumption* studies and, more recently, its *TGI Volumetrics,* an annual report giving special analyses of BMRB's TGI data showing market shares accounted for by different demographic and readership groups.

It is rare for a media-owner to undertake research to disprove the information provided centrally, although such action might be taken if he considered the findings presented an unfair picture of his medium. More usually, media-owners seek to provide additional information which might persuade advertisers and agencies to view their medium favourably.

Media-owner's own surveys can provide much useful information and often venture into fields untouched by central research. As examples, media-owners have undertaken research into the effect of advertisement size in relation to page size, into the effect of advertising on retailers, and into page traffic and the 'life' of advertisements in publications which are kept for reference rather than read and thrown away.

Media-owners who are not, for some reason or other, included in the central reports may commission research to provide comparable information to permit their medium being assessed on the same basis. Where no central research exists, media-owners may have no choice but to provide details of their medium's coverage and to undertake research to obtain this information.

Media-owners' information activities are many and varied, and this aspect of the media-owner's work is discussed again in the later chapter devoted to 'The Media-Owner'.

A major difference between central research and media-owner's own information is that whereas the former is provided on a regular basis, media-owners undertake research activities often on a more *ad hoc* basis, from time to time whenever they wish to prove a point about their medium. Another difference is that, somewhat understandably, advertisers and agencies are likely to suspect it of being biased in favour of the medium sponsoring it. In this respect it is worth noting that the Research Committee of the Institute of Practitioners in Advertising provides a service for member agencies in appraising such published surveys and sends out its report in the form of an appraisals bulletin. The IPA also welcomes advance consultation in regard to any surveys proposed by media-owners.

Some media-owners undertake a great deal and do so frequently, whereas others provide very little information. This makes it difficult to include within this book any formal list of the additional research information available from this source. Nevertheless, any executive concerned with the effective use of media should be aware that some extremely valuable research has been undertaken and should certainly check out this source of information.

Agency- and client-sponsored research

This field of research is comparable in many ways with media-sponsored research, in that it is aimed at providing additional information. It may suffer from the same drawbacks: failure to cover all the media in the group, or being carried out at irregular intervals. A further disadvantage (other than to those directly concerned) is that the information may not be freely available, which is understandable since the advertiser or agency incurred considerable research expense to gain a competitive advantage. Such research is, in fact, a business investment and is rightly regarded as confidential information.

Other information sources

In addition to the wealth of useful information contained in reference publications, relevant 'news' information and articles of interest are featured in the editorial columns of various publications (those asterisked should be considered as essential reading). In alphabetical order, those most relevant to our field are:

* *Admap* Published monthly by Admap Publications of 44 Earlham Street, London WC2H 9LA.

Advertising A quarterly review published by the Advertising Association of Abford House, 15 Wilton Road, London SW1V 1NJ, in conjunction with the CAM Foundation and the Institute of Practitioners in Advertising.

Advertising and Marketing incorporating *Industrial Advertising and Marketing,* published quarterly by Business Publications of 117 Waterloo Road, London SE1.

Advertising Age — Europe, published monthly by *Advertising Age.* UK contact is Bill Carnahan, Room 411, International Press Centre, 47 Shoe Lane, London EC4A 3JB.

* *Campaign,* published weekly by Haymarket Publications of 22 Lancaster Gate, London W2 3LY.

Marketing   This weekly magazine succeeded two earlier Haymarket Publications — the monthly *Marketing* and the weekly *Marketfact*. It is circulated to defined classifications of marketing personnel responsible for significant levels of MEAL-monitored expenditure, as well as to Institute of Marketing members.

Marketing Week, published by Michael Chamberlain of 60 Kingly Street, London W1R 5LY.

Media International   A monthly international advertising and marketing magazine, published by Alan Charles Publishing Ltd. The Editorial and Head Sales Office is at 27 Wilfred Street, London SW1E 6PR.

  * *Media World*   A monthly magazine published by Media World Ltd of 111/113 Temple Chambers, Temple Avenue, London EC4Y 0DT. A regular copy is available free of charge to anyone who is directly responsible for the planning, buying, selling and researching of consumer media with an advertiser, media-owner or advertising agency. Those not meeting these requirements may receive a regular copy on subscription.

Other publications   It would be wrong to leave this section without reference to the fact that some media-owners and trade and professional bodies have their own publications which they use to communicate items of interest and that, in addition to these special interest publications, articles of specific interest appear from time to time in a host of other publications, both newspapers and magazines.

Books   There are, of course, a host of books of immediate advertising and marketing interest. Two must be singled out, however, for their immediate practical application to the effective use of media. These are:
  * *Media Planning* by James Adams, published by Business Books.
  * *Spending Advertising Money* by Simon Broadbent, published by Business Books.

Reference works   There are also various reference books that can assist you in making effective use of advertising media. These include:
  Advertiser's Annual (Kelly's Directories)
  Benn's Press Directory (Benn Publications)
  Willing's Press Guide (Skinner Directories)

Activities   There are also various conferences and courses at which useful information and details of new developments can be gained. Mention should be made here of the workshops and seminars of *Admap, Campaign* and *Media World*, the ESOMAR (European Society for Opinion and Marketing Research) Seminar on 'Media Management and Media Choice: ten years of progress ... or stagnation', the meetings of the Media Circle and the Media Research Group, the conferences and activities of our own trade organisations and professional bodies, the Media Industry and Media Business Courses organised by the CAM Education Foundation, and other events, including a wide range of seminars and short courses of media interest, run by colleges, institutes and commercial organisations.

3

MEDIA EVALUATION — CRITERIA FOR COMPARISON

To use media to full advantage, it is clearly essential to evaluate them to select those most suitable, and many criteria exist by which you can compare one medium with another. There are various factors you must take into account when making decisions. Part 3 will review criteria for evaluating complete advertising schedules, but this chapter looks first at how you can compare individual media. These factors can vary in priority according to each advertiser's marketing objective and so, in reviewing them below, they are not necessarily in your order of importance.

Who will your advertising message reach ?

One major consideration is the market covered by the medium in question. Market investigations have a high priority in the work of advertiser and agency alike, both of whom will make a straight cross-check between the market covered by the medium and the market they wish to reach. Clearly the closer the approximation, the more effective the medium.

The term used here is *demographics,* commonly defined as a means of analysing an audience by sex, age and social status or other classifications. Information about age is usually given in fairly broad groupings, e.g. 15—24, 25—34 and so on. The social grades commonly used are those pioneered in the National Readership Surveys and are normally based on the occupation of the head of the household. There are six such grades:

Social grade	*Social status*	*Head of Household's occupation*
A	Upper middle class	Higher managerial, administrative or professional

B	Middle class	Intermediate managerial, administrative or professional
C1	Lower middle class	Supervisory or clerical and junior managerial, administrative or professional
C2	Skilled working class	Skilled manual workers
D	Working class	Semi and unskilled manual workers
E	Those at lowest levels of subsistence	State pensioners or widows (no other earner), casual or lowest grade workers

Many of the data sources described in Chapter 2 include a wide range of other demographic classifications (such as terminal education age, or ownership of consumer durables) but in some cases, e.g. with industrial or technical products, your interest may be in the job description of the people your advertising message will reach, the industry in which they are employed, or their special interests, rather than their personal attributes. In other instances, your interest may be in product-related data. Are they heavy or light users of your product? Or in their attitudes. Are they conservative in their buying habits, or are they likely to respond favourably to new products? Are they in need of your product and *ready* to buy? Whatever the categories, the fundamental question is a basic one. Who do you wish to reach, and to whom will the medium in question deliver your advertising message?

Where?

This cross-checking procedure applies equally to geographical location, since this aspect of the media audience is just as important as its composition. This information may be available in terms of the Registrar-General's Standard Regions, or perhaps by television area. Marketing areas vary, and there must be strong correlation between your own marketing area and the area to which the medium would deliver your advertising message. For local advertisers the two areas should coincide as closely as possible. Even so-called 'national' media vary in intensity of coverage across the country and you should clearly take account of these variations.

How many?

In evaluating media you need to know not only the composition and location of the media audience covered but also its size, together with the number of individuals in each of the various categories. How many of each type and in each area? Breakdowns may be required for several categories simultaneously, to show how many people of a given sex, age and socio-economic group receive your advertising message within a defined area.

There may be different stages of answer to this 'how many?' question. With press media, for example, you may have at your disposal circulation figures and also readership — but much depends on definitions and research methods. To illustrate this point, contrast the differences in the data available about television audiences and press readership.

For television advertising, measurements can be made at the time of transmission, and numbers may be quoted to you in terms of TVRs or Television Rating Points. A television rating is the percentage of ITV homes tuned to a particular transmission and can apply to any time period such as one minute, a quarter of an hour or a rate card segment, and also to individual commercials, to commercial breaks or to programmes. TVRs may also be expressed in terms of individuals viewing rather than homes with sets switched on, so that 1 TVR represents 1 per cent of the potential TV audience. A person who is in the same room as an operating television set for 8 out of 15 minutes is counted as a viewer for that particular quarter of an hour. You should note that the 'viewer' does not have to be present for the full 15 minutes, and that the term 'in the same room' covers anything from attentive watching to a casual glance while undertaking some other activity.

With press media, by way of contrast, advertising contact can be made over a considerable period, and the definition of a 'reader' is equally important. With the National Readership Surveys, a key concept is the *issue period*. Average readership is the number of people who claim to have read or looked at one or more copies of a given publication during a period dating back from the date of interviewing equal to the interval at which the publication appears — a daily newspaper is thus held to have an issue period of one day, a weekly publication has an issue period of seven days, a monthly publication between 28 and 31 days and so on.

You should note that the term 'reading or looking' covers anything from thorough reading to a casual flip through, and that it does not matter *which* issue — any issue will do. Readership may also be affected by other problems of definition:

(a) Parallel readership   This refers to people who read more than one issue within the issue period prior to interview. No matter how many back issues had been read, it would still be counted as reading one issue, and average issue readership would thus tend to be deflated.

(b) Replication   This refers to the re-reading of old issues (perhaps 'specials' which may have been kept for reference) by people who may have actually seen later issues. This would inflate average issue readership, since it does not truly represent additional readers.

You should also bear in mind that any figures are necessarily dated in themselves: readership surveys, for example, are 6–12 months old before new data is published. This, ironically, benefits media in decline (unless you arbitrarily reduce readership pro-rata according to the latest available circulation figures which, for national newspapers and consumer magazines, are published with greater frequency). When considering the number of people your advertising message will reach, you should therefore always remember that, whilst numbers are important, the research methods which produce them are by no means perfect. This statement is not made with a fault-finding attitude, but simply to set matters in context. Furthermore, it is always comforting to reflect that in many countries of the world even authentic circulation figures are not available, let alone readership (or viewing or listening) figures. Under such circumstances, we must be grateful for the wealth of data at our disposal, and not cavill at any minor imperfections. Furthermore, we should remember that with television and press the research needed to provide such information is well established but, as Chapter 2 made clear, with a number of other media you will not have all the data you need.

Penetration versus profile

In discussing the number of people your advertising message reaches, you need to know the degree of penetration or coverage represented by the number reached. In simplest terms, penetration means the *proportion* of the total market covered. If you seek to reach housewives, for example, it will interest you to know that by using a certain medium you can reach 20 per cent, 50 per cent, or some other proportion of *all* housewives.

Later, when considering advertising planning, we will consider the coverage achieved by a full media schedule but within this chapter the term 'penetration' is restricted to the proportion of the total market to which any given medium will deliver your advertising message.

A medium's 'profile' typifies the categories of people reached. Profiles differ from penetration in always adding up to 100 per cent. A simple example which illustrates the difference between the two terms is that of women's magazines. A women's magazine read by half the women in the country has a 50 per cent penetration. If you look at the magazine's profile, however, this will be 100 per cent women. (In point of fact, the profile might well be 95 per cent women and 5 per cent men, since even women's magazines have some male readers). This is of course an oversimplification since profile information may be broken down into numerous different age-group, area or product usage categories but, however many sub-groups are detailed, the total profile always adds up to 100 per cent.

Wastage

It is unlikely that any advertising medium will give you perfect coverage of your market. Some potential purchasers will not be covered and so you will not achieve 100 per cent penetration. Equally, some of the people you *do* reach will not be in the market for your product. Since you nevertheless have to pay a charge based on the medium's total circulation, readership or viewership, you will clearly want to assess what proportion of its audience is likely to constitute less valuable coverage. Such considerations will clearly influence your choice of media, but should not lead you to under-value that part of the total coverage which *is* of your target group. If coverage of the people you want to reach is properly evaluated, then coverage of others can be a bonus rather than 'wastage'.

Mood

Your prospective customer's state of mind when receiving your advertising message can directly enhance or weaken your campaign effectiveness, so this consideration should be well to the fore when you contrast the media available to you. In this respect you should distinguish between media where advertising is an intrusive element and others where it is acceptable or, better still, has positive interest value. By advertising in women's publications, for example, your advertising message will reach women — the 'Who?' question tells you this — but you know that it will reach women when they are in a receptive state of mind. They will be relaxed and seeking information about homes, beauty, fashion or food, and thus receptive to advertising messages about merchandise in these product fields. Special interest publications similarly offer you the double benefit of reaching a selected group of likely purchasers and of delivering your message when they are in a receptive mood, and the same is true of many exhibitions. This principle can be extended to specific positions within a medium: an advertisement on the gardening page of a newspaper selects gardeners out of the total readership and delivers the advertising message when they are mentally 'tuned in' to the subject of gardening.

In that editorial reflects readers' interests, any advertiser is advised to check previous issues to see how frequently there has been editorial relating to his particular product area, since this should give a further indication of whether readers are likely to be in the market for his product.

A medium's editorial content may influence mood in another way by lending an atmosphere of authority or expert knowledge of a subject, with consequent benefit to the advertiser and his product.

In preparing advertising campaigns, many people make the mistake of concentrating on their own activities, rather than thinking in terms of their potential buyers. An extension of the mood question can place the emphasis where it should be — on the consumer. Rather than asking 'What will my advertisement do to people?' you should ask 'What will people do to my advertisement?' The answer to this question depends not only on the creativity of your advertising campaign (which is of course beyond the immediate scope of this book) but, equally, on the state of mind they are in when they receive your advertising message. This question thus links back with the 'who?' question — if a medium reaches people ready to buy your product, and delivers your advertising message when they are likely to respond favourably to it, the medium is likely to be highly effective.

The extreme example is advertising in certain directories or works of reference, the very nature of which indicates that those people consulting them are not only potential customers but are in the market *now* and thus ready and eager to buy — why else should they be consulting the directory?

When?

Timing your advertising message is a vital consideration. For some advertisers this is a question of seasons: promoting summer goods in the summer and winter goods in the winter. Others may need to be more precise, and deliver their advertising messages on a given day of the week. Some media, such as point-of-sale displays, deliver your message seconds before the purchase is made. Again, this is a straight cross-checking procedure — when is the most effective time for your advertising message to be received, and when will the various media deliver it?

Frequency

A second aspect of timing concerns repetition: the regularity with which your advertising message can be delivered. Some media permit you to stimulate your market only once a month, while others enable you to give weekly or even daily reminders. Consumer-buying habits — day and frequency of repeat purchases — thus directly influence your use of media.

Speed

A third aspect of timing relates to speed of operation rather than when and how often your advertising message is delivered, since some media must receive advertising material far in advance of publication date. Should you need to deliver an urgent sales message such as a price reduction, you would choose the medium with the shortest copy date in order to make your announcement as speedily as possible. Similarly, if your future plans are subject to constant change, you might be averse to using media with long copy dates (perhaps months in advance of actual delivery of your advertising message) since this means you have to decide your message on a long-term basis, whereas immediate short-term considerations are of major importance. You might equally be wary of using media that demand notice of cancellation long in advance of publication date, and thus do not permit flexibility in planning.

Span of attention

The attention that prospective purchasers pay to your advertising must be considered from two aspects: the duration of your message and the amount of time for which it will receive attention.

Some advertising messages have a very brief existence: a 15-second television or radio commercial, for example, clearly cannot receive attention for more than 15 seconds and, once transmitted, the prospective purchaser cannot refer back to it (unless and until it is broadcast again). Newspaper and magazine advertisements exist for a longer period, and so can be studied at leisure.

Equally important is the amount of time prospective purchasers will devote to your advertisement. Posters exist 24 hours a day, seven days a week (even if they are not at work all that time) and thus have a longer life than most media. Nevertheless, your advertising message must be kept short, since posters are usually only glanced at by people hurrying past. Posters on stations or in buses and trains, where there is a 'captive audience', may be studied for longer periods.

These two aspects of attention must be considered from the communications standpoint, for brief duration is neither good nor bad until related to a specific advertising task. Hence, you must consider how much information you need to convey. Is your message brief enough for a 15-second commercial or poster, or do you need to convey details about prices and sizes and so on?

A balance must be struck between the amount of time needed to convey your message and the duration of interest the message will receive. The decision you reach has direct media implications.

Life

Some media repay their use within a very few days, while others give you full value for money only over a much longer period. From the advertisers' point of view this means you may receive results in one short burst or spread over weeks, months, or even years. Since this affects the period for which the market for your product is stimulated, the life of any medium is an important consideration. A television or radio commercial, for example, delivers its full impact at the time of transmission, whereas a magazine with extremely long life may go on bringing results until it literally falls to pieces. Here you should distinguish between publications that are read once and thrown away and those that are kept for reference.

The medium

A factor of prime importance in media selection is the means by which your advertising message is delivered. What form does it take — do people read it, watch it or listen to it? Television gives you the benefit of movement to demonstrate your product in use, together with sound in the form of music, and the human voice to speak the advertising message. Cinema advertisements, too, have movement and sound. Both can have the advantage of colour. Posters have colour and size but not movement. Most newspaper advertisements are printed in black and white. In magazines, colour is frequently available to attract attention and show your products in their natural colours as they appear on retailers' shelves. Colour availability is not enough in itself, however, for quality can vary considerably, and this will influence selection within the range of colour media.

Indirect influence

Some media bring results through their effect on important groups other than the main media audience. Such influence frequently bears on retailers, who stock and display merchandise in the belief that advertisements in a given medium will stimulate consumer demand from which they can profit. Manufacturers place tremendous importance on obtaining good distribution and display, and any medium that helps in achieving this has a marked advantage over others. The example most frequently quoted is television, which exerts a strong influence on retailers as well as the main media audience. Co-operative press campaigns, where your stockists' names and addresses are featured in advertisements, can be equally effective in influencing retailers. Where this is the case, you should clearly take account of it in reaching media decisions.

A quotation that illustrates the importance of this point is taken from a respondent who stated, as an important rule to follow in order to produce the best media plan:

● *in assessing consumer coverage, impact, etc., always bear in mind that trade impact is very important too.* (ad)

Availability

This heading in fact covers three criteria for media selection. One is fundamental and governed by the rules and regulations relating to certain media, which might categorise certain types of advertising as unacceptable. Products or services that are not acceptable for advertising on television, for example, include cigarettes and cigarette tobacco; matrimonial agencies and correspondence clubs; fortune tellers and the like; and undertakers or others associated with death or burial. Television as a medium is thus not available to such advertisers.

A second availability criterion that links with the question of *how* the medium will deliver your advertising messages, relates to creative scope and thus could be asked under either heading — what colours are available (specials or publisher's choice only)? More directly under this heading of availability, however, what precise sizes and positions does the media-owner accept? It is beyond the scope of this book to list all the standard transport sizes and positions, for example, or to detail the various sizes and positions available in newspapers and magazines, and you would of course want to study these when making a more detailed review of those media of interest to you. In making this review, the fundamental question is a simple one. What advertisement 'units' — or choice of units — must you think in terms of when preparing your creative proposals? To give an extreme example, there would be little point in preparing a campaign based on diagonal half-pages, only to find this size totally unacceptable when you attempt to make your bookings.

Clearly your creative proposals must be put in hand in a practical manner, in a form acceptable to media-owners. The range of units is considerable and most media-owners are keen to co-operate, so this need be no creative straightjacket. And it is always worth asking the media-owner if odd shapes will be accepted.

Thirdly, under this general criterion of availability, you will most certainly need to know what advertising spaces or positions are actually available. Should all the best positions be already booked, or only a limited number of transmissions available, you have little choice but to consider spending the balance in other media.

Reliability

How certain can you be that your advertising message will in fact be delivered? Any advertiser who has based his selling efforts on the belief that his market will be stimulated at a particular time will naturally be wary of any medium that omits his advertisement for some reason or other. Equally important, how reliable will the delivery *quality* be — in terms of, for example, colour?

Competitive activity

This overall heading covers various criteria for media selection. First, before booking with any medium it is advisable to check if rival manufacturers appear regularly, and in what sizes and positions and with what frequency.

Secondly, you should also consider the general weight of advertising, and in a publication carrying a vast amount of advertising you may think it necessary to book a larger advertisement or a special position, to ensure that your advertising message receives attention.

Thirdly, there is the matter of the company you will be keeping: the fact that a medium carries (or does *not* carry) well prepared advertisements for leading firms can, in itself, influence the mood of the media audience.

Facilities

The range of facilities offered by media is wide. However, they can all be grouped together under the general theme of what the media-owner will do in addition to delivering your advertising message.

Some magazines, for example, include reply-cards which readers use to obtain further information about the products advertised. One television contractor's rate-card, selected at random, featured telephone-answering and reply-handling facilities, supporting press advertisements, promotional 'trailers' to stimulate viewer action, a retail sales force available to help sell-in to stockists, a 'Merchandiser' circulated to grocers giving the trade advanced details of major advertising activity on TV, direct mail facilities for advertisers to promote their campaigns to distributors, sales conference assistance, research facilities and help with production of television commercials.

The provision of valuable research data by media has already been mentioned. This can extend to provision of computer runs and help with media scheduling. Less ambitious, but nonetheless vitally important, is the assistance given to inexperienced advertisers by media representatives in preparing and producing effective press advertisements.

Some of these facilities may be provided free as part of the media-owner's normal service, whilst there may be an 'at cost' charge for others. Such facilities can be most useful and you should most certainly check them out and use them as necessary. You should, however, beware of 'letting the tail wag the dog'. Media-owners, quite understandably, want repeat orders: hence the range of additional facilities to help you achieve a successful campaign. The prime reason for using any advertising medium is, however, to deliver your message and, in evaluating media, the answers to the questions listed above are of greater importance than any secondary facilities that the media-owner might offer. Of even greater importance is the answer to the next question.

Cost

The factor left until last, though it is of course a prime consideration in media selection, is cost. Much depends on the size of your appropriation, for some media call for large expenditures and may thus be out of the question for advertisers with small budgets. Cost is basically a straightforward question but nevertheless presents considerable problems in terms of booking unit, size, position, amount of advertising booked and other considerations discussed below.

Booking unit

The complication here is that advertising is sold in different units, making straight comparisons impossible. Newspapers, for example, are usually sold by the 'single column centimetre': one centimetre in one column costs £X and space is sold in multiples of this. A 20 cm X 2 cols advertisement simply means 20 centimetres taken in two adjacent columns, or 40 cm, and the cost of this advertisement is thus 40 times the basic unit cost. Similarly, a 25 cm X 4 cols advertisement is charged at 100 times the unit cost. Media planners often make cost comparisons of charges for the same-size advertisement in two publications, but a straight comparison is not possible. Even when advertisements in two media are the same size, they may appear in publications of different page sizes. It is known, for example, that an advertisement in a tabloid newspaper is more effective than in a broadsheet, because it is more dominant in the smaller page than the larger and will thus attract higher readership.

Research can overcome this problem, but comparison of media on a straight cost basis is still difficult to achieve, especially when the basic unit differs. Magazines, for example, are usually sold not by the single column centimetre, but by the page or fractions of a page: half-page, quarter-page, eighth-page, etc., whereas cinema and television and radio advertising is sold by time — 15, 30, 45 or 60 seconds and so on.

The problem of contrasting media that sell advertising in different units is further complicated by the fact that cost varies with three factors: size, position and amount of advertising booked.

Size

There are three basic advantages to large advertisements — more people see them, there is scope to include more information and better creative work, and the advertisements themselves usually have greater impact. The bigger your advertisement the higher the cost, but the complication arises that cost does not always vary in *direct* proportion to size, when calculated on the unit rate. Some media offer large advertisements at a 'bargain' rate to encourage you to take such sizes: other media, where larger sizes are in heavy demand, may charge higher premium rates so that, for example, a 25 cm X 5 cols advertisement costs more than 125 times the single-column centimetre rate. This is a straightforward matter of supply and demand for the media-owner, but for the advertiser and his agency it makes more complex the already difficult problem of comparing competitive media.

Position

The cost of an advertisement also depends on its position. An advertisement on the front page is seen by more people than one inside the publication: similarly, a 'solus' advertisement receives more attention than one that has to compete with other advertisements. A poster on a main road is seen by more people than one in a side street, and the same is true of a television commercial transmitted at peak viewing time rather than in the afternoon. Good position results in high coverage of the total potential audience and there is accordingly a higher charge, which advertisers try to evaluate in relation to what they are getting for their money.

Your advertisement's position affects not only the number but also the type of people who see it. An advertisement on the motoring page is more likely to be seen by motorists, and a similar argument applies to advertisements on sports pages, fashion pages, home hints pages and so on, which select likely customers for betting shops or football pools, fashion houses and food products. The editorial content of such pages also influences the mood of the media audience, who will be more receptive to the advertising message. With other media, position can equally well influence the type and mood of the media audience.

Size and position

Size and position may be fixed jointly by some media-owners, so that no choice is offered. The position on the front page of a newspaper, for example, may be guaranteed to be solus, but the publisher restricts it to a certain size and may, in effect, be offering a 20 cm X 2 cols front-page solus. Similarly, the publisher might offer a 25 cm X 2 cols, facing TV programme page. Both these advertisements would be charged at special rates, since they are important sizes and positions. With other media, the same reasoning may apply.

The effect of size and position

Size and composition of the media audience directly affect media selection, yet surprisingly there is, for some media, very little information available about the different audiences that will be reached by varying sizes and positions. The National Readership Surveys, for example, give only overall readership figures for publications. Common sense tells you that more people see large advertisements or a front-page solus, and that an advertisement on the women's page selects women out of the total readership, but this is by no means precise enough: you need to know exactly the size and composition of the audience you will achieve with a given advertisement on a certain page, rather than a general picture of the medium's readership.

Similarly, with television, you do not know what difference it will make to your audience if you have a 15 or 30 second or some other length of commercial, but the television audience surveys do indicate, on the other hand, both the size and composition of the media audience you are likely to achieve if your commercial is transmitted in a particular time segment. Similar information could be made generally available for press media, but some practitioners have questioned the research techniques used to measure page traffic and the effect of advertisement size and, in addition, there are the usual problems of agreeing, organising, supervising and — above all — financing such research.

Amount of advertising booked

Cost varies not only with size and position but also with a third factor — the total amount of advertising booked. This is because most media-owners, in order to encourage repeat bookings, offer some form of discount to advertisers who support them regularly.

Series orders bring direct advantage to the media-owner, since it is most helpful to know what bookings are in hand for future issues. Furthermore, there is a considerable economy in time, salary and selling expenses if, say, 12 orders are achieved through a single call instead of the representative having to make 12 separate calls to achieve the same results.

Newspapers and magazines frequently offer a 'series' discount if the booking is for a minimum number of insertions. There is a similar 'volume' discount for television, and other media usually decrease their rates as the size of the total booking increases. Media-owners may also offer 'package' deals through which you book, at an advantageous rate, a number of advertisements to be delivered within a given time period.

Special discounts

Cost varies with size, position and total booking, and most variations appear on published rate cards, but other types of discount may also be featured. A rate card selected at random included a 'first-time' discount to encourage new advertisers to use the medium, test market discounts, expenditure investment discounts, limited expenditure investment discounts, limited expenditure discounts, limited expenditure development discounts and cash-with-order rates.

These and many other variations may be featured on standard rate cards, which clearly merit detailed study.

From time to time, however, media-owners often find it expedient to extend other special offers to boost sales in otherwise slack periods. These offers are many and varied but divide into two basic groups — a discount offer to sell the same amount of advertising at a reduced charge, or alternatively a bonus offer of more advertising at no additional cost. These offers may be made known by special mailings and sometimes, when the offer applies for an extended period, special rate cards may be issued.

Furthermore, some or all of these offers may be linked with the third question raised above — how many? — in that the advertising offer is linked with a guaranteed minimum audience, as revealed by research. With television advertising, for example, you may encounter GHIs — Guaranteed Home Impressions — when the contractor guarantees to transmit a given number of impressions. This is defined as the gross number of homes receiving exposures. As these packages usually consist of more than one spot and many homes receive your commercial more than once, consequently the *net* coverage of homes is likely to be less.

Finally media-owners may find themselves called upon to negotiate special arrangements at top level, particularly where big advertising expenditures are involved. Basically, this amounts to hard bargaining between the media-owner and the advertiser or his agency, both sides seeking to conclude arrangements to their own best advantage. The advertiser and agency seek lower rates or, what amounts to the same thing, premium positions without paying a higher rate. The media-owner, naturally enough, seeks the maximum amount of revenue he can secure.

Cost and value for money

1 Cost per thousand Cost is frequently considered together with quantity, and one medium compared with another, by what is termed CPT or 'cost per thousand' — the cost of reaching each thousand of the target universe (homes, housewives, adults, etc). It is usually expressed in pence, and is used as a general yardstick of media cost and efficiency. Cost per thousand is calculated by dividing, for example, the single-column centimetre rate of a publication by its circulation. To illustrate this with simple hypothetical figures, a newspaper charging £1 per s.c.c. and with a circulation of 20,000 thus has a cost of £1.00/20 = 5p per thousand circulation. Another newspaper might charge £10 per s.c.c. and have 500,000 circulation and here the cost per thousand circulation is only 2p. The second paper costs more in outlay — £10 instead of £1 per s.c.c. — but the circulation is larger, and so in this respect you get more for your money.

The cost per thousand concept is frequently used in evaluating different media and is, therefore, one with which you must be thoroughly familiar. It is also perhaps the most misused: it can be treated as a precise measuring instrument but in many cases it is used much too loosely. To quote 'cost per thousand' is meaningless unless it is made clear just what is being measured. Before accepting any cost per thousand figure for one medium in comparison with its rivals, you should ask a very basic question — 'Cost of *what* per thousand *what*?' Costs per thousand are most frequently quoted per s.c.c. for newspapers (or per page for magazines) per thousand circulation, but very few advertisers are interested in total circulation, and few, if any, plan in terms of single-column centimetres. Their interest lies in the advertisement size required, and only that part of the total media audience likely to buy their product. For this reason, cost per thousand calculations are frequently extended to compare actual advertisement costs — the cost per thousand of a 20 cm X 2 cols insertion or of a solus position in one publication rather than another. Equally, it may be calculated not for circulation but for readership, or for readership of a particular category — cost per thousand housewife readers in the 16—24 age group and in a stated socio-economic category. Similarly, television cost per thousand is sometimes based on numbers of homes and the cost of a 30 second commercial: many advertisers, however, use commercials of a different length and calculate cost per thousand on the composition of the audience, rather than the number of sets switched on.

2   *Weighted values*   Cost per thousand calculations are useful in comparing one medium with another as regards value for money in terms of the audience numbers you are likely to reach, but the approach is sometimes extended to allow for subjective as well as statistical values, through including 'media weights' in your calculations. A media weight is necessarily subjective and reflects the importance you place on intangible factors. If you think colour or high-quality printing of particular importance to your advertising, or feel that the mood of the potential customer receiving your message through a magazine is of greater or lesser value in comparison with the same message received through a newspaper, you may wish to allow for this in your calculations since this would provide a more relevant measure of cost effectiveness than cost per thousand alone.

The concept to be used under such circumstances is called Valued Impressions per Pound, or VIPs:

VIP = (Media audience x Media weight)/Cost

The media weight is the value you place on intangible factors such as colour, expressed in numerical terms.

Quite apart from allowing for subjective views as well as statistical information, there is another important difference between VIPs and cost per thousand. One calculation is the inverse of the other, i.e. the *higher* the VIP index then the *more efficient* the medium, whereas with cost per thousand calculations you seek the lowest possible figure. The two different methods, nevertheless, have the same underlying aim — they are simply alternative methods you can use in assessing value for money.

Production costs

Another factor that indirectly affects media planning is production costs, as distinct from the charges levied by media-owners. With some media, production costs constitute only a small proportion of total costs, while in others they are important enough to demand major consideration. In some cases, such as direct mail or display material, production charges are of course inseparable from media costs.

4

SUMMARY AND QUOTATIONS

Chapter 1 outlined the wide range of media available to deliver your advertising messages; Chapter 2 reviewed the data sources from which you can obtain information about these media; and Chapter 3 explained the criteria by which you can compare them:

Who will your advertising message reach?
Where are these individuals located?
How many will receive your message, in total and in each category?
What penetration will you achieve, and what is the *profile* of the media audience?
How much *wastage* is involved?
What will be the *mood* of the media audience, when they receive your message?
When will it be delivered?
With what *frequency* can you contact potential purchasers?
How quickly does the medium operate, and how far in advance must you decide your advertising message?
What *attention* will your message receive?
What is the *life* of the medium?
How will your message be delivered?
What *indirect influences* does it have?
What advertisement sizes and positions are *available* on the rate card and in actual practice?
How *reliable* is the medium?
What *weight of advertising* is carried, generally and for rival brands in particular?
What additional *facilities* are offered?
What is the *cost* of using the medium, when related to size and position of advertisement and overall extent of booking, and how does it compare with others in terms of value for money, as distinct from total outlay?

Clearly there can be no such thing as the 'best' medium. The benefits offered by the various media must be contrasted with the requirement of your advertising task. All advertising media have their various advantages and drawbacks and any medium, or combination of media, could be 'best' in certain circumstances, depending on the objective. The various objectives which might underlie your advertising campaign, and the construction of an effective media schedule to achieve your chosen objective, will be discussed in Part 3. What is certain, however, is that to evaluate the various possible media against your advertising objectives, you must have the facts and figures about them at your fingertips, you must understand this data and you must be able to use it properly. The vital importance of a thorough knowledge of media and media data can best be illustrated by the following quotations, which appeared on respondents' forms as replies to the question 'What, in your opinion, are the most important rules that should be followed in order to produce the best media plan?'

Knowledge of media

Many respondents stressed the need for knowledge of media: comments made included

● *detailed knowledge of all available media forms* (ag)

This is very general, however. *What* should you know about media, if you are to use them effectively? Many commented on the need to understand media as such.

● *appreciate how your advertisement will project in a given medium* (ad)

● *planner/buyer should study the contents of the media in greater depth to understand why the consumer likes them — he will then be better able to use these vehicles for his client* (ag)

● *a deeper understanding of how media work. A clearer knowledge of the way the media operate in the communications industry and the purpose they fulfil* (m-o)

Knowledge of media research available

Others were concerned about the data available — or lack of it — rather than the media themselves. What they felt essential was:

- *availability of suitable media appraisal such as readership breakdowns etc* (ad)
- *usage of audited and authentic medium/market research* (ag)
- *stress the use of valid and up-to-date media research* (m-o)

This last quotation raises two further points — keeping up-to-date and the use you make of the data.

Keeping up-to-date

Not only do media statistics change as new data is published but the media themselves change — keeping yourself up-to-date under these circumstances is no small task. It is no wonder that a media-owner suggested that:

- *Everybody in every agency plus those to whom it is relevant at the clients' should see a presentation from every media no less than once a year, and definitely not all on the same day* (m-o)

The use made of research

Having up-to-date information is one thing — using it correctly is another. The correct use of research data arose mainly as a negative one, in comments on practices to be avoided. These included the following:

- *lack of understanding of media research data* (ad)
- *failure to evaluate available research data* (ag)
- *insufficient study made of media-owners' research, especially as regards the market covered* (m-o)

One media-owner went even further: in his opinion

- *there is a great deal of inexperience in the use of media data and a good deal of blinkered thinking. As agencies have become more creatively oriented, my experience is that the standard of media planning in the press area primarily has declined drastically since the early 1950s* (m-o)

If this is true, hoefully this book will help reverse the trend.

Quality of research

The quotations above stressed the use of *valid* or *audited* or *authentic* research. This clearly implies that some research is not valid, audited or authentic as it should be. Some respondents questioned, in varying degrees, the *quality* of the research available. One respondent, with strong views, suggested that there should be

● *sanctions on those who mislead in their data (circulation, standing with readers, etc.)* (ad)

Others commented on

● *lack of circulation information from media in comparable terms* (ag)

● *inadequacies of media information (reliable) on readership* (ag)

● *poor media research and old-fashioned socio/economic stratification of population* (ag)

The queries about research quality came mostly from advertisers and agencies, but media-owners also had reservations: one media-owner passed the ball straight back when he suggested that:

● *if advertisers targeted their markets more exactly, i.e. not bland ABC1s, then media would make available more qualitative research to enable advertisers to understand readers/viewers better* (m-o)

Chapter 9 covers research and investigations, including the various ways in which you may analyse your market, so we will revert to this important matter later in the book. The message, at this stage, is nevertheless clear

● *the need to match media and market.* (ad)

The practical application of research

The final quotation selected to end this Part appeared under the heading of comments on other matters which respondents considered important for the effective use of advertising media:

● *information about coverage, circulation, reader status, duplication and competitive activity is vital in arriving at correct media decisions and are as important as a clear understanding of the potential market for the product and of the advertiser's marketing policy* (ag)

This quotation provides an ideal link with the next part of the book — The Organisation of Media — which examines not only the advertisers, but also their agencies as well as the media-owners.

Part 2

THE ORGANISATION OF MEDIA

Having considered the range of media, this Part turns attention to those organisations and individuals responsible for their use. I have made clear my view that you cannot separate media planning principles from the people applying them or the firms in which they work: the first chapter in this Part therefore covers the media-owners and subsequent chapters concentrate on the advertisers and their agencies.

Each chapter is in two parts: the first is descriptive and outlines the structure of the organisation whilst the second half, which features quotations from current practitioners, concentrates on what the individuals should — or should not — do for the effective use of advertising media.

Any media representative must fully understand how advertisers and their agencies operate if he hopes to gain an order, and it is equally essential for advertisers and agencies respectively to appreciate the working of the other two parties to the advertising contract, if they hope to use media to best advantage.

Any reader who wishes to skip the chapter describing that part of the industry in which he is employed — on the premise that he knows its contents from everyday working experience — is welcome to do so, *but for the descriptive half of the chapter only*. The second part, giving the practical views of others on what he should or should not be doing, must be considered essential reading.

A fourth chapter in this Part outlines some of the specialist services available.

5
ROLE OF THE MEDIA-OWNER

The media-owner's structure

All media-owners differ in their precise organisational pattern, but it is nevertheless possible to describe a basic structure around which individual media-owners make those variations best suited to their particular operation. This chapter discusses the media-owner's various departments, the inter-relationship of their activities and how they can best work with advertiser and agency respectively for more effective advertising.

The editorial department

With most media, advertising is not their reason for existence but only a means of helping them exist. Newspapers and magazines are read for their editorial content and television watched largely for entertainment, and it is editorial skill in interpreting and satisfying target audience taste that determines the size and type of media audience. This in turn influences the possibilities for using these media as effective means of advertising.

The editorial side is frequently sub-divided, with special sections appealing to particular groups within the overall media audience. Newspapers, for example, have special gardening or motoring features, or pages written expressly for women readers. On television and radio, there are similar specialist programmes. Some features appear regularly (whether daily, weekly or monthly) while others appear only on particular occasions. The latter category could include features giving special coverage to, for example, the Boat Show or the Royal Academy Summer Exhibition.

Editorial is not always the reason for the existence of an advertising medium, however. Outdoor advertising, for example, has no editorial content and justifies itself solely as a publicity medium. With some media, advertising also serves as 'editorial': the 'editorial' of an exhibition for example, is of course the advertisers' stands. It is worth bearing in mind that advertising serves the media audience just as much as the advertisers and media-owners. Exhibitions provide a clear example of this but the same point applies equally to press media. Fashion advertisements in women's magazines are — at least to the male eye — virtually indistinguishable from editorial pages.

The production department

The writings of the editorial staff together with relevant illustrations must be put into print, and readership depends not only on the editorial being of interest but also on it being well printed. Printing quality also affects advertising effectiveness and is one of the factors that advertisers and agencies should consider when selecting media.

Similarly, television and radio programmes must be produced and transmitted. Poster sites must be constructed and the posters themselves pasted up. For some media, such as point-of-sale display material, production is of major importance and constitutes the main part of the advertising: the same applies to direct mail and to exhibitions.

The circulation department

There is more to successful publishing than writing and printing alone, for printed copies are of little use until they are delivered to actual readers. This is the task of the circulation department and the sheer physical work is often under-estimated. The flow of printed copies coming from the press must be bundled and addressed, and special transport is frequently necessary: fleets of delivery vans, special trains, or even aircraft. A few minutes' delay in the delivery chain may lead to missing a vital connection, and thus to loss of sale of thousands of copies. A whole network of wholesalers and newsagents is involved and the media-owner must ensure that his publication is available in sufficient quantities and well displayed. In this respect, the work of the circulation representative is similar to that of most consumer goods salesmen. In addition to the routine circulation operation, complex enough as it is, the circulation department may often arrange special distribution facilities for extra sales at important events or exhibitions.

With a number of publications, magazines particularly, a considerable proportion of copies are not distributed through the newsagents, but posted direct to readers on a subscription basis. By contrast, with some media there is no 'circulation' in the sense of a separate physical activity. With direct mail, for example, circulation is really only an extension of production work and, with television and radio, building of audiences depends not only on production and transmission of the programmes but equally on their promotion. To this end, many media-owners develop promotion departments. Circulation, subscriptions and promotion departments may operate as separate units, or may be joined to form an overall publishing department.

The subscription department

Many publications rely to a great extent on subscriptions for their distribution. Subscription circulation is important not only as a source of revenue, but also because it implies regular readership, which is of prime importance to potential advertisers. Indeed, analysis of subscriptions, as a form of research, can provide valuable information about the type and location of readers. With magazines on controlled circulation, where copies are sent (free of charge) addressed by name to individuals in certain defined categories, this research aspect is dominant, and the subscription revenue foregone. Publishers of controlled-circulation journals count on the assurance they can give potential advertisers about circulation and thus readership to bring them an advertising revenue which more than compensates for the loss of subscription income, so that in this respect the readership aspect is all important. The same applies to specialist journals received by members of various professional bodies, as part of the service they receive in return for their membership subscription.

The promotion department

With subscription copies of publications, or those sold through newsagents or booksellers, the promotion department plays a key role. Other media, which do not have the equivalent of circulation or subscription departments, rely equally on the promotion department. The size of audience that views a television programme, for example, or attends an exhibition, turns on the skill of the promotion department. This department may also sponsor special events such as rallies, races or exhibitions, as part of the medium's overall promotional programme.

In considering the promotion department's activities, any media-owner should be considered a manufacturer in his own right, with merchandise to sell, who must plan his advertising with as much care as other producers. It is not unknown for a media-owner to have an advertising manager (responsible for promoting the medium) as well as an advertisement manager (responsible for advertising revenue).

The advertising manager may plan a number of distinct campaigns. There may be a promotional campaign aimed at the public, persuading them to buy a publication, to watch a television series or attend an exhibition. Just as manufacturers usually have a second campaign aimed at retailers or wholesalers, so the media-owner will mount promotional campaigns aimed at wholesale and retail newsagents, with the object of persuading them to stock up and display his publication. Media-owners differ from other producers in needing a third campaign to potential advertisers, to bring in advertisement revenue. Most media-owners undertake a great amount of promotional activity, to back up the efforts of their media representatives. These campaigns include a whole range of material: direct mail shots, trade press advertisements and sales aids for media representatives to use in their presentations. The promotion department will also devote considerable attention to making known the work of ancillary services such as a research department.

The research department

Much research is undertaken centrally: the readership surveys and television audience reports described in Part 1, for example, provide information about reading and viewing habits which is readily available to all advertisers and agencies, and serves as an important tool in media evaluation. Given the existence of this central research information, you may wonder why a media-owner should run his own research department. Quite simply, the main purpose is to provide additional information not contained in the central research, which might persuade advertisers and agencies to view the medium more favouably. In describing the data available, Part 1 pointed out that much valuable information was available from media-owners' own surveys, and such work is the province of the research department which may also subscribe to the various research services available: all this activity has the common aim of providing information that might be useful to you in your planning. Much of this information will equally be of assistance to the media representatives in their selling tasks, but there is however a major problem underlying such research activities by media-owners.

The surveys commissioned centrally and those sponsored by media-owners complement rather than duplicate each other. There may be areas of overlap and differences may arise through use of varying research methods, but these problems are of minor importance in comparison with the underlying question of whose responsibility it is to undertake and finance the research.

Advertisers and agencies can justifiably claim that the media-owner has a responsibility to provide information about the coverage of his medium. No difficulties arise when a medium is included in the central research, but where the media-owner starts to provide additional information a fundamental problem does occur.

An overall review of media-owners' research shows that most of it is at one of two levels. The first level of research provides information about the medium's coverage, to enable media planners to judge the medium's power to reach that market. But should the market not be worthwhile, no amount of research will persuade manufacturers to use the medium. Hence some media-owners tend to provide 'second stage' research information to show the value of a market — and thus persuade manufacturers to mount a campaign in that market, in which case the media-owner should get his share of the advertising expenditure, and can use his first-level research to ensure inclusion in the schedule. Some media-owners go even further, into what can be termed 'stage three' research, by checking into sales in their market of particular groups of products, to show manufacturers of these products the desirability of mounting a campaign in the area. In short, the media-owner researches the market he serves, rather than the medium itself.

Such research is really aimed at providing marketing information and this is where the controversy arises. Why should it fall to media-owners to provide costly marketing information which advertisers or their agencies should have collected themselves, if they are to mount successful marketing campaigns? And, again, to *whom* should the media-owner make the information available? The marketing information was collected to influence marketing policy, and it is only *after* this is decided that media planners make their contribution — selecting media to reach the market that is the target of the campaign. Yet many marketing surveys are sent to media planners, to whom they are not of immediate *media* interest. The same problem arises where media-owners promote their areas as ideal for test marketing. The decision to mount a test campaign is a marketing decision and not a media one, yet media planners are frequently bombarded with such information, just as they are mailed about merchandising services. Media-owners thus have the problem of distinguishing between the tasks of selling the market and that of selling the medium, since these call for selling activity directed to different individuals. This problem, however, is relatively easily resolved in comparison with the more controversial one of who is

85

to finance the research, and the answer to this has yet to be agreed.

Returning to less controversial but perhaps more interesting matters, it is worth noting that some media-owners are moving into 'stage four' research — providing information about the ability of their media to *communicate* and whether the same message received through Medium A is more effective than if received through Medium B.

The need for marketing information has resulted in some media-owners' research departments operating to an entirely different end, acting as an internal service organisation for the advertisement department. The research role here is to assemble facts and figures that advertisement representatives will find helpful in their contacts with advertisers and agencies. In addition, research staff may analyse current advertising to predict future trends. Where research is entirely devoted to securing additional business, the department may be known by another name, such as 'Sales Research' or 'Business Development', and operate independently of the research department, which devotes itself to field research.

Marketing and merchandising departments

In many cases, a research department marketing survey is linked with an outline of the various merchandising services provided by the media-owner to assist advertisers in ensuring the success of their campaigns. The one 'Marketing and Merchandising' document thus includes details of activities such as trade mailings, conference facilities, reprints, display material and many other aids which, when criteria for media comparison were discussed in Part 1, were grouped under the general heading of 'Facilities'.

The advertisement department

The advertisement department has the vital task of obtaining maximum advertisement revenue. For some media such as television, radio or posters, where there is no income from sales or subscriptions, advertising is the sole source of revenue on which the medium depends for its existence. (There may, of course, be income from sale of editorial material to other media-owners, but our concern here is with advertising rather than editorial.) Even where a medium does not wholly rely on advertisement revenue, such as a publication sent to association members in return for their subscription, advertisement revenue is still of importance in that it permits publication of larger issues with better quality printing. Never forget, also, that the advertisements communicate information and are thus a service to readers.

The individual controlling sales of advertising within a medium is usually known as the advertisement manager or director (a very different individual from the advertising manager, whose responsibility is to buy advertising). Before starting to sell, the advertisement manager — and his representatives — must know exactly what is available to sell. For press media, the advertisement manager must negotiate with editorial and production staff, and agree precisely what advertising space he can sell. He must then decide the units into which the total advertising space can best be broken down, and obtain agreement on precise sizes and positions. The advertising rates at which these spaces and positions will be charged must also be decided.

This exercise, which must be performed for every issue of the medium, is not a one-way process with the advertisement manager asking what is available. The degree of advertising support achieved by the advertisement side directly influences the size of the issue and the number of pages of editorial that can be included. With other media, a similar process will apply. Television and radio representatives must know how many minutes of advertising time are available, in what units, and the precise positioning of the commercial breaks. Exhibition organisers must know what stand space can be accommodated within the exhibition area, and the location and size of individual stands. Once advertising availability is known, the advertisement manager can set about achieving sales.

The advertisement manager as head of a department   The advertisement manager is head of a department in just the same way as the editor, the production manager, the circulation manager, or a manufacturer's advertising manager. He must evaluate the amount of selling to be done, the number of calls to be made, their geographical location, and the level at which contact must be made, since some selling jobs call for representatives with special experience and skill.

Assessing the market and division of work   A list of potential advertisers must be built up, and a careful analysis made of each. Once the list of potential advertisers and — if appropriate — their agencies is built up, the advertisement manager's next task is to divide it among his various representatives and provide each with a call list. There are various ways in which this can be done and the advertisement manager must decide the most suitable division for his medium. It may be a straightforward sharing of work, each representative having a list of advertisers and agencies on whom to call. Alternatively the division may be by type of advertising, some representatives being responsible for classified advertising, for example, and others for display. There may be further special-isation within each division, with one representative having special responsibility for, say, car or fashion advertising. Again, calls may be split by area, each representative being responsible for all advertising within his defined territory.

Where division is by area, this reflects the advertisement manager's responsibility for predicting levels of activity, for such division assumes that there is adequate potential within each area and sufficient work to support, say, a Northern representative. Should there not be sufficient work to justify full-time employment, the advertisement manager may arrange for his representatives to make field trips from time to time to various areas. A final point is that some media-owners find it preferable to contract out of advertisement selling altogether, and to appoint space-selling agencies to undertake the work. Naturally, these methods of dividing the work are not mutually exclusive, but frequently overlap.

The advertisement manager must also bear in mind possible future expansion and increase his staff in good time to meet it. For even when the new man arrives he cannot be put to work immediately and, however experienced, will still need training to acquaint him fully with the new medium he is selling. The advertisement manager thus has a major responsibility in the selection and training of representatives, as well as their control. Some media-owners now pay more than lip-service to this matter and have appointed training officers, but the advertisement manager still remains directly concerned, as the type of training given will depend upon his view of future requirements.

Staff training   Staff training is of great importance, and it might be helpful to review briefly the knowledge required by a representative, if he is to make his contribution to effective use of his medium. This knowledge reflects the tasks of the advertiser and agency described in Part 3 of this book, on the effective use of media:

1   *His product*   The representative must be fully acquainted with the physical means by which his medium delivers your advertising message, advertisement sizes and positions and rates, copy dates, and all the mechanical production data regarding the advertisement material required.

2   *Editorial policy*   Though the physical format remains the same, editorial content changes with each issue and may open up prospects of attracting advertisers previously not interested. Hence the representatives must be fully conversant with overall editorial policy, and with all future details: in this respect, training is a never-ending task.

3   *Media audience*   Potential advertisers are directly concerned as

to the audience they can reach through the medium. One of the first tasks of advertiser and agency is to define their market and, in evaluating media, they make a straight cross-check — with what certainty will the medium reach the defined target market? Accordingly, the representative must have at his command readership or viewership figures, or other research information.

4 *Potential advertisers*   Representatives must understand thoroughly the marketing and advertising problems of the advertisers and agencies on whom they are to call. What type of advertising do they undertake, in what sizes, with what frequency, and on what dates? What are their marketing objectives? When does their season start? Which groups constitute their market, and what coverage of these groups does the medium offer? Which agencies are employed, and how is the work shared with the advertising department? Who plans the media schedule, and when? Part 3 discusses these investigations in more detail but here it is sufficient to point out that if media representatives are to be of service to potential advertisers and their agencies — and thus obtain the orders they seek — they must have this knowledge at their fingertips.

5 *Media selection and planning*   Understanding the potential advertiser's objective, and the principles by which media are evaluated and schedules planned, the advertisement representative can then help ensure that his particular medium makes its maximum possible contribution to the success of the overall campaign.

6 *Creative skills and constraints*   With some media, it is not sufficient for the representative to merely sell space. Where advertisers are inexperienced, it may be necessary to create and produce advertisements for them to use, for without this help it would be impossible for them to use the medium. This aspect of the advertisement department's work is discussed in more detail below, as are the legal and voluntary constraints affecting creative content.

7 *Selling techniques*   Even when representatives have full knowledge of the physical format of their medium, its editorial policy, the market covered, the potential advertisers and the contribution which the medium could make to achieving their advertising objectives, there still remains the basic task of selling. While 'salesmanship' is important, it must be based on sound knowledge and reasoning, for all the sales talk in the world cannot compensate for lack of basic reasons for advertising in the medium. This is stressed because there are still a few media representatives who believe that string-pulling will bring orders.

A well-stocked wardrobe and superficial charm will not alone induce a media planner to include a medium on his schedule. The same applies to lavish entertainment. Advertisers and media planners are busy people, with better use for their time than wasting it on unwanted hospitality, and are unlikely to accept invitations from media which do not merit serious consideration.

Supervision and control   While the representatives are making calls, the advertisement manager must keep himself informed of their progress. With some media the representatives, like their colleagues on the manufacturing side, are required to submit regular call reports, so that the advertisement manager knows what orders have been received or are pending, and can maintain up-to-date records.

The direction of selling   The advertisement manager and his representatives must decide the best direction for selling. Should their sales effort be directed to the advertiser or his agency or both, and which individuals in these organisations should they contact? Here the detailed structure of the advertiser and his agency, described in the following chapters, becomes significant.

The direction of selling is affected by client/agency relationships. Deciding which individual should be the target for sales effort may be a problem as sometimes more than one individual, or even a committee, is concerned. Advertisers employ agencies for their expert advice and experience, but this generalisation masks numerous possible variations. Division of the budget into 'above the line' expenditure handled by the agency and a 'below the line' budget handled by the client can vary from case to case, depending on each client's expertise and inclination, and the expertise of his agency. Even with 'above the line' expenditure by agency planners on the more conventional advertising media, client/agency relationships can vary, thus influencing the media-owner's selling activity.

Much depends on the relative dominance of the advertising department and agency. In some relationships the agency is the dominant partner, planning and executing the campaign, the client playing the more passive role of briefing the agency on the problem, and checking and approving the proposals. With a number of companies, however, particularly those with strong marketing orientation, the tendency is for the advertiser to adopt the more dominant role. Where a company's marketing manager is responsible for the full range of marketing activities (including advertising, selling, merchandising and sales promotion, research and even product policy and pricing) it follows that the client/agency relationship must differ from cases where the advertising manager is responsible for advertising alone.

Marketing-orientated companies are not necessarily dominant in every aspect of advertising and marketing: all depends on the relative strength and expertise of the individuals in both advertising department and agency. Furthermore, a change in staffing on either side could result in a shift in this pattern of dominance: another reason why it is so vital for media-owners to keep up-to-date with staff changes.

The background and experience of the individuals concerned influences the approach as well as the direction of media selling. When calling on an advertising manager, for example, much depends on his specialist expertise (or any weaknesses in his knowledge). By definition, an advertising manager should have an all-round knowledge of advertising matters, but clearly any individual must be more expert on some topics than others, and will therefore be more searching in his questions on his special advertising interest. An advertising manager who trained originally as a copywriter or visualiser is bound to have a different outlook from one whose background is research or media. One will be influenced by the creative possibilities of the medium, while the other will make a far more statistical assessment. Clearly the approach made by the media representative must vary accordingly, and for this reason a thorough personal knowledge of prospects is essential. The same is true when calling on an agency account executive.

On contacting a manufacturer's advertising manager, the media representative will frequently be referred to the agency. The key figure through whom the client makes contact with all the agency specialists is the account executive and so, naturally enough, his is the name mentioned when referring representatives to the agency. Many representatives make the understandable mistake of insisting on speaking only to the named executive, and virtually refusing to accede to his request to contact the agency's media department. This practice is likely to upset both parties: the executive wants the expert advice of his media department and not constant phone-calls from the media representative, however well-meaning he may be; and equally the media planners are unlikely to view favourably any media representative unwilling to speak to them initially, and then doing so only with an attitude of 'second best'. By all means media representatives should maintain contact with the account executive, but they should remember that he relies on the advice of his media department and directs their selling effort accordingly.

When contacting the agency's media department, many representatives find themselves unable to decide *who* to speak to — group heads, media planners, media buyers, media assessors, media researchers or any of the other titles that abound in agencies. The various media department structures and the wide variety of organisation patterns described in Chapter 7 make it difficult to give general advice, but many media-owners have found it helpful to extend their central records to include information about advertisers and agencies. Thorough and continuous investigation into which people are influential in media decisions can build up a 'structure chart' for advertiser and/or agency. In this way, the record can show the names of the advertising manager, the account executive, media planners or buyers and so on. More important, 'weights' can be allocated to each (just as media planners often assess media) according to the relative influence each has on media decisions. Where different representatives from the same medium call on the same agency, media-owners often build up a structure chart for each agency in the same way, based on the combined view of all the representatives concerned.

Media/agency/client contacts

There are occasions when the representative feels that his medium has not received the attention it merits in the client's media schedule, and he therefore seriously considers that his case could not have been adequately presented to the client, or was insufficiently considered by the agency. It is usually advisable for the representative to be open with his views, rather than go to the client 'behind the agency's back'. A clear statement of his case to the agency, with adequate reasoning as to why the schedule should be revised to include his medium, will have more effect than complaining to the client, quite apart from any ill will that may be caused. Agencies do not often make mistakes, but they do occur from time to time, and an agency would naturally prefer to correct its own error, rather than have it pointed out by their client at a media-owner's prompting. If, after requesting the agency to review the position, the media-owner feels that his case has not received due consideration, the representative should most certainly go direct to the client, but should pay the agency media staff the courtesy of notifying them of his intention to do so. And the media representative should make sure he *has* got a case to present. Advertising managers do not like to have their time taken up reviewing situations that have already been considered by their agency. The media representative may see the advertising manager the first time but, unless he feels the visit was justified, the chances are that the media representative will not be so lucky on the next occasion. All going well, however, all this selling activity will result in an order being placed, and attention should now be focused on the media-owner's next task.

Confirming the orders

Most media-owners keep some form of 'space register' showing the amount of advertising space available for sale in future issues. This shows the total amount and sub-divides it into run-of-paper and special positions (or their equivalent for other media). The register must be kept up-to-date so that the advertisement manager and his representatives can see at any moment what space has already been sold and what is still available. Leaving space unsold, through oversight rather than through lack of effort, means loss of potential advertising revenue.

Immediately an order is received it must be checked carefully for accuracy of vital facts such as size, position, cost, discounts, etc., and to ensure that the order has been duly signed and is correct in every way. This done, the order must be checked against the register to see if the space requested is in fact available. For run-of-paper insertions this is a straightforward operation, a simple check that total bookings do not exceed the amount of space available. For special positions, however, the operation is more complex since it means placing a named advertiser in a particular position in the medium. Such positions can be sold only once, and considerable ill will would result if the same space were promised to two advertisers. It might even lead to future business from one advertiser going to another medium, perhaps less suitable, but where it was certain to appear as promised. Reliability was one of the criteria for comparison discussed in Part 1.

The space register is of vital importance even before an order is received, for its accuracy may determine whether or not the order is placed. With many media the space register is used by representatives who telephone in during discussions with advertiser and agency, and make immediate bookings based on the information given. Under such circumstances, information must be literally up to the minute.

Space registers are maintained by publishers, and owners of other media have similar systems. Television and radio contractors, for example, have 'time registers' showing the booking position for commercial breaks between programmes. Poster contractors must know their site bookings, and be able to say which will become available and when. Even where the medium has a high production and service content, such as direct mail, and there is no top limit to the amount of advertising that can be sold, the direct mail houses must know when their various machines are fully occupied, and when they have capacity to accept further work.

Immediately the order has been checked against the register, an approriate entry must be made and the order duly acknow-

ledged, either by returning the tear-off slip which may be incorporated in the order, or by sending the media-owner's own acknowledgement form. Some media-owners have put the detailed record-keeping
aspect of their work onto computers and, in this general area, most
media have administrative and 'paperwork' systems just as thorough
as those in advertising departments or agencies, which will be
described later. Two actions then follow: the production staff must
obtain the necessary material, and the advertisement department
must consider where best to place each advertisement, and decide
upon the most suitable 'make-up'.

Production and creative services

Advertising material must be obtained from the advertiser or his
agency. Even when this is received well in advance of copy date,
the prudent media-owner checks all material immediately it arrives:
is it of the right size and type, and does the advertisement conform
to the various voluntary codes and legal restrictions, and to any
rules that the media-owner himself imposes? Advertisers and agencies
have thorough administrative systems but the possibility of errors
still exists, so material must be checked without delay. Should the
material be at fault, prompt notification enables the client or his
agency to recify the mistake and supply correct material. It will be
too late to check at the last minute, as there would then not be time
for errors to be corrected. For other media, similar action is involved,
according to the production process.

Even where the advertiser or his agency supplies a complete
advertisement, its appearance in the medium still involves some
production work. With press media, for example, the advertisement
must be inserted in the appropriate place in the medium and correctly printed. For other media, similarly straightforward production
work is involved.

Frequently, however, additional services are called for, particularly
by smaller advertisers. Where a complete advertisement is not
supplied, but only typed or even hand-written copy, the media-
owner must undertake typesetting and is thus involved in more
production work. Indeed, without this production work it would be
impossible to accept the advertisement.

The service may extend to creative work and some media employ
special staff to prepare creative suggestions for prospective advertisers, so that their representatives can submit copy and design proposals. Alternatively the representatives themselves may prepare
these creative suggestions.

Creative and production services may equally be provided by

other media. Many television and radio contractors offer facilities for special 'budget' commercials, quoting special low all-inclusive rates covering scripting, actors, studio and production. The same applies to the cinema, where stock films may be available which local advertisers can purchase at much less expense than they would incur in producing a film for themselves, and which they can personalise by including their own name and address. Direct mail houses similarly extend their services beyond production alone, and offer creative advice to those using their medium.

It is not only for inexperienced advertisers, who for lack of expert staff might be precluded from advertising, that media-owners provide these creative and production services. In other cases, media-owners have virtually been forced into such activity to safeguard their own interests. Some media-owners, for example, have encountered advertisers who do not take full advantage of the creative possibilities of the medium and, in extreme cases, produce advertisements that are actually *negative* in effect. Clearly the advertiser would receive little or no benefit from his campaign in such circumstances and would decide, wrongly, that there was no point in using the medium, since it had 'proved' itself ineffective. Incredible though it may seem, this was the case in the early days of television, when many advertisers withdrew from the medium for this very reason. Direct mail houses still find the same thing today. Some media-owners therefore extend their facilities, taking the more positive attitude of ensuring that their advertisers produce effective advertisements, and no longer take the more passive role of providing help only when asked. Action such as this is, of course, self-defence for the media-owner since if the advertisements do not bring results he will not get repeat orders.

Preparing the make-up

Where advertisers have booked special positions the problem of make-up does not arise, since the location of such advertisements is determined by the booking. Many advertisements, on the other hand, are booked on a 'run of paper' basis and it is left to the advertisement department to place these in the most suitable position. And to do so is in the advertisement department's own interest as well as being a service the advertiser expects, for a well-placed advertisement results in better response, and thus greater likelihood of a repeat order. Clearly an advertisement for a garden product is better placed on the gardening page and a car on the motoring page, than *vice versa*. Such obvious cases speak for themselves but, in practice, positioning is usually more difficult and the advertisement department finds it a problem to satisfy all the calls for right-hand page, top of column, outside edge, front half of publication, and similar requests. Once the detailed make-up is decided, however, the media-owner can then proceed to the next stage.

Final proofs

The production staff proceed simultaneously with two separate tasks — editorial and advertising. The advertisement department's make-up, placing advertisements next to the most favourable editorial, serves as production's guide in placing the advertisements in position. Further proofs are usually produced but not circulated to advertisers, since they are for internal use only. Their purpose is to ensure that all is in order and that no mistake has slipped through the previous careful checks. The advertisement department may, for example, have sold space in the belief that a 25 cm X 2 cols advertisement is to appear on a given page, while the editorial staff have designed on the assumption that space was needed only for a 20 cm X 2 cols advertisement. Or perhaps, through a production slip by advertiser and agency, an advertisement of the wrong column width was sent in error and, through an equally unfortunate error, this was not noticed on receipt. Again, page proofs may reveal that two advertisements containing coupons have been placed back to back: under such circumstances neither advertiser could get maximum results and the advertisement department would lose revenue by having to give both advertisers a rebate.

Page proofs may also bring to light unfortunate positioning which may have to be corrected: the advertisement department's make-up may have placed an advertisement for holidays abroad on a general news page, but if the news of the day happens to describe riots or some other unfortunate event in the country concerned, the travel agent would not be at all happy to see his advertisement next to news that must inevitably reduce response to his offer. Events or mistakes such as these are rare, but the possibility that they may occur nevertheless exists; hence the rule for the media-owner — just as much for the advertiser and agency — is meticulous checking and double-checking to remove all possibility of error. If all goes well, no last-minute changes will be necessary and publication can proceed.

Publication

Copies must be printed and physically distributed to newsagents or subscribers. Television and radio programmes and commercials must be transmitted, and cinema films screened. Although the advertisement department is not directly concerned with this side of affairs, its activities still depend on the successful completion of this vital stage: the actual communication of advertisements to the media audience. Immediately the advertisements appear, the accounts department must be given all the information they need to invoice advertisers correctly.

Invoicing and voucher copies

The advertisers or their agencies must be invoiced before they will pay, and the invoicing task is to ensure that every advertiser is charged at the correct rate for each appearance of his advertisement. A smoothly operating accounts department avoids any loss of advertisement revenue through failure to invoice, and directly affects the speed of payment. Invoice queries by advertisers or agencies often cause ill-will or frayed tempers, and hold up payment. Delayed settlement can cost money in bank charges, and if settlement of many invoices is held up the consequent shortage of funds could place the media-owner in a difficult financial position.

Equally important is an efficient voucher service, for before the advertiser or agency will settle the invoice they will want to check that their advertising appeared as booked. The voucher may sometimes take the form of a 'tear sheet' rather than a full copy of the publication. With some media it may not be possible to provide a voucher copy or physical proof of appearance, in which case the media-owner may send a 'certificate of transmission (or of posting)' or some other assurance that the advertising has appeared. Failure to send the necessary voucher copy or certificate means that payment of the invoice is delayed until this omission is rectified. The smooth functioning of the voucher section is just as important as an efficient accounts department: the purpose of all this activity is receipt of advertisement revenue.

Follow-up

Once the advertisements have been invoiced, do not imagine that the operation is complete and the way now clear for further selling. Adequate follow-up of the issue just published is essential. The representatives who obtained each advertisement must check them with as much attention as the advertisers and their agencies will devote to them. Did the advertisements print well? What ratings did the television commercials receive? Did the exhibitor have an attractive stand? Evaluation of results, with a view to improving future performance, is of major importance to both advertiser and agency, and advertisement representatives, in selling future issues, must be equally concerned with the advertisement which has just appeared. This also provides them with the ideal opportunity to seek repeat orders.

The new issue

Every new issue presents opportunities to follow-up previous advertising and affords scope for new sales, which means we are now considering the operation of the advertisement department from the same point at which we started. We can now turn from an examination of structure, to reviewing the media-owner in actual practice.

The media-owner in operation

This second part of the chapter concentrates on comments made by current practitioners when asked about media-owners' relationships with advertiser and agency, and what they should and should not do, for effective use of media. Numerous interesting points were raised; so many that it is impossible to include them all. What I have done, therefore, is to select those topics raised most frequently, and illustrate them with appropriate quotations.

Quality of the medium

Many respondents' comments reflected the fact that advertising effectiveness depends directly on the value placed on the medium itself. They recommended that the media-owner should

● *pay attention to the long-term quality of his product* (ad)

● *recognise his primary role of producing the medium.*

● *Examples of the results of* over-*selling are the colour supplements/daily papers inundated by direct response and retailers* (ag)

Understandably, most comments on this theme came from the advertisers and their agencies, rather than media-owners.

The market served

Other practitioners developed this theme, extending it to the audience reached by the medium. Their advice was for the media-owner to

● *try to develop media that hit specific targets* (ad)

● *act responsibly as custodian of a market* (m-o)

Client/agency contacts

As you would expect, practitioners from all sides of the business commented on the need for media-owners to maintain contact with advertisers and agencies, when they advised representatives to

● *cultivate the advertisers as well as the agencies* (ad)

● *work closely with client and agency* (ag)

● *maintain regular contact with both agency and advertiser* (m-o)

The more controversial matter of media contact with client *versus* agency is discussed separately below.

Information: general

Other comments related to the *content* of the representative's calls, rather than the act of making contact, and here again there was considerable agreement that the media-owner should

● *aim to keep both advertiser and agency informed — with facts* (ad)

● *provide detailed information on his medium* (ag)

● *sell his medium to both agencies and advertisers. They will have to justify the decision, so the media-owner should provide the arguments and the information to back them up* (m-o)

The need for representatives to provide information was thus generally accepted, and is perhaps self-evident. The question is — what kind of information?

Information: editorial

Many stressed the need for advance information about forthcoming editorial, when they advised that the media-owner should

- *try to improve communication of forward editoral content* (ag)

This point was however more often made in reverse — and more vehemently — by respondents commenting on practices to avoid. They urged that the media-owner

- *should not keep coming to client with (always) unrepeatable offers of super features/supplements/specials with one-week copy dates!* (ad)

Not so surprisingly, there are no quotations from media-owners in support of the need for more advance notice. Most would probably agree, but no doubt point out the practical difficulties involved.

Editorial and advertising

The relationship of advertising to editorial was the subject of more specific comment by practitioners who urged the media-owner to

- *ensure balance between editorial and ads* (ad)

As with the previous point, the matter was raised more often in a negative context, by those who urged that the media-owner

- *should not go in for special features (with associated advertising) unless there is a clear opportunity and occasion for this, e.g. an exhibition — in which case the editorial must be of high standard, not just something to pad out the advertisements* (ad)

- *should not barter editorial space for adverts. This lowers the tone of the medium to everyone's loss. A barter deal is easy to spot and devalues* all *editorial* (This does happen!) (ad)

- *should not start aiming editorial at advertisers to try and ingratiate himself with them* (ag)

Information: audience

The need for details of the audience to whom your advertising message will be delivered was stressed by many practitioners, who advised the media-owner to

- *be more informative towards advertisers about what his medium delivers in the way of audience — as distinct from just mailing rate cards* (ad)

- *provide clear and factual information about his medium to all interested parties* (m-o)

The widely recognised need for audience information raises the somewhat controversial matter mentioned earlier — who should fund this research? One agency man pointed out that the media-owner should

● *be prepared, from time to time, to invest in research of relevance to marketing in specific fields* (ag)

The need for investment in research was, however, recognised by media-owners themselves. One pointed out the need for media-owners to

● *recognise that the bulk of revenue is not mediated by personal selling, and thus allocate more funds for audience measurement and definition* (m-o)

The *accuracy* of some information provided by media was questioned by a number of respondents who advised that media-owners

● *should not represent facts in a totally distorted fashion* (ag)

Media-owners were not unaware of this possible danger: one advised that the media representative

● *should not knowingly misrepresent the reach of his medium* (m-o)

Information: background

Other practitioners felt there was need for media to provide 'Proof of results' information, when they requested representatives to

● *offer advertisers case study information* (ad)
● *demonstrate effectiveness* (ag)
● *contribute case histories, research and other evidence of success* (m-o)

This was thus another area in which there was general agreement.

Preparation prior to call

Having information is one thing — being able to use it to best advantage is another. Respondents from all sides of industry emphasised the need for 'homework' prior to any call, when they advised the representative to

- *do his research before he makes his call in an effort to learn a little about the client's business* (ad)

- *familiarise himself, as far as possible, with a brand's history and marketing background as a prelude to any discussion with the agency* (ag)

The fact that media-owners equally appreciate this need for prior research is illustrated by a quotation taken from one who pointed out that he

- *should not expect business unless he has sussed out the advertiser's problem* (m-o)

The purpose of the call

Quite apart from prior preparation, other respondents stressed the need for a *purpose* for the representative's call, when they commented on practices to avoid. They advised that the media-owner

- *should only visit a client when he has something to offer or discuss, rather than making a 'courtesy' call in order to put in expenses!* (ad)

- *should not send reps for the sake of calling* (ag)

- *should not waste the time of busy client and agency personnel* (m-o)

The need for a purpose to the representatives call was thus widely accepted by all parties.

Quality of representation

Various respondents commented on the media representative's selling expertise (or lack of it!). In their opinion, the media representative should

- *listen occasionally instead of boring the pants off his prospect* (ad)

- *get more expert at media selling* (ag)

- *communicate the advantages they have to offer more professionally* (m-o)

There is more to this than 'salesmanship' alone, however. Some practitioners pointed out the need for the media representatives to

- *take a more intelligent view of agencies i.e. the salesmen should be able to handle all the data put out by their research departments. Frequently good research done by media-owners is ignored or misunderstood by salesmen who only seem able to haggle over trivia* (ag)

This need was well appreciated by many media-owners, who made the same point in reverse when commenting on practices to avoid. Their advice included the following

- *media-owners should not send out untrained personnel* (m-o)

- *should not insist on quantity of calls rather than quality* (m-o)

Rates and deals

There was general agreement on the matter of rate increases, as illustrated by recommendations that the media-owner

- *should not raise prices at short notice* (ad)

- *should not issue rate increases at short notice* (ag)

- *should not increase rates without adequate notice* (m-o)

On the matter of deals, however, opinions were divided. One advertiser advised that the media-owner

- *should not offer high discount to ensure revenue — especially where the medium is not an exact or ideal fit* (ad)

It would appear from this comment that not all media follow the advice of one media-owner, who felt that he

- *should maintain a sensible business 'face' on which client/agency can reply, i.e. not suggesting he is giving a marvellous 'discount' or service when in fact he is not* (m-o)

Contradictory views were expressed by other practitioners, one of whom advised the media-owner to

- *bend the rules for clients who will invest more* (ag)

A totally opposite view is the advice that the media-owner

- *should not 'deal' with favoured customers* (ad)

A media-owner's view of this controversial matter was that he

- *should not bow to agency or advertiser pressure to make special deals just for him* (m-o)

Clearly then, this is an area in which you will not find unanimity of views.

Advertisement facilities

The range of advertisement positions available was the subject of comment by many respondents, who urged media-owners to adopt a more flexible approach. Advice was that they should

● *be flexible in accommodating special requests* (ad)

● *recognise that positioning is important, and editorial make-up should allow for as many and varied positions as possible* (ag)

The matter of positioning run-of-paper insertions, once the order is placed, is discussed separately below.

Accepting and implementing the order

Many respondents urged that media-owners should make agreements and then stick to them. Obvious perhaps, but many thought it sufficiently important to stress that media-owners should

● *not sell out to a higher bidder once a firm contract for a spot/ place has been agreed* (ad)

● *accept a requirement for firm days/firm positions* (ag)

● *make clear the advertisement position, agree the rate − and stick to it* (m-o)

Once agreed, the order should be implemented. Again, obvious perhaps, but many felt the need to point out that media

● *should not make promises they cannot keep* (ad)

● *should not fail to read orders (general policy by certain TV contractors)* (ag)

● *should not omit advertisements without notice* (m-o)

Problems may of course arise which prevent the media-owner from implementing the order, however much he would wish to. This was the subject of comment by one respondent, who advised that the media-owner

● *should not put his relationship and image at risk by not talking directly and effectively to the advertiser on day-to-day problems* (ad)

Advertisement position

Many were concerned with the normal process of media-owners' positioning of advertisements once the order was placed, and urged that they should

● *be more aware of the advertiser's reasons for using their particular medium, and the importance of positioning e.g. in relationship to advertiser's competitors using the same medium* (ad)

This point was appreciated by media-owners, one of whom pointed out the need for

● *sensible placing of advertisements* (m-o)

Production quality

The success of an advertisement depends on the effectiveness with which the medium actually delivers the message. Many respondents were therefore understandably concerned with production quality when they urged media-owners to

● *print the desired colour!* (ad)

● *monitor more closely the standard of reproduction* (ad)

Service

What services should the media-owner provide, in addition to delivering your advertising message? This was the subject of comment by many practitioners, who were unanimous that the media should

● *ensure total client satisfaction – remember after-sales service* (ad)

● *be keen on following up the business he has already got* (ag)

● *spend more time on after-sales service* (m-o)

Others extended the service concept to emphasise long-term relationships. They advised the media-owner to

● *be concerned with building up a long-term business relationship with the brand as opposed to merely benefiting from short-term profit* (ag)

The need for after-sales service was thus widely accepted, but the question then arises of what *kind* of service? When it came down to detail, the various parties to the advertising contract did not always see eye to eye.

Schedule improvement

Part 3 explains in detail the importance of revising a schedule as circumstances change after the original booking is made, and many respondents felt that the media-owner has a responsibility in this respect, when they recommended that he

● *should not accept bookings without attempting, during the campaign, to improve positions, offers 'deals', etc.* (other)

Special circumstances

You may have to alter your schedule unexpectedly and some quotations related to such events, in advising that the media-owner should

● *respect the real problems of clients and accept short-term changes as necessary, e.g. allow cancellations if product not available* (ag)

The last word on this topic goes to the media-owner who pointed out the media

● *should not be liable for client/agency problems which result in loss of advertisement revenue for insufficient or poorly explained reasons* (m-o)

Use of the medium

The likelihood of repeat orders for the media-owner depends directly on the success of the campaign he carries. It is not surprising therefore that media-owners recommended that they should

● *be prepared to back up the selling operation with creative facilities* (m-o)

● *Develop ideas and concepts related to their medium* (m-o)

Campaign planning

Others went even further and looked at the campaign as a whole.

They recommended the media-owner to

- *encourage effective collaboration between agency and advertiser. There are real opportunities to enhance relationships to achieve more effective advertising* (ad)

- *consider advertiser's requirements constantly. It is the joint responsibility of the media-owner and agency to ensure successful campaigns. This includes rates, position, timing and editorial environment* (ag)

- *be ready to assist an agency in producing a media plan, with, for example, statistical information* (m-o)

Back-up service

As pointed out earlier, most media-owners realise that unless the campaign they carry is successful, the prospect of repeat orders is unlikely. In consequence, quotations emphasising the need for media-owners to involve themselves with their advertisers' profitability came mostly from the media-owners themselves. Here is one example of what they felt they should do:

- *be prepared to help and assist advertiser and agency in all aspects of marketing to help ring the till of advertisers!* (m-o)

Others went further, in suggesting how this profitability might be achieved, when they advised the media-owner to

- *seek closer involvement in merchandising operations* (m-o)

- *offer total marketing service, where applicable, via support promotional material, bill displays at point-of-sale, etc.* (m-o)

This viewpoint was not restricted to media-owners alone, however. Other quotations came from other sources:

- *the agency and media-owner may work in partnership in some cases, i.e. below-the-line promotions, competitions, etc.* (ag)

Evaluation of results

The media-owner carrying a successful campaign can presumably hope for repeat business, so again it is not surprising that media-owners recommended that they should:

- *join with advertiser in researching effectiveness of plan* (m-o)

- *improve monitoring of response to client's advertisements to assist future decision-making* (m-o)

Media services: the negative side

Most comments suggesting after-sales service came from the media-owners themselves, but other parties did not always see eye to eye with them when it came to the detailed aspects of this service. Where did the criticisms come from? Various respondents commented as follows, pointing out practices that media-owners must avoid:

● *should not tell clients how to create advertisements — they haven't got a clue* (ag)

● *should not overdo promotional activities to influence business* (ag)

● *should stop purporting to be marketing experts* (ag)

These critisms came from agencies, and the comments suggesting types of service came from the media-owners. It is not surprising therefore that the next topic — the media-owner's contacts with client *versus* agency — is a controversial one.

Client versus agency contacts

The need for media-owners to maintain contact with advertisers and agencies was made earlier, but this general statement masked widely differing opinions. on whom should the media-owner concentrate his selling activities — the advertiser or his agency, or both? All shades of opinion were represented.

One group of respondents took the 'client plus agency' stance, in advising that the media-owner

● *is entitled to approach the client without permission but should inform the agency what he is doing* (ad)

● *should keep agency informed of meetings with clients* (ag)

● *should not approach the client direct without* advising *the agency of its intention* (m-o)

Other respondents took a different stance — instead of the client plus agency approach, they were in favour of the 'agency only' practice, as the following quotation illustrates:

● *media-owners should not solicit the client but should address their information to the agency* (ad)

Two agency respondents explained why they took this stance, pointing out that:

- *media-owners can be very helpful to clients generally in co-operation with agency — problems arise if agency feels media-owner is going behind his back. Media-owners should not approach client without agency permission. It can only lead to problems — and client will probably ask agency's advice anyway, after the visit* (ag)

Another agency man commented that

- *I have no objection in principle to media talking directly to clients, but I consider it unnecessary and a complication in practice. It is useful in very broad cases, particularly at the start of a new medium (commercial television and radio for instance), where it can help prepare clients for agency recommendations. But the essence of being an agency is that it is not necessary for all media to talk to all advertisers — which would leave no time for anything else* (ag)

As you would expect, a third group disagreed with either stance. Instead, their advice was that the media-owner should

- *establish and maintain relations with client* (ad)

- *the media-owner is free to approach whoever he likes. The better agencies are always approached first!* (ag)

- *should be free to approach client without agency permission* (m-o)

The final quotations on this controversial topic come from two media-owners who made the identical point, in their different ways. They stressed that

- *the media should always retain direct contact with client. Accounts switch frequently from agency to agency, and the client/media relationship is vital for continuity* (m-o)

- *the media-owner has every right to see client and probably does not need agency permission. The client has probably been 'his' before the agency's — and may continue for years after client has left agency* (m-o)

Divide and rule?

Quite apart from the controversial matter of the *direction* of media selling, a number of respondents felt that some media adopt a 'divide and rule' approach. Their dislike of this is illustrated by quotations relating to practices media-owners should avoid in their selling operations:

- *should not try to play client off against agency — or vice versa* (ad)

- *should not divide and rule* (ag)

Other respondents were more specific, citing just *how* some media-owners create conflict between agency and client. Practices they disliked included the following, which they urged media-owners to avoid:

- *should not offer a deal cutting out the agency and their commission. (This really does happen!)* (ad)

- *should not quote different prices to client and agency* (ag)

Others suggested another practice to be avoided:

- *should not offer deals to the client which are not available to the agency* (ad)

- *should not offer to clients something which he has not already offered to the agency* (ag)

The back-door approach

Some practitioners disliked representatives who tried underhand means to obtain an order. They advised that media

- *should not use undercover method of influence* (ad)

- *should not approach the Chairman, sales manager or other back-door influence* (ag)

The rejected medium

There is never sufficient money to include *all* candidate media in a schedule, and various respondents commented on what action the excluded media-owner should — or should not — take. Various agency men suggested that media

- *should not denigrate to the client an approved media plan which excludes him* (ag)

- *should worry about getting his own house in order rather than constantly telling us what's wrong with our media dept, client's marketing, client's advertising, etc.* (ag)

- *should not sulk if the selection decision goes against him* (other)

The fact that media-owners are aware of this danger can be illustrated by a quotation which recommended that the media representative

- *should accept that his medium is not necessarily right for every schedule, let alone essential (small esoteric magazines are especially bad at this)* (m-o)

Other respondents commented on media which, if not rejected, felt they had a 'right' to be included, or to a larger proportion of the budget than they had in fact received. Again, these comments appeared under the heading of what the media-owner should *not* do:

- *should not assume that advertising is his by divine right* (ad)

- *should not query an advertisers's spread of money e.g. between TV contractors if there are good marketing reasons — too often TV contractors are concerned with 'share' when this is of no relevance to the advertiser* (ad)

Although most comments of this nature came from advertisers and agencies, some came from media. As one pointed out, media-owners

- *should not assume that any business is theirs 'as of divine right'* (m-o)

It would be unrealistic to think that media which genuinely merit a place on the schedule are *never* rejected. The possibility of error was recognised by practitioners who suggested that the media-owner

- *should not approach the advertiser direct without first consulting the agency. However, if there is a serious fault on the agency side it may be necessary to state their case* (ag)

- *should not avoid presentation to client direct if this is the only way to get entrance to proposals through unreasonable 'blocking' by agency* (m-o)

- *should not be frightened of criticising a poor campaign* (m-o)

Even if this does not bring the media-owner the immediate result he hopes for, there is always the future. One suggested that he

- *should not take NO for an answer* (m-o)

The final question in this chapter is from the advertiser who advised that the media representative

- *should not assume that because he has told him once the buyer/ advertiser knows all the media can or cannot do* (ad)

6

ROLE OF THE ADVERTISER

The actual tasks of the advertising manager which, overall, make for good advertising, are:

1   *Research and investigation*   Gathering the company, product and market data essential for effective planning.
2   *Problem analysis*   Deciding your campaign objective, which directly effects both media selection and the creative approach to be featured.
3   *Budgeting*   Fixing the advertising appropriation, so that you spend the right amount in achieving your chosen objective.
4   *Preparation of advertising proposals*   Planning an advertising campaign, creating advertisements and selecting media, to achieve your determined objective.
5   *Approval of proposals*   Checking, prior to executing the campaign, that your proposals are likely to be successful.
6   *Execution of these proposals*   Putting your plan into effect.
7   *Evaluation of results*   Checking that you received value for money, and seeing what lessons can be learned for the future.

This process is a closed loop, and evaluation of the results of this year's campaign should provide additional information on which to base next year's planning. All these tasks will be examined in detail in Part 3. This chapter, however, reviews the role of the advertising manager and how he can best tackle them.

Advertising in perspective

Before examining how the advertising manager sets about his tasks, consider for a moment the goods or services to be sold. Advertising will *not* sell poor merchandise: if it does, buyers will soon realise that the goods are of poor quality and the harm done goes beyond your initial sales. Advertising should therefore never be used to sell 'mistakes'. If customers will not buy goods when they see them on

112

the shelves, why on earth should they buy them just because they are advertised? This point is stressed because manufacturers or retailers do sometimes try to clear dead stock through advertising, and then blame advertising when no sales result. Clearance items can be featured with profit from time to time, at attractive bargain prices, but these are special cases. For advertising to be effective, it must offer customers a benefit, such as a new or improved product, lower prices, or newly arrived stocks. Thus a first essential for effective advertising is a good product.

The second essential is that your products must be made known to the right people. This is, perhaps, obvious, but there is no point in telling people about goods which are of no use to them, however much of a bargain is offered. So careful consideration of your 'market' is another essential. If potential purchasers do not know of your merchandise they will not buy it, hence effective advertising means telling the right people about the right goods.

With the right merchandise and the right people to inform, a third consideration is the right means of conveying information to these people. There are many ways to reach prospective customers with your advertising message (and this book concentrates on how to use them effectively). There is no *one* medium that is best — they all reach different markets by different methods. So it is vital for you to select the advertising medium that reaches the people you want, and which will deliver your advertising message most effectively. Correct media selection is therefore vital to effective advertising.

A fourth essential in planning advertising is to get the right message. If you have the right goods, know who your prospective purchasers are and have the means of contacting them, then for successful advertising your message must attract their attention and convey your product's benefits. Hence great care must be paid to the wording of your advertisement, the choice of illustration and the overall layout.

Fifthly, but of equal importance, is timing. Advertisements that appear too early or too late, before your customer is in a position to think about buying or after the purchase has been made, are wasteful.

Finally, your goods must be readily available in the shops when the customers go to buy. Any weakness in distribution will result in your advertising merely increasing your *competitor's* sales, for the retailer — rather than lose his profit — will recommend an alternative brand.

In short, for your advertising to be effective, careful planning must ensure that several factors are right:

Right products — which people would buy if they knew about them.

Right people — to whom your product is of interest.
Right media — which reach these people effectively.
Right message — which conveys your product's benefits.
Right time — when your potential customers are likely to buy.
Right distribution — when your goods are available in the shops.

A Jewish colleague once illustrated this by remarking that there was no point in trying to sell bacon to Jews by advertising in the Catholic Herald on a Friday! Amusing though this anecdote is, it does not cover *all* the essential 'rights' — it stresses wrong product to wrong market in wrong medium at the wrong time, but ignores the vital matter of message. This omission nevertheless only reinforces the importance of right product and right market, for *no* advertising message, however brilliantly created, could ever persuade people to buy a product that is forbidden them. Another omission is right budget, so you do not spend too much or too little on achieving your objective.

This planning of 'rights' is an oversimplification, but it does make clear the need for planning. It is vital that your advertising is carefully planned. Advertising is not a separate operation unconnected with your company's other marketing activities: advertising, sales and display effort must all be co-ordinated. With careful planning, advertising expenditure is controlled and spent to best advantage, and ensures results that bring profits which more than pay for the advertising. Part 3 describes how this planned advertising can best be achieved.

The changing structure of the advertising department

The structure of the advertising department will vary with the firm and with circumstances, and the background to such changes must now be considered. Advertising is no longer treated in isolation: advertising and marketing activities now pay an increasingly dominant role in determining overall policy rather than merely reflecting it. Advertising and marketing men are found on Boards of Directors and the status of their departments has changed accordingly.

Another aspect of change relates to the range of work carried out by the advertising department, whose manager may find himself with responsibilities such as public relations, merchandising, marketing and market research. Again the structure varies: in some firms, one individual controls all these activities and his title (and that of his department) changes accordingly, while in others they are divided among two or more executives, each the head of his own department.

Whatever the structure, it is essential that all these activities interlock: unless advertising ties in with merchandising and public relations in aiming to achieve the identical marketing objective, it is impossible for advertising media to be used to maximum effect. For this reason, we should examine these allied activities.

Public relations

The Institute of Public Relations defines PR as 'the deliberate, planned and sustained effort to establish and maintain mutual understanding between an organisation and its public'. Advertising is one of the tools used to achieve mutual understanding, but public relations is another far broader one which covers every contact made by the organisation in every field.

To illustrate its wide scope, take the launch of a new product by your company. Certainly you would need to inform the public and forewarn retailers, and public and trade press advertising would play a key role in ensuring public and retailer acceptance of your new product. Public relations activities, however, operate on a much wider front, for the new product is also 'news' and the editors of consumer and trade publications need information to keep their readers up-to-date. The same applies to other media such as television and radio.

It would be a great mistake, however, to regard editorial mentions as 'free advertising' and to set about public relations work with the intention of 'getting something for nothing'. Instead, you must consider the special requirements of each editor and what will interest his readers. The art of good press relations is knowing just what is of news value to different media, and so presenting the editors with the information *they* want, in the form they want it, and in good time for them to use it. Sending out extra copies of a press release to all and sundry publications in the belief that 'they may use it, and it only costs a stamp' will, in fact, do your firm a disservice. Editors who repeatedly receive useless press releases from the same source will, before long, no longer bother to read them. Then, when something occurs which is of genuine interest, your press release will not get the attention it would otherwise have received. Editors are busy people, working under pressure against the clock, and cannot be expected to waste their time reading releases in the hope that one in a hundred will be of interest.

Public relations activity does not end with the issue of press releases but covers any contract, on any topics of interest, with the different sections of your public. Many people will be personally affected by the new development, and should be told directly of its implications rather than being left to read about it by chance. Those on the factory floor will want to know about the new product and the sales staff will be equally interested. Many other staff divisions — such as warehouse, despatch and accounts — will want to know how the new product affects their work and, even outside the firm itself, there will be many sections of the community affected by or interested in your new product. Retailers and wholesalers, for example, will be directly interested, as will be the suppliers of raw materials or machinery, while your company's shareholders will most certainly want to know how their money is being spent. In each of these cases there is need for public relations activity to ensure a flow of clear information — a flow which, in the Institute's definition, is deliberate, planned and sustained. Failing this there could be lack of mutual understanding and, in extreme cases, even ill-will, all of which could have been avoided had you taken the trouble to inform people of what was going on, rather than leaving them to find out for themselves.

Public relations activity covers *every* contact, and not only those made as a result of paid-for advertising. Playing a vital part in your firm's operations, it demands top-level attention and in some organisations public relations work is linked with that of the advertising manager. In others, it is developed to such a scale that a full-time public relations officer is necessary, often with his own department. Alternatively public relations consultants may be employed, or the advertising agency's PR service used. Clearly then there is a variety of ways in which your company's public relations can be safeguarded and promoted: the important thing is that this must never be neglected and must interlock with other activities, if advertising media are to make their full contribution to achieving your business objective.

Merchandising and sales promotion

The advertising manager's responsibilities may be extended further to merchandising and sales promotions, since an advertising campaign's success depends as much on your goods being in the shops at the right time as on the effectiveness of the creative work and the media schedule. Many companies therefore devote special attention to backing up their advertising campaigns with striking displays of the product at point of sale. This may be undertaken by the advertising manager as an additional responsibility, a separate merchandising and sales promotion manager may be appointed, or the work may be shared with the appropriate section of the company's advertising agency or with outside specialist services.

When display material is produced, considerable effort is needed to ensure that retailers use it effectively, and before retailers will stock or display new merchandise they must be convinced that the line will sell. This means stimulating their enthusiasm by telling them of the forthcoming advertising and the demand it will create, and persuading them to stock and display the new product. In short, in addition to the public advertising campaign there should be a second campaign aimed specifically at securing maximum co-operation from distributors.

Your 'dealer campaign' might include advertisements in the trade press, sales letters telling of future consumer advertising, and the provision of display material. There may also be arrangements for 'co-operative' advertising in which the retailer joins your firm in local media advertising, perhaps on a shared-cost basis, to announce that he stocks the advertised brand. For retailers who are unskilled in display, you may provide a special window dressing service. All this activity can be grouped under the heading of merchandising and sales promotion, in that it is aimed at making sure there is adequate distribution of your products and they are well displayed in the shops when your advertising campaign breaks on the public.

Merchandising can also help your company's sales force in persuading retailers to stock and display the goods. General sales promotion may include a sales conference at which the production manager talks about the new season's products, the sales manager talks about sales targets, while the advertising manager — aided perhaps by the agency — outlines the advertising support. The advertisements and the media schedule will be shown to the salesmen and the thinking behind your advertising campaign explained. The purpose of these conferences is to make sure that every representative knows of and understands the advertising campaign that will be backing up his sales efforts. And it is of vital importance that the salesmen do understand the advertising, for even though a product is widely advertised it cannot be bought until it is in the shops, and the shopkeepers will not stock it unless the salesmen have convinced them that it will sell. The consumer advertising campaign can thus provide your salesmen with an effective means of persuading retailers to stock and display your lines, and each salesman may be provided with a portfolio containing specimen advertisements and details of your media schedule, which he can use as a sales aid in making his presentation to the retailer.

For effective advertising, therefore, you should in fact have three distinct campaigns: one to persuade the public, a second to inform retailers, and a third directed at your own salesforce to put them fully in the picture.

Marketing

The Institute of Marketing has adopted the following definition:

'Marketing is the management process responsible for identifying, anticipating and satisfying customer requirements profitably'.

Marketing thus directly influences the work of the advertising manager. Sometimes his work is linked with that of the marketing manager, or both functions might be united in a single post — perhaps with the added responsibilities of public relations, merchandising and sales promotion, and market research.

The modern concept of marketing has in fact revolutionised production and selling. In the early days of large-scale production, a firm manufactured a product, the sales manager sold it and the advertising manager devised a suitable campaign. Their joint effort was aimed at achieving sales of a product already in production. Salesmen perhaps passed back any comments they received from retailers regarding public reaction to the product or, more recently, there may have been some research to define the market and to learn consumer attitudes to the product. Then, on the basis of this somewhat meagre information, the company or its agency designed the pack and planned the advertising campaign. In essence, however, all this activity was aimed at selling a product already produced: in other words, the product came first and was followed by the selling and advertising decisions.

This brief description over-simplifies the process, but serves to illustrate how the modern concept of marketing has meant a complete reversal of this attitude. Instead of manufacturing a product and then selling it, marketing now attempts to locate and define a need and to ascertain in advance in what size, shape, colour, packaging and at what price consumers would most want the product. Only then does marketing assess how best to produce, distribute and promote the product itself. Thus, long before any production facilities exist, and when the idea is still at development stage, marketing plans the complete production and selling operation. Research ascertains the form and quantity that will best suit the market: an obvious prerequisite to production, for how else can management decide what facilities are necessary to manufacture the product in the right quantities, and in the packing and at the price required? Marketing also considers distribution of the product, the type of retail outlets, trade discount and sales force structure, and the degree of emphasis to be placed on advertising and personal selling.

Today, most marketing plans go even further: they look to the future by attempting to predict your product's life circle (introduction, growth, maturity and decline), and also include research and development activity to improve existing products as well as providing new products for your company to market in the future.

Marketing unites advertising, selling, market research and many other activities. None of these is new: the only new concept is linking these various activities under the common heading of marketing. The marketing man must have a full appreciation of the parts played by market research, production, packing, price, advertising, personal selling, merchandising and distribution in successfully producing and selling his company's lines and in planning future products. In many companies marketing has become the hub of all activity. Sales and advertising departments have always been complementary, but the new concept of marketing is leading to these 'separate' activities being united under a single marketing director, who controls a number of executives responsible for various aspects of the marketing mix, or brand managers responsible for individual products within the range. Even in companies where sales and advertising remain separate, the concept of marketing implies that the staff in both departments must work in close co-operation, fully 'market-orientated' and conscious that the all-important factor is not what they wish to sell but what the customer wants to buy. The two are not necessarily the same and, where there is a difference, it is increasingly rare for the manufacturer to regard his view as the dominant one. The consumer is sovereign and has freedom of choice: maximum profitability to the company must be balanced by a corresponding satisfaction for its customers.

Marketing research

The purpose of market research is to provide information which will help manufacturers anticipate consumer needs so that they can decide how to satisfy these needs in a profitable way, and the need to adopt a marketing approach has already made clear the vital role of research in locating and defining consumer needs. The many different applications of marketing research, and the various ways in which information can be obtained, call for major attention and cannot be covered within the scope of this book. All that need be said here is that research may be an additional task for the advertising manager, or it may be the responsibility of the marketing manager, perhaps through a specialist market research manager, through the research department of the advertising agency, or through an independent market research company.

Administration of the advertising department

The advertising manager as head of a department

The advertising manager is head of a department just as much as the head of production, sales, transport or any other section: he thus has responsibility for staffing his department, and its size depends to a great extent on whether or not any advertising agency is employed.

Where the firm does not use an advertising agency, the advertising manager must have in his department creative staff to prepare the advertisements, or be in touch with freelance workers on whom he can call. Similarly he must be able to deal with the work of media selection, planning and booking, and the physical production of advertisements.

Even where this work is undertaken by an advertising agency (or by the creative workshops and media independents described in the next chapter), it does not follow that there is no staffing problem for the manufacturer's advertising department. Careful control must still be kept of schedules, accurate records maintained of the company's advertising, and voucher copies and invoices checked. Perhaps the advertisements call for readers to fill in a coupon. This simple request involves a vast amount of work in sending out booklets, sorting out the coupons and perhaps passing them on to the firm's representatives as sales leads, and analysing the response to the campaign. Responsibility for advertising involves a great deal of executive, creative and purely routine administrative work, even when an agency is employed. Division of work between advertiser and agency varies but, whatever the circumstances, the advertising manager must ensure he has staff to cope with whatever work he accepts as his responsibility.

Agency selection and liaison

The advantages and disadvantages of using an agency will be covered in the next chapter, but clearly the decision whether or not to employ an agency rests largely with the advertising manager and he will be called upon to advise his Board of Directors accordingly. If it is decided to do so he will be responsible for selecting a suitable agency, negotiating arrangements for handling his advertising, and for briefing the agency on his company's requirements. After this briefing he will throughout the campaign work closely with the agency team in the preparation and execution of proposals, and the evaluation of their results.

The importance of agency liaison must never be under-estimated and, in fact, it largely depends on the client's advertising manager whether or not the agency produces a good scheme. There is no question of the advertising manager sitting back and leaving everything to the agency, for even the finest agency, staffed by experts in every specialist branch of advertising, can give of its best only if it receives full backing and co-operation from the advertising manager.

Division of work

Some advertisers rely on their agency for the full range of advertising media, while others undertake part of the work themselves. More usually press, television, radio, cinema and outdoor advertising come within the agency's orbit, while control of other media may rest with either party. Exhibitions, direct mail, print and display material are frequently retained under the advertising department's direct control, even when an agency is employed. Some advertisers adopt a policy of dividing their appropriation into two parts: an 'above the line' budget to be spent by the agency and a 'below the line' budget which is retained by the advertising department. There is no uniformity about where the client's work ends and the agency's starts, and much depends on the staffing arrangements the advertising manager considers most effective under the circumstances in which his firm operates.

The structure of the advertising department

There is no limit to the variety of structures within different companies' advertising departments. A firm may or may not employ an advertising agency and, either way, the advertising manager may rely on only a few staff or alternatively he may have a large department containing numbers of expert staff, equivalent to a fully-equipped agency. The advertising manager may in fact have in his department a number of specialists who are the counterparts of the agency experts. In such circumstances, agency media proposals will be checked by the advertising manager's own media expert, creative proposals by his creative staff, research by research specialists and so on, with the advertising manager in overall control and taking an overall view. Alternatively, these experts may undertake the full advertising task without outside assistance.

Where a company has several different divisions or products, there may well be separate advertising departments, each under its own advertising manager and co-ordinated by an advertising director. Each of these departments may produce its part of the company's advertising without agency assistance, but in other cases the advertising departments may employ one or more advertising agencies.

There is thus a wide variety of organisational patterns, but there is certainly no question of one business structure being 'better' than others: each firm adopts the organisational pattern most suited to its circumstances and adapts itself as the business world, and the firm itself, changes. The advertising manager must consider future expansion, perhaps caused by additional products to be marketed and, reverting to his role as head of a department, must recruit and train new staff and/or review his agency arrangements accordingly.

The advertiser in operation

As in the previous chapter, this second part features comments made by current practitioners when asked about practices to be followed — or avoided. Now, however, attention is turned on the advertiser and his relationships with the other two parties. As before, it is impossible to cover all the many interesting points raised, so analysis is restricted to those topics raised most frequently.

Client knowledge

Many respondents commented on the body of knowledge the advertising manager must have at his command in order to do his job to best advantage. The full range of this knowledge will be detailed in Part 3: all that is necessary here are a few quotations to set it in context. Respondents recommended that the advertising manager should

- *be well supplied with marketing information about his product or service* (ag)

- *be the expert in his own market, and be crystal clear about the target audience* (other)

- *be very clear about advertising objectives* (m-o)

In addition, many respondents pointed out the need for thorough knowledge of media, when they advised the advertising manager to

- *learn as much as possible about media selection himself, to understand what the media and his agency say to him* (ad)

- *learn/understand media characteristics* (ag)

122

- *develop a good working knowledge of the media that are/or might be relevant to his business* (m-o)

Numerous respondents made the same points but in reverse, when commenting on practices to avoid. The most succinct came from the advertising manager who pointed out that he

- *should not expect miracles if he has not done his homework properly* (ad)

Forward planning

This 'homework' must be done well in advance, and there was unanimity on this point among respondents who recommended that the advertising manager should

- *initiate planning well in advance of campaign date* (ad)

- *allow time for a professional job to be done* (ag)

- *provide sufficient time for the media planning/buying operation* (m-o)

Others wanted to look even further into the future. An example of this viewpoint is the respondent who urged that

- *planning should look beyond the immediate campaign, to the next and even further* (ag)

Some respondents had reservations about whether planning should be put in hand as far ahead as the last quotation suggests. Two quotations which illustrate these doubts come from respondents who advised

- *plan ahead, but don't allow too much time (best judgements are made under pressure)* (ad)

- *insufficient time often leads to hastily drawn-up plans. However, too much time leads to theoretical plans which do not reflect current influences, e.g. TV strikes* (m-o)

While there were differences of opinion about just how far ahead you should plan, practitioners were unanimous on the danger of *not* planning for the future. Many, pointing out practices to be avoided, urged that the advertising manager

- *should not believe a good media plan can be prepared quickly* (ag)

There were also practical problems, to which others drew attention:

123

- *should not forget about copy dates, and early booking discounts, etc., and then moan about the high cost of media* (ag)

- *should not expect prime media opportunities – print colour/ airtime – to be available short-term. Similarly premium positions or guaranteed days or issues* (ag)

Media-owners endorsed this view, in urging that the advertising manager

- *should certainly not leave planning late as so often happens, since this inhibits proper media planning immediately* (m-o)

Before leaving this topic, you should note the words '. . . as so often happens . . . ' in the last quotation. Although there was un-animity about the dangers of late planning, it would appear that the advice to plan ahead – although universally accepted – is not always followed in practice.

Contacts with agency and media

The media-owner chapter revealed the controversial nature of client/ agency/media-owner relationships and, as you would expect, these differences of opinion are reflected within this chapter – particularly as regards the advertiser's contacts with his agency *versus* the media-owner. Before considering opposing views on this topic, however, the less controversial need to give information to agency and media-owner can be illustrated by a few quotations. These are taken from respondents who advised the advertising manager to

- *share his whole problem (not hold back)* (ad)

- *contribute to the agency and media-owner's knowledge of his market* (ag)

- *know his marketing objectives, know what he wants from his advertising, what he expects it to achieve, then communicate this to both agency and medium* (m-o)

Other respondents extended the advertising manager's responsibilities beyond providing information, in urging him to

- *lead the other two. Such leadership is as effective by collaboration as by authority – and perhaps more so. The advertiser should provide a firm system to permit free collaboration, i.e. a free flow of information and ideas* (ad)

For some, this 'free flow of information' was extended to include other contacts than the basic trio of advertising manager, agency and media-owner, to include others within the advertiser's company. Their advice was that he

- *should not divorce agency/media-owner from other contacts in his company* (m-o)

- *should plan with all concerned including not only the agency and media-owner but also the advertiser's marketing and outside sales staff whose knowledge of the customer is important to the advertising plan. The expertise of* all *concerned should help produce the best results* (ad)

- *where a media co-ordinator is employed by the advertiser, he should work in unison with media department and media-owner* (ag)

The trio

Some practitioners recommended a three-way working relationship (others quoted later took a very different stance). Their advice to the advertising manager was that he should

- *aid and abet the agency through regular discussions with media-owners* (ag)

- *trust media-owners and agencies to work together to solve media problems* (m-o)

Client/agency contacts

Others favoured a client/agency working relationship which largely excludes media. One advertising manager stated that

- *there should be no need for media-owners to contact clients if an agency is employed. A proper briefing to an agency obviates the need for direct media contact* (ad)

As you would expect, some agencies took the same stance. A quotation to illustrate this came from the agency man who advised that the advertiser

- *should have confidence in his agency team without having to go direct to media-owners* (ag)

It is not surprising that no media-owner was in favour of the 'agency only' approach. Some, however, felt that the advertising manager

- *should not deal direct with media without the agency's knowledge* (m-o)

Client/media contacts

Other practitioners took a totally different view. Far from recommending an 'agency only' approach, they advised the advertising manager to

● *establish a close 'relationship' directly with media* (ad)

● *meet the media-owner regularly and let him know how his medium is being used* (ad)

Others extended this beyond a 'contact' relationship: their advice was that the advertising manager should

● *work with media as a specialist/adviser* (ad)

It is not surprising that there are few quotations from agencies in full support of this direct client/media approach.

Make it clear

One advertiser at least was more than aware of the conflicting approaches to the controversial matter of client/agency/media contacts. His advice was that the advertising manager should

● *define the nature of the relationship with media and agency, i.e. media prefer to approach the advertiser direct. This is acceptable to some advertisers but not to others* (ad)

Media too would like the position clear. One media-owner's advice to the advertising manager was that he should

● *brief his agency clearly and agree in advance his interest in direct contact with media-owners, within agreed confines* (m-o)

Media briefing

With many respondents in favour of close client/media relationships, there are — as you would expect — a number of quotations which recommend giving media a detailed briefing. These came from respondents who advised the advertising manager to

● *in conjunction with the agency gain the co-operation of potentially useful media-owners by familiarising them about brand marketing background and company expectations of forthcoming campaigns* (ad)

An agency man with the same viewpoint cited as one of the common errors militating against effective use of media

● *lack of media involvement in and access to marketing data* (ag)

Most quotations supporting the view that media-owners should be given a fuller briefing came — as you would expect — from the media-owners themselves, who recommended that the advertiser

● *should provide the media with relevant data so that they can put forward sensible proposals* (m-o)

This is clearly what media-owners would like, in order to make their contribution. One media-owner at least had however clearly encountered a very different attitude. He urged that the advertising manager

● *should not tell media a pack of lies just to get rid of them* (m-o)

The media contribution

Many respondents felt that media-owners could and should help ensure more effective use of media. They advised the advertising manager to

● *ensure that media have the opportunity to contribute at an early stage* (ad)

Most quotations suggesting closer media involvement came, as you would expect, from the media-owners themselves who advised that the advertising manager

● *should certainly work with his agency but should never over-look the fact that media personnel are much more likely to be in possession of vital local knowledge* (m-o)

● *should work with media-owners as partners. This is most important — media-owners can be of great assistance providing computer runs and other information* (m-o)

The conflict of interests

Before turning to client/agency contacts, the overall relationships between all three parties should be examined. Whilst it is all very well to talk of advertiser, agency and media-owner jointly striving for perfection, many respondents were fully aware of the realities of life. They pointed out that

- *partnership is a lofty ideal. It is not a reality because of vested self-interest* (ad)

- *the best solutions do come from working as partners, but remember that this is not an* equal *partnership. Ultimately each partner has different business objectives* (ag)

My favourite quotation on this topic came from the media-owner who advised that the advertising manager

- *should not forget that agencies and media-owners are profit-making businesses just like his own — not the National Health* (m-o)

Client/agency briefing

The need for the advertiser to pass information to media, and to both media and agency has already been illustrated. The parallel need for the advertising manager to brief the agency in its own right is illustrated by the following quotations. These respondents recommend the advertiser to

- *give a clear, easily understood briefing. The client should make sure his agency thoroughly understands his product, his philosophy and his business* (ad)

- *give complete background information, subject to confidentiality* (ag)

- *involve the agency in the total marketing strategy* (m-o)

As the importance of sound agency briefing is so fundamental, it is not surprising that an even larger number of respondents cited poor briefing as a common mistake militating against effective use of media. The quotation which made this point most concisely was that the advertising manager

- *should not demand a media plan without providing an adequate brief* (ad)

General client/agency relationships

The need for a close relationship between advertiser and agency was recognised by both parties. One quotation from either side will be sufficient to illustrate this point. These come from respondents who advised the advertising manager to

- *work, as a team, at all stages of development, with the agency*

128

- *work with agency as his experts* (ag)

The second quotation leads neatly into the comment made by a media-owner whose observations indicate that this ideal situation does not always work out in practice. He pointed out that

- *advertisers employ agencies as experts or hod carriers. I suspect that those that employ them as experts get the best and most effective advertising* (m-o)

Client/agency working relationships

Other respondents were more specific about these relationships, and recommended that the advertising manager should

- *be in close contact with the media department of the agency rather than relying on a second-hand contact via the team* (ad)

Many agency men endorsed this view, in recommending the advertiser to

- *maintain contact with service departments in addition to account handling department* (ag)

The strongest view on this topic is the advice that the advertising manager

- *should not give the media brief to anyone other than the media planner or buyer* (ag)

Who does the job?

According to many respondents, it is vital that the agency be left to get on with the job for which it is employed. This seems too obvious to merit comment, but the point was raised so many times it demands quotations to justify its importance. Advice given was that the advertising manager should

- *fix the budget and target audience and media objectives then leave it to the agency* (ad)
- *leave media planning to the agency experts — or change agencies* (ag)
- *after giving the agency full information, let the agency make the final decisions* (m-o)

129

As you would expect, the same point was made in reverse by respondents who advised that the advertising manager

● *should not keep a dog and do his own barking!* (ad)

Others took this approach even further, to include warnings against 'telling the agency what to do' and 'interference'. The need to avoid the first error is illustrated by a respondent who urged that the advertising manager

● *should not dictate media planning to the agency* (ad)

It is significant that most quotations on this theme came from the advertising managers themselves — but that criticisms implying that they *did* interfere, in the various ways described below, came from the other two parties.

Trust and confidence

A logical extension to the 'leave it to the agency' and 'don't interfere' viewpoint is of course for the advertising manager to place greater trust in his agency. A number of respondents made this point when they recommended the advertiser to

● *place more trust in his agency* (ad)

● *have full confidence in the planning and buying ability of the agency* (ag)

● *select an agency he trusts and listen to it* (m-o)

Interference

Some respondents were specific on the matter of interference in commenting on practices to avoid, and various levels of interference became apparent — talking too early to media, direct booking, involvement in deals, and subsequent changes.

Talking too early to media

A number of practitioners felt this was harmful: their advice was that the advertising manager

● *should not discuss rates for airtime/space with media-owners without first entering into talks with the agency* (ag)

Another agency man gave his reason for this standpoint, in advising that the advertiser

● *should always discuss his objectives together with agency media department not first with media-owners as this can lose negotiating points for the agency* (ag)

Direct booking and involvement in deals

Some advertisers apparently do more than just talk to media, and buy space direct despite the fact that they employ an advertising agency. This was a practice to be avoided according to many respondents, who advised that the advertising manager

● *should never deal direct, excluding agency from booking* (ad)

An agency respondent pointed out the drawbacks, when advising that the advertiser

● *should not deal direct with media, as he may well not be aware of competitive activity, etc.* (ag)

Other advice on practices to avoid was that the advertising manager

● *should not interfere in agency/media negotiations on discounts, etc.* (ad)

● *should not try to beat agency by dealing with media, i.e. making deals* (ag)

There were numerous quotations on these lines, but not *everybody* took this stance. One respondent — perhaps a maverick? — suggested that the advertising manager

● *should not leave media handling entirely to the agency. By dealing direct he may get a better deal (and keep agency on toes!)* (ad)

This quotation would seem a suitable one on which to turn to the more positive matter of the advertising manager ensuring that he has an effective advertising campaign.

Quality control

Various respondents from all sides of the business recommended action to ensure high-quality advertising. From the client side came advice that the advertising manager

- *should largely take the advice of agency media experts, but be in a position to challenge that advice* (ad)

A similar viewpoint is that of the agency man who advised that the client should

- *trust the agency's selection ability, but be experienced enough to debate and challenge* (ag)

A media-owner's viewpoint was that the advertiser should

- *work primarily with agency or specialist media buying operation, but should be prepared where possible to have experienced personnel within his own organisation to question the agency's recommendations* (m-o)

Some advertisers apparently 'control' quality in a different way. One advertising manager commented that

- *in contrast to the way we operate, I have come across advertisers who are surprisingly passive and accept the agency's recommendations with little, if any, questioning, presumably on the basis that 'the agency knows best'. In contrast, I have come across people who will ignore the agency's recommendations, but will rely on 'gut' feelings. I have never discovered what 'gut feeling' actually is, but a surprising number of people apppear to have it.* (ad)

The most outspoken comment on this matter came from the advertising manager who stressed that

- *the advertiser should not assume that his agency will always strive to achieve the best possible media selection. Media buyers are inherently lazy and overworked, so will do the least work possible. Challenge their choice and demand that they evaluate alternative media or they will churn out the same schedule time after time* (ad)

This might be an opportune time, therefore, to mention another factor directly affecting the quality of any advertiser's campaign: one practitioner advised that the advertising manager

- *should reward the agency and recognise that agencies want to make a profit* (ag)

The final quotation on quality control refers to the ultimate sanction, and comes from the advertiser who advised that the advertising manager

- *should not be afraid to take business away from an agency if the performance is not to target* (ad)

132

Quality control: the negative side

It is disappointing that some respondents found it necessary to comment on what the advertising manager should *not* do, if he is to hope for high-quality advertising. As practices to avoid, it was recommended that he should NOT

● *side with media against agency* (m-o)

● *play one off against another* (ag)

● *BULLY* (m-o)

● *be rude, arrogant, and think he knows more about advertising than anybody* (m-o)

● *mess his agency about — and then pretend he did not* (ag)

Flexibility

Few advertising plans are implemented *exactly* as planned, and various respondents commented on the possible need for changes when they advised the advertising manager to

● *be flexible concerning tactical changes in the plan subject to keeping objectives* (ag)

● *be flexible enough to take advantage of media-owner offers* (m-o)

Changes to brief

Various practitioners pointed out the negative aspects of changes in plan, when they commented on practices to avoid. They urged that the advertising manager

● *should not change the rules in the middle of buying* (ad)

● *should not allow plans or budgets to be altered in the short term without being aware of the implications in terms of reduced media efficiency* (ag)

● *should plan ahead and, short of major disasters, stick to the plan* (m-o)

Campaign changes

Most readers will know the apocryphal story of the advertising manager who said 'Let's take this campaign off — they'll all be tired of it by now' only to be told 'It hasn't appeared yet — you've only seen it at internal meetings'. Various advertising managers were aware of this danger, when they advised that you

● *should give the media schedule time to do its job* (ad)
and
● *should not pull out of a campaign half-way through* (ad)

A final quotation touches on changes but also covers the whole client/agency relationship. This comes from the agency man who commented that

● Of course *the client has the final say in media selection: it's his money. But he should (a) approve the final schedule as early as possible, (b) not make changes thereafter. (The same golden rules apply equally to creative work.) The other golden rule is that, since clients have the final say, they should pay their bills promptly, but this probably comes under the heading of effective use of agencies, rather than media!* (ag)

I have already made clear my view — you cannot separate use of agencies from use of media.

Miscellaneous

The final tongue-in-check quotation has nothing whatsoever to do with media planning and buying, but I could not resist including it. One practitioner advised that the advertising manager

● *should also pay for lunch occasionally!* (other)

7

ROLE OF THE ADVERTISING AGENCY

Whether undertaken by advertiser or agency or shared between them, the various component tasks which overall make for good advertising remain the same. These tasks are listed at the start of Chapter 6. The aim of this chapter is not to consider these tasks as such, but to review how the agency sets about them, in partnership with its client.

It is interesting to recall that agencies were originally media-owners' service departments, not independent organisations. In the early days of advertising, agencies acted as representatives for newspapers and sold space in them to advertisers. At first, the agencies bought space in quantity, and made their profit by selling it in smaller units for as much as they could get. Later still, agencies started to sell space on a commission basis, and a commission system is still the current basis for agency remuneration, agencies taking their profit from commissions granted by media-owners rather than from advertisers.

Finding it easier to sell space if they suggested how it should be used, the agencies started a copywriting service, and soon afterwards design and art services were added. By this time, agencies were really working more for the advertisers than for the newspaper proprietors, and before long they became fully fledged service organisations giving their clients a complete range of advertising services. They also became independent, and bought space in whichever newspapers or other advertising media they thought best served their clients' interests. Today, the term 'agency' no longer applies in the legal sense, since the agency makes contracts in its own right — with its clients on the one hand and with media-owners on the other — and remains a party to the advertisement contract, which it would not were it an 'agency' in the legal sense of the word. Agencies are thus liable in law for debts to media, even though they made the bookings on their client's behalf.

The advantages of using an advertising agency

There are a number of reasons why a manufacturer employs the services of an advertising aganecy instead of relying on his own advertising department.

1   A team of experts   Primarily, agencies justify their existence by providing a team of experts to work in closest co-operation with the client's own advertising staff. The team includes specialists in all the many aspects of advertising practice including, of course, media. There are, however, many other advantages to agency service.

2   The work load problem   The advertiser could no doubt recruit experts on his own staff, but there might be insufficient work to keep an expert on, say, media, fully occupied. The agency, on the other hand, can afford to employ the specialist, since he will be working full-time for a number of clients, according to their varying needs for his expert advice. Alternatively, the client might himself employ a number of independent consultants (as discussed later in this chapter), but, here again, they would not be accustomed to working together, whereas the agency has the experts immediately available and already working as a team.

3   A new approach   A further advantage of employing an agency is that it brings a fresh approach to a problem, since its staff are detached from the company's day-to-day operations, whereas an advertiser's own staff often become so involved in detailed work that they no longer see the wood for the trees.

4   Experience in allied fields   Again, since they are handling different products for a number of clients, agencies have wider experience and their personnel, not being restricted to any one company's problems, are unlikely to take a narrow view. Besides, the knowledge and experience gained from one marketing problem can frequently be adapted to meet another, and in this way each client derives benefit from the agency's experience in other fields — an advantage of particular importance today when trading patterns are changing so rapidly. An agency keeps abreast of new developments through direct contact with the marketing problems of a number of advertisers, and can advise its clients in the light of its wide knowledge and experience. Advertisers, of course, also keep themselves up-to-date but, because they operate in only one product field, their experience is inevitably limited.

5   Buying power   The advertising agency's total expenditure must necessarily be larger than any one client's individual budget. Accordingly, when buying on its clients' behalf, it can bring considerable pressure to bear on suppliers and media-owners — far more pressure than most advertisers can exert on their own. This buying 'muscle' can be exerted by the agency not only on media purchases but on all other items, such as print or artwork, that the agency buys on its clients' behalf.

6   *Reduced cost*   A further advantage of agency service arises directly from the commission granted by the media-owners, which helps reduce the costs of using the agency's team of experts. Media-owners grant commission, usually ranging from 10 to 15 per cent, to recognised advertising agencies, and agencies get commission on almost everything they buy on a client's behalf. If an advertisement costs £1000, that is the amount the client spends whether he makes the booking direct or through his advertising agency. But by booking it through his advertising agency, though it still costs him £1000, the agency receives 15 per cent commission, or £150. Where the commission granted by media-owners is less than 15 per cent, the agency may 'round up' the charge made to clients, at +17.65 per cent of the net cost, to recoup the difference in income from that advertisement.

For some clients, where the commission is enough to cover costs and provide a sufficient profit, the agency will work on commission alone, and the advertiser then reaps the benefit of agency service without charge. On the other hand, if an agency finds its expenses in handling the client's advertising exceed the commission received, or leave an insufficient margin of profit, it will charge a 'service fee' to obtain the additional income necessary. Even where the advertiser pays a service fee, however, this is usually still less expensive than taking all the experts onto his own staff.

For many years there has been talk of the commission system breaking down but, despite much discussion of alternatives, it still survives — even if in changing form.

Commission was originally granted only to 'recognised' advertising agencies, and the financial vetting of applicant agencies was usually undertaken by the appropriate media-owners' trade organisation, as a central service for its members. Following the extension of restrictive practices legislation to services, however, the recognition system came under review.

After discussion with the Office of Fair Trading, it was agreed that joint financial vetting of applicant agencies was an essential area for continuation of collective action, and thus acceptable within the terms of the legislation.

Other matters formerly incorporated in the joint recognition system have however now been excluded: these are the agreement to pay commission, the former ruling about non-rebating of commission to clients, and the granting of recognition to certain categories of agency only (with requirements as to their equipment/ staffing and ownership). It is now considered that these areas primarily concern the individual relationships between media-owner and agency and between agency and advertiser, and should therefore not be covered by the revised recognition system.

All matters relating to payment of commission are thus now for the individual decision of each media-owner. Accordingly, under the new arrangements, recognition no longer carries with it any entitlement or conditions regarding the payment of commission. Recognised agencies do, however, benefit from the central trade body's recommendation to its members that such agencies should receive credit terms.

Further legislation or new rulings by the Office of Fair Trading may lead to other modifications, and alternative methods of agency remuneration or internal business pressures within the advertising industry may still lead to the commission system breaking down and so, when considering the advantages of using an advertising agency, the other — and main — benefits of agency service should be the prime consideration.

7 *Other savings* Other benefits of agency service, though of less importance, can nevertheless result in considerable administrative savings. Any company placing its advertising direct receives individual invoices from all media on the schedule, as well as accounts for artwork, production of press advertisements, printing of leaflets, and for making television, cinema or radio commercials. When an agency is employed, however, the advertiser receives comprehensive accounts covering all these many and varied items, which he can then settle with a single payment. In addition, there are clerical savings in that typed copies of media schedules and other documents are provided as a normal part of the agency's service.

The drawbacks of agency service

Employing an advertising agency is not without its drawbacks, though in most cases these are outweighed by the advantages.

1 *Divided attention* One disadvantage is that agency personnel work on several different accounts at the same time, and clearly cannot give their undivided attention to all of them simultaneously.

If something urgent crops up with one client, agency personnel may be prevented by other commitments from devoting all their time to dealing with it, whereas a manufacturer employing his own advertising staff knows that his problems receive undivided attention all the time.

2   *The time lag*   Again, agency service is not always as speedy as direct working, and a manufacturer whose advertising is constantly subject to unexpected changes might prefer to do the job himself. If the content of the advertising is under continual review, this could well apply: a mail order firm, for example, might wish to drop one item from an advertisement immediately stocks were exhausted and replace it with another line. Similarly, a travel agent might wish to stop advertising his Italian holiday tours just as soon as all places were booked, and to substitute another country where he still has vacancies.

3   *Cost*   A further drawback arises from the commissions received by the agency, the service fee charged, and the amount of work involved. For some types of advertising, the commission may be so small and the service fee so high that it becomes more economical for the advertiser to engage his own experts and to set up an advertising department which amounts to a small agency. Much depends on the nature of the advertising, for where media costs are low the agency receives little income from commission. On the other hand, it takes just as much effort to prepare an advertisement for a technical journal as for a national newspaper, yet the former task will bring the agency far less revenue than the second, simply because it receives commission on a smaller sum.

4   *Built-in 'inertia'*   The income *versus* workload problem can be extended, since the agency receives roughly the same commission on £1000, whether it is spent on a single advertisement or on hundreds, but its costs will vary considerably. A travel agent, for example, might get far better results from classified insertions than from display advertisements and would consequently want to advertise in this way. From the agency standpoint, however, this could be extremely uneconomic — imagine how many classified or semi-display advertisements you could buy for £1000 — and each one would necessitate typing an order, preparing copy and type mark-up, checking proofs and vouchers, and paying an invoice. The administrative costs would leave little or no profit from the commission. The commission system thus has a 'built-in' temptation for agencies to achieve maximum income with minimum effort.

The same argument can be applied to changes in advertisement content. The agency incurs lower staff costs by preparing one advertisement and letting it run week after week for a year than if it changes the content each month. The income from commission remains the same, yet monthly changes of copy mean 12 times as much work, with consequent higher staff costs and lower profits.

Agencies rightly need to make a profit, and to some extent this can be achieved by charging a higher service fee to recoup the additional staff costs involved. The higher the service fee, however, the more attractive it becomes for the advertiser to run his own advertising department, or to transfer to an agency charging a lower fee.

Agency directors are of course more than aware of all these drawbacks, and take the necessary steps to overcome them. Agency management is thus of great importance in ensuring that advertising skills are used to maximum effect, on behalf of the agency's clients.

Agencies and media owners

Employment of an advertising agency should bring benefits to media-owners as well as to advertisers. Ideally, it means that a media representative presents his sales argument to an advertising expert who will appreciate his medium's various selling points, evaluate them in terms of the client's marketing strategy and prepare a schedule in which all the media dovetail in a carefully planned campaign.

With companies which have little experience of advertising — particularly small firms — media representatives often find selling a difficult task, because before they can present the case for their medium they must devote considerable time to selling the need to advertise. With some inexperienced advertisers the media representative has to go even further, even to the extent of writing copy and suggesting layouts. This point brings to light another benefit that media-owners receive from agency service: when an agency is employed, there are expert staff to create advertisements and the media-owner's production staff can expect to receive the necessary material in good time. In many cases, media-owners receive from agencies complete advertisements, and are not involved in any typesetting expenses. Furthermore, when proofs are submitted, they are returned promptly with alterations indicated with the accepted proof correction marks instead of the crossings-out and arrows used by the inexperienced layman.

As every media-owner knows, there are times when the agency does not deliver as promptly as it should (perhaps because of pressure caused by rush campaigns for a number of clients simultaneously) and the media representatives find themselves chasing the agency for material or the return of corrected proofs. For the most part, however, the media-owner's life is made easier by the smooth functioning of agency procedure.

There can also be financial benefits, since the media-owner is dealing with an advertising agency he recognises (either directly or through his trade association) rather than a number of perhaps little-known clients into whose creditworthiness he would otherwise have to make individual and time-consuming investigations. The agency is liable in law for space or time booked on its clients' behalf, and the media-owner can thus look to the agency direct for payment.

Agency procedure

When a company appoints an agency, the first task of the agency personnel is to find out all about their client's activities and problems. The agency's investigations, discussed in detail in Part 3, necessarily duplicate those undertaken by the advertising manager when he was first appointed, since the agency staff need an equally clear under-standing of the client's company background and marketing objectives. The agency will spend considerable time making a thorough investigation, for not until the advertiser's problem has been accurately defined can the agency attempt to solve it. The size of the appropriation and the period to be covered are also important to the agency, as are precise instructions on what the appropriation covers. Are production charges included or only media costs? Is the client undertaking part of the campaign himself and keeping back a 'below the line' budget for this purpose? Practice varies with the firm, as we have seen, and there are no hard and fast rules. Obviously, however, the agency must know what money is available and what it has to cover.

Ideally, the client will give the agency *all* the information it needs when he gives his advertising 'brief': the quality of work produced by the agency to a considerable extent depends on the client's skill in giving his agency all the information it needs in order to prepare advertising proposals on his behalf.

Once the agency is confident that it has a correct understanding of the situation, it can start the vital work of preparing an advertising campaign to help its client achieve his marketing objectives. In many cases, to ensure that its understanding of the problem is correct, the agency will prepare a 'facts book' detailing the marketing situation, which the client will double-check for accuracy. One respondent recommended, as a basic rule for the effective use of advertising media

- *agency/client agreement in writing on product positioning, market strategy and target audience* (ad)

Planning the campaign

An important person in defining and solving the advertising and marketing problem is the agency's account executive. This title is rather misleading, since the executive has little to do with accounting as such, although he certainly bears responsibility for expenditure of the appropriation. The account executive is, in fact, responsible for *all* aspects of handling the client or 'account'. He is usually selected soon after the agency is appointed and attends the meeting at which the agency is briefed on the problem. It is true to say that no client, however well-intentioned, ever gives a 100 per cent perfect briefing and it is up to the executive to ensure, by asking the right questions, that his agency has all the facts it needs to solve the problem.

The account executive has a two-way role, in that he represents the agency to the client and the client to the agency. He is the individual to whom the agency staff in all departments turn for information: equally, it is through him that the client's problems are channelled to the appropriate agency specialists, and their work co-ordinated. Frequently you may encounter different levels of account executive. Some larger agencies have account executives backed by assistant executives who handle the day-to-day work on each account. At a higher level, there may be account supervisors, each responsible for a number of account executives handling a similar number of accounts. Again, there may be account directors at a still higher level, with overall responsibility for the campaigns handled by their account supervisors. Another variation is that an individual on the executive side may be responsible for a number of accounts rather than just one. For greater cross-fertilisation of ideas, and to prevent them getting into a rut, many agencies deliberately give their executives varied responsibilities. You may also meet agencies where the term account executive' is not used, executive staff being referred to as 'representatives' or 'managers'. Finally, mention must be made of the widely debated question of the *need* for account executives, and the fact that some agencies have been established with the deliberate policy of ignoring the traditional function of the account executive. For the sake of simplicity, however, the term 'account executive' is used from this point on, to identify the executive function.

Once the problem is clearly defined, the agency staff can start to solve it, and here the account executive plays a key role. He may start by calling a meeting of a 'Plans Board' (formal or informal) on which will be representatives of all the important agency departments. Creative staff are present to consider the theme to be featured in the advertising, and the media department to advise on whether the prospective customers could best be reached by press, posters, television or some other medium. Both media and creative departments *must* be represented on the plans board, since the decision of one department directly affects the other.

One agency respondent felt extremely strongly on this matter, as the following quotation proves:

● *this agency strongly believes that close liaison between the media and creative departments is vital in the development and implementation of really effective advertising. It is inconceivable to us that either function should be carried out independently with only nominal or infrequent communication between the two. And yet in some agencies the two departments are not even located in the same building!* (ag)

Use of any medium also involves *production* considerations, for there is obviously no point in booking space if the advertisement cannot be prepared in time to meet the media-owner's copy date or if the medium's ability to *deliver* your advertising message is not utilised to full advantage. Production costs, too, are important and can influence media selection. The agency production staff are thus directly concerned in media decisions, and will give their views at plans board meetings. Others beside creative, media and production staff may also be represented on the plans board, including any experts in the agency's team who can contribute to solving the particular problem. The plans board may also include other account executives, in addition to the one handling the particular client, for the benefit of their experience and advice. Similarly, other senior members of the various departments may sit on the plans board, even though they are not involved in the day-to-day running of the account. Thus the client gains maximum benefit from the combined talents of the agency.

The plans board discusses the client's overall marketing problem from every angle and finally agrees on a basic solution. Since any advertising campaign represents a combination of interlocking decisions regarding marketing, media, creative, production and other aspects of advertising, clearly broad agreement must be reached by the board as a whole.

The research department

When agency staff attempt to define their client's marketing problem they may decide that they lack sufficient information to reach a sound and reasoned judgement and will call in the research department. This department may already have a representative on the plans board, for the benefit of his general advice, but when more detailed information is required the research department starts to function in its own right.

A tremendous amount of information is readily available in published form, so before any 'field' research is undertaken there is always 'desk' research, which involves checking through existing sources of information. In some agencies desk research staff form a separate department and may be known by another title such as 'Information' or 'Library', while a second department — usually with the formal title of 'Research Department' — looks after field research.

Desk research is carried out before field research, as a matter of form, but if some vital questions remain unanswered, or if some of the information available was published some time ago and is thus out-of-date, then field research becomes essential and the agency research department takes action. Its task lies in planning the operation rather than undertaking the actual 'fieldwork', which is usually carried out by a specialist market research organisation. The agency selects and works with the most suitable market research company in planning the research and supervising the fieldwork. Equally, it gives much thought to interpreting the results and making recommendations for action.

As soon as the information collected has been carefully checked and interpreted, there are further meetings of the plans board to consider the advertising and marketing campaign. Once the overall campaign strategy has been agreed, the individual departments set to work to crystallise their ideas and to produce detailed proposals in accordance with the agreed broad plan.

The media department

The media department is represented when the overall campaign is discussed at plans board level. Once the general strategy is agreed, it is then up to the media department to get down to detailed planning with the aim of spending the client's appropriation in such a way that his advertising message reaches prospective buyers as effectively and economically as possible. The media planners are experts on the full range of media and have at their command all the relevant statistics about press, posters, cinema, television, radio and other media.

There is often considerable specialisation within the media department. At its head there may be a media director who represents the media viewpoint on the plans board and agrees the overall strategy. Immediately responsible to him may be media planners whose task is to take the broad strategy and go into the detail of specific media, size, position, number of insertions, dates and so on. Once this stage is agreed, specialist media buyers may take over to put the plan into operation. For example, specialist television time-buyers may negotiate with the programme contractors for the best possible implementation of the media planners' proposals and decide in exactly which breaks, at what times and on which days the client's television commercials will appear. The time-buyers keep this schedule under constant review, adjusting it in the light of changes in BBC or commercial programmes, statistics on audience size and composition, or any additional information likely to influence the schedule's effectiveness.

The time-buyers may also be responsible for radio and cinema advertising, or these two media may be the province of separate specialists. Even in the field of press media, specialisation may occur, one space-buyer concentrating on national newspapers, and another on, say women's magazines. In some agencies outdoor advertising might be the responsibility of specialist staff, as might be exhibitions. These different experts have, however, a common aim: to communicate the client's advertising message as effectively as possible through the media which are their own particular responsibility. Other agencies find it more effective to avoid over-specialisation and require their staff, at all levels, to handle the full range of media.

Some agencies have specialist media research staff, sometimes called 'media assessors'. Media-owners issue a great deal of useful research material and the flow of information is such that some agencies appoint staff whose main task is to evaluate these documents, thus leaving others free for their main function of planning and buying.

In larger agencies there may be many experts and the media department may operate on a 'group' system, each group containing both planners and buyers, with the media director exercising general control over all groups.

Whatever the agency structure, the experts' skill lies not so much in their detailed knowledge of media (although this may call for years of experience) but in applying this knowledge to their client's advertising problems. If the media specialists are to match the advantages (or drawbacks) of the wide range of advertising media with the requirements of each client's individual marketing problem, they must fully understand that problem. A full briefing of the media department is, therefore, essential if it is to come up with the right answers.

Given this efficient briefing, the media department can then evaluate the range of media, select those most suitable in the light of the client's requirements and prepare detailed proposals. This work is complex and merits more attention than can be given in one chapter dealing with an advertising agency's overall operation. Media evaluation, selection and planning are, therefore, the subjects of later discussion in Part 3.

The creative department

While the media department interprets in detail the broad approach agreed at plans board level, the creative staff take their work to a more advanced level. Copy is written for press advertisements or printed material, and layouts prepared. For posters or display material, roughs or dummies are made, and storyboards drawn up for television or cinema commercials. Detailed discussion of these activities is outside the scope of any book on media, although clearly the creative content of advertisements is vital: there is little point in spending hours on devising a complex media plan only to have it deliver the wrong message. The reverse is just as true — even a superb advertisement cannot work to best advantage if delivered to the wrong audience. Creative and media aspects of campaign planning are of equal importance if you are to use advertising media effectively.

Review of proposals

As soon as detailed media and creative proposals are ready, the plans board meets again to review the work. Possibly there may now be a formal change of title, and the committee becomes known as the 'Review Board'. In some agencies, the review board comprises precisely the same individuals as the plans board and would therefore probably continue under the same name. In others, the individuals as well as the name are changed. Whatever the practice, the purpose is to check meticulously, point by point, the proposals to be submitted to the client to ensure that there are no discrepancies in the work of the individual departments, that all the various aspects of the campaign interlock, that the proposals conform to the basic strategy agreed by the earlier plans board, and that the quality of the work matches up to the agency's standards.

146

This, then, is the pattern of agency work — investigation, analysis of the problem, agreement on a basic solution, working out a detailed plan, and careful checking to ensure that the proposals are faultless. The various stages involved are an indication of the care which agencies take in their work, even though the procedure may not always be on a formal basis. Indeed, a plans board meeting may sometimes be completely informal, with the account executive talking over the problem with individual members of the various departments, after normal office hours and away from the interuptions of the telephone and other distractions. Some practitioners argue strongly against formal plans or review boards on the grounds that they stifle individuals and impose an agency style on all clients regardless of their requirements. For this reason, meetings may sometimes be completely informal.

Presentation of proposals

Once the detailed proposals have been approved by the review board, they are made ready for presentation to the client. The media schedule is typed out in its final form, as is the advertisement copy, and finished versions of designs are prepared by the creative staff. These are then presented to the client, and the inter-relationship between copy, design and media explained. It is essential that these three are presented together, for the client would be unable to approve a media schedule without knowing the advertisements to be featured, nor could he approve creative work without knowing the media in which it was to appear. Creative and media proposals are accordingly presented together, with other parts of the plan.

The presentation of campaign proposals is of major importance and should not be viewed as 'selling' the proposals to the client but rather as careful explanation of the individual parts of a complex plan and how they are related. Presentation of proposals is, in fact, the very reverse of the agency's first task. When the problem was first discussed, it was broken down into individual components for detailed work by the various departments, whereas in the formal presentation the specialist proposals are joined together and presented as a co-ordinated plan.

At the presentation, the account executive usually outlines the market situation and the agency's approach to the client's problem. He then introduces individual members of the agency team who, in turn, present their own sections of the campaign and explain the reasoning behind them. The research staff outline how prospective customers were defined: the media planner in his turn presents the schedule designed to reach the market defined by research: and the creative staff show and discuss the suggested advertisements. Experts from other departments may also be called on to clarify their particular part of the plan. Finally, the account executive concludes the presentation by summarising the major points made and the reasoning behind them.

An effective presentation is of major importance, because the client's acceptance of an agency's proposals depends on a clear understanding of the many complex and interlocking sections of the campaign plan. Cases are not unknown where a campaign has been rejected, not because the plan was a bad one but because the agency failed to explain adequately the thinking behind it. For this reason, agencies often go to considerable lengths to ensure that the client has a clear understanding of the proposals. On the media side, charts are prepared (some often very elaborate) to present visually the proposed schedule and further charts are used to clarify the reasons why this particular media pattern has been selected. Some agencies even have 'charting departments', set up solely to prepare the visual aids necessary for perfect presentation of their proposals.

Where the presentation is on a major campaign, the agency may call on all those concerned to make a 'dry run' beforehand, amounting almost to a rehearsal, and may go to the extent of preparing scripts for the entire proceedings, showing the order of speaking, the words to be spoken by each individual, and the charts, films or other visual aids to be used. Some agencies even put the entire presentation on film or video-tape and screen this to the client, rather than risk the possibility of error that is always present in a 'live' presentation. This sounds an elaborate procedure, as indeed it is, but it could be well worth while in ensuring that the campaign is faultlessly presented. It is all too easy when speaking to overlook some point or fail to express it clearly, or to take points out of order and so destroy the logic of an argument. The more complex the scheme, the greater the need for the details and the reasoning behind them to be made completely clear. As marketing problems and advertising planning become more complex, so the need for lucid presentation becomes even more vital.

Execution of proposals

Before giving the agency formal approval to proceed, the client checks the proposals to ensure that they are sound and that they dovetail with his company's marketing activities. Once the agency has the client's agreement, the advertising proposals can be put into effect: the media schedule must be converted into actual orders to media-owners and parallel action must be taken by creative staff and other departments to bring their proposals to finished form. The detail of this work is described in Part 3.

The control department

The control department is often described, and with justification, as the nerve centre of an agency. Its function is evident from the various titles by which it may be described — 'progress', 'traffic', 'control', or 'copy detail'. It controls the progress or traffic of detail work, and the smooth functioning of the agency turns to a great extent on the efficiency of this department.

Copies of media orders come to the traffic department and set in motion the complex procedure of producing an advertisement. Take, for example, the task of handling a straightforward insertion in a Christmas issue. The booking may be made many months in advance, but it would be foolish to wait until the last minute and then do a rush job, since this rarely results in effective advertising. The control department, therefore, undertakes the complicated arithmetic of routing the advertisement through the agency. The copy detail staff must prepare a detailed time schedule, working back from the media-owner's copy date, which may be weeks or even months in advance of publication date. Time must be allowed for typesetting and production and for correction of proofs by both client and agency. Account must also be taken of the time needed to produce artwork, and to mark up copy for typesetting. Before this work can be done, the copy must be written and a visual prepared, and adequate time must be allowed for these to be submitted to the client and approved. Even before the creative team can start work, the account executive must contact the advertising manager, to see if there are any special requirements for this Christmas advertisement, and this, too, must be allowed for in the time schedule.

The control department must anticipate the time needed for each of these stages and build in a safety margin to allow for unexpected delays and, if necessary, the revision of copy, visuals, or proofs. A time-schedule must be prepared, allowing so many days for each stage, and careful watch must be kept to ensure that no delays occur anywhere along the line. If there is delay on the part of someone early in the chain, some other unfortunate individual will, later on, have to race against time. Too much haste seldom produces good work, as well as greatly increasing the possibility of error — and mistakes in advertising tend to be expensive. A good control department thus makes for efficiency and prevents costly errors, as well as directly affecting the quality of the agency's work.

In addition to press advertisements, the control department is frequently responsible for the progress of television and radio commercials, printed material, exhibition stands — in fact all agency work, whatever the medium. With a major campaign, where media and creative proposals are submitted together for approval, the work of the department even extends to ensuring that the proposals are ready in good time for submission (and prior checking by the review board). Once the proposals are approved, the control department also supervises their execution.

Vouchers and accounts

Just as the advertising manager checks to see that his company receives value for money spent on advertising, so does the agency. The voucher section checks that the correct advertisement appeared on the appointed day, in the position booked and that the printing quality was up to the required standard. Not until the voucher copy has been checked is the media-owner's invoice passed through for payment. The location of the voucher section varies: in some agencies it is part of the media department, in others it is attached to the production or control departments or is an extension of the accounts department.

Other departments

The general pattern of agency operations remains the same whatever the variations in size and agency structure: problem analysis, preparation of media and creative proposals to solve that problem, and execution of the approved proposals. The proposals are based on the three functions of advertisement creation, media selection and production work, and these three form the essence of agency service.

In the course of time, however, and reflecting the increasing complexity of marketing problems, many agencies have extended the scope of their services by developing other departments, staffed with experts capable of solving specialist sections of their client's marketing problem. Some agencies, for example, have a special research department, and other activities such as television, marketing, merchandising, public relations and international operations may also merit the status of separate departments, each under its own director. Some agencies develop these activities in another way, by establishing subsidiary or associated companies which operate on a commercial basis, and offer their services to all, rather than restricting them to the agency's immediate clients. As well as being profitable in their own right, such companies can also play an important part in attracting new clients to an agency.

Television   The specialist nature of television advertising led some agencies to group the various specialists together in a working unit, rather than leave them in the various departments that would normally house them. Production of television commercials calls for different expertise than for printed media; the agencies therefore include specialist television producers on their staff. Similarly, on the creative side, the agency's staff may include specialist storyboard artists and scriptwriters, who think in terms of moving rather than still pictures, and the spoken rather than the printed word. On the media side, as we have seen, specialist time-buyers may be employed.

Whatever the agency structure, the aim is to create effective television commercials and to screen them to best advantage. It is becoming less customary now to concentrate all television staff in a single department and, where separate television departments do still exist, they tend to concentrate on the creative and production sides, and to leave time-buying to the media department.

Merchandising   In reviewing the advertising manager's work the point was made that, as well as stimulating public demand for his company's products, he must also ensure that they are on display in the shops and readily available for customers to buy. In consequence, a considerable amount of merchandising or sales promotion activity is aimed at retail outlets and the company's sales force to ensure that the public campaign is well backed-up at point of sale. Some larger agencies have specialist staff to advise clients on this vital work or, where the advertiser does not have experts in this field, to mount complete merchandising campaigns for him.

Marketing   Marketing, like merchandising, may be the province of the agency as well as the advertiser. Some agencies have special marketing staff who co-operate with clients in analysing and assessing consumer wants and needs and devising marketing programmes to satisfy them.

Some agencies have even gone to the extent of establishing their own retail outlets which operate independently on a profit-making basis. Such shops provide the agency with invaluable first-hand information about the market, and can be used for testing products, packaging, or other elements of the marketing mix.

Public relations   As we have already seen, PR may be added to the responsibilities of the advertising manager or may be delegated to a specialist section of the agency. A number of agencies have a PR department, fully staffed by experts who work in co-operation with their clients: others may provide a similar service through associated or subsidiary companies. Either way, the aim is still a 'deliberate, planned and sustained effort to establish and maintain mutual understanding between the organisation and its public'.

International   With so many organisations tending to operate internationally, a number of advertising agencies now extend their services to include advising clients on business activities overseas. This is done in a variety of ways. Some agencies have set up branch offices in a chain of overseas centres, staffing them with both local personnel and head office experts. Others have forged financial links by taking over the ownership of an existing overseas agency. This method has the advantage of acquiring an established business organisation which is already operating successfully with an expert staff and avoids the many problems of starting from scratch. Other agencies extend their services more informally by teaming up with similar agencies in important overseas centres, which are then described as 'associate companies', each agency helping the other, and its clients, by advice on its own market. Though each associate agency benefits from the association, the other methods described afford certain advantages that cannot be achieved by such informal links. Financial control ensures that better liaison and common thinking can be achieved than through 'associateship' alone, and there is the further assurance that the agency's operation will be kept in line with what is required.

Specialist agencies

Some agencies, rather than expand by diversifying their departments, prefer to concentrate their abilities, as in the case of an agency specialising in technical advertising. Copywriting for industrial products demands a degree of technical knowledge that the average consumer-product copywriter does not possess. Similarly, technical illustrations such as cross-sections of machinery may prove outside the average agency creative expertise. Specialist agencies, whose staff have the necessary technical knowledge and skills, thus take their place on the agency scene. Similarly, the particular needs of recruitment advertising have led some agencies to concentrate on this specialist area.

Other 'agencies' concentrate their abilities in a different way. Rather than provide the full service of advertisement creation, media planning and buying, and production work, they restrict their expertise to one of these three functions, and it is thus possible to call on specialist services for creative work only. On the media side, the 'buying shops' or media independents — the companies that undertake responsibility for buying media on behalf of advertisers (independently of the agency providing the creative work) — are now an important feature of the current advertising scene.

Some advertisers, rather than use a conventional full service agency, prefer to rely on creative consultancies and media independents, working alongside their own advertising staff. Some small agencies also use media independents, either for their media buying or as a substitute for a complete media department, and may equally call on creative consultancies in the same way.

Agency systems

Quite apart from departmental variations, agencies also differ in their system of operation. Some operate on the 'group' system whereby the agency is divided into two or more separate units, each of which amounts to a self-contained agency. Others use the 'pyramid' system, under which directors are responsible for a group of accounts (rather than for staff members) and the executive, media, creative or other staff may all work on several accounts, each of which may be under the control of a different director. The media department may operate on either system.

The agency in operation

As in the previous two chapters, this part concentrates on how the agency should set about its tasks, rather than examining the tasks themselves. Similarly, since it is impossible to include all the points raised, emphasis is given to those mentioned most frequently, which are illustrated by relevant quotations.

Three-way relationships

Before considering the agency's working relations with client and media, respectively, there is the matter of their three-way relationship. Respondents from all sides of the business advised the agency to

● *not only allow but encourage direct contact between all three parties* (ad)

● *communicate regularly with clients and media-owners* (ag)

153

- *encourage contact between client and media-owner* (m-o)

Other respondents extended this to media presentations, when they recommended that the agency should

- *give media reps opportunity to present new information — present to advertiser at same time* (ad)
- *outside of planning periods encourage* ad hoc *presentations by media to agency and client personnel* (ag)
- *give media representatives the opportunity to contribute and put forward any sound proposals to client* (m-o)

The matter of three-way contact was raised (in reverse) by those commenting on practices to avoid. As you would expect, it was media-owners who suggested that the agency

- *should not be fearful of the influence that media personnel can bring to bear. Client/agency/media should be encouraged to work together* (m-o)

The final word on the three-way relationship goes to the agency man who pointed out that

- *this is not a* menage a trois, *but two separate couples: client/ agency and agency/media. (I won't pursue the analogy though it could be fun!) The agency is the go-between, listening to media, making up its own mind, and making recommendations to its client. As in so many other respects of the advertising business, the essential role of the agency is to be in the middle* (ag)

Let's look in more detail at these two separate couples, starting with agency media.

Agency/media-owner relationships

Agency/media contacts   There was unanimity on the need for close contact with media, when respondents advised the agency to

- *develop a good working relationship with media-owners* (ad)
- *adopt an open-door policy with media-owners* (ag)
- *maintain close contacts with media* (m-o)

This was developed by other practitioners who urged the need for close *personal* links. Their recommendation was that the agency should

154

- *have close personal ties with media. In a high-demand situation,* my *agency should be given preference* (ad)

- *establish contact with media-owners at every management level* (ag)

- *see media people at correct level* (m-o)

Information from media   The fact that media-owners are a source of valuable information was widely recognised, as the following quotations illustrate. It was frequently suggested that the agency should

- *recognise the value of the media-owner's knowledge and maintain flexibility so the information can flow freely to the benefit of client* (ad)

- *involve media representatives in providing market/media data* (ag)

- *always be aware of the information readily available to them from media — both collectively and individually* (m-o)

Some advertisers, however, had reservations about the information supplied by media. Their advice was that the agency

- *should filter information from media-owners and where necessary ask for further information in order to present facts to client* (ad)

It was not only the advertisers who had reservations — comments were made also by the other two parties, of which the following two are typical. Advice was that the agency

- *should insist on ever-improving reader/viewer data from media-owner* (ag)

- *should not believe more than 25 per cent of an unauthenticated circulation figure* (m-o)

Information to media   The flow of information should be a two-way process — two media-owners made this very point when they urged the agency to

- *be open with and to media representatives* (m-o)

- *. . . ensure a general two-way communication with media* (m-o)

Even if the other two parties did not make this point in so many words, the need to provide information to media-owners was widely recognised, as the following quotations illustrate: they recommend the agency to

- *ensure creative considerations are understood by the media* (ad)

- *give media-owners full planning background* (ag)

- *fully explain to media the objectives of a campaign* (m-o)

It is distressing that, when the same point was made in reverse, it was worded more vehemently by other respondents, who advised that the agency should NOT

- *lie to media-owners about budgets* (m-o)

- *mislead media reps with irrelevant information* (m-o)

The media contribution   Many respondents went beyond stressing the need to maintain contact with media-owners and using them as information sources. They urged that media be permitted to make a more positive contribution. Advice given was that the agency should

- *give media-owners opportunity to contribute* (ad)

- *encourage the media to take part in creative media thinking* (ag)

- *make full use of media facilities/runs/research, etc.* (ag)

As you would expect, it was the media-owners themselves who raised this matter most often, in advising the agency to

- *allow various media to tender their own media plans and consider these alongside their own requirements* (m-o)

One suggested when such a contribution would be most important: his view was that the agency should

- *give media representatives opportunity to contribute — almost total involvement particularly where new or innovative plans are afoot* (m-o)

Another media-owner suggested a different contribution when he advised the agency to

- *give media the opportunity to contribute to the creative and production process, so as to achieve the best reproduction possible* (m-o)

One agency man, however, had a distinct reservation. His advice was to

- *keep reps at arm's length after all possible facts, as opposed to bullshit, have been got out of them* (ag)

Media contacts with agencies   A point made earlier was that the agency staff should know their personal contacts *within* media, and some media-owners pointed out it was in the client's interests to extend media contacts reciprocally within the agency, to include both account and creative staff. Their advice was that the agency should

- *always give media representatives access to account handling executives* (m-o)

- *encourage media to present their case to* creative *people, not just time-buyers* (m-o)

Debate   The desirability of permitting media to contribute was extended by some practitioners to beyond the initial planning stage. Their advice was that the agency should explain — and debate — its planning approach with media-owners. They suggested that the agency

- *should not refuse media-owners access to contribute and challenge* (ad)

- *should where possible without jeopardising client confidentiality or exposing deal arrangements be prepared to debate its media approach if requested by any potentially useful media-owner* (ag)

The agency's duty to media   Although in the usually stronger position of being buyer rather than seller, the agency nevertheless has obligations to media-owners: these can be considered under 'before' and 'after' headings.

The need for knowledge of media is stressed in other chapters, and so only one quotation is necessary to illustrate how this applies to the agency in the 'before' situation. One respondent's advice to the agency was concise: it should

- *make sure it understands the medium before talking to the rep* (other)

The 'after' situation imposes other duties on agencies, once the orders have been placed. Media-owners pointed out the need for agencies to

- *supply copy in time and in a form to ensure good reproduction in the particular medium to be used* (m-o)

Agency/media relationships — the negative side

Various respondents mentioned difficulties which arise in every-day practice. Some drew attention to problems with which media-owners must contend, and suggested that the agency

● *should understand media-owners' problems (strikes, etc.)* (m-o)

Others pointed out that agency and media-owner approaches to solving their mutual client's problems were necessarily on a different basis. One quotation from either side will be sufficient to illustrate this. Advice to an agency from an agency man was that it

● *should always be prepared to listen to the sales 'pitches' of media representatives. In general, however, they have little if any knowledge of the marketing considerations and cannot be truly objective because of their vested interest. In certain directions their contribution can be extremely important — major research studies, consumer surveys* (ag)

The media advice which reflects the different standpoint is that the agency

● *should make full use of the facilities which media-owners make available, e.g. better analysis, and at the same time be aware of the danger of misuse of these facilities, i.e. trying to get the media-owner to do the agency's thinking for it* (m-o)

Agency/client relationships

The client's briefing   Many respondents commented on the vital role of information in the agency/client relationship — information both to and from the agency's client — and this is of course a reflection of points made in the earlier chapter on the advertiser. The importance of obtaining full information *from* the client was raised by respondents who urged the agency to

● *make sure they know the overall marketing plan for the brand* (ad)

● *be skilful in producing right information from the client* (ag)

● *establish parameters of brief* (m-o)

Information to the client   Other respondents stressed the need for information to flow in the other direction, from agency to client. Their advice was that the agency should

- *keep the client well informed of all changes in the media scene* (ad)

- *try to expand media knowledge of advertisers* (ag)

- *should not avoid 'educating' the client if he is ignorant of media* (m-o)

Working relationships   Many comments were made on the working relationships between the agency and its client. First came the obvious essential: that the agency should

- *work as closely as possible with the client* (ag)

Others pointed out the need, within this relationship, for the agency to respect the client's knowledge and

- *remember in specialist markets the client often understands the needs of his customers better than they do* (ad)

This point was however made more strongly in reverse by respondents who urged that the agency

- *should not object to advice and information from client, who must know a great deal about his own business, and here again the outside sales force are aware of the customers' reading (or viewing) habits, etc. This knowledge should be welcome by the agency even if it may mean revising the plan* (ad)

An agency man who accepted this view was concise in his recommendation. His advice to the agency was that it

- *should not assume it knows all there is to know about the client's own market* (ag)

Information vs Advice vs Instructions

There is no clear dividing line between accepting information and advice, and giving advice can turn imperceptibly into giving instructions. Accordingly, there was a wide range of opinions when this general area was raised by respondents. Views expressed ranged from advice that the agency

- *should not forget client's views on media matters* (ag)

to, slightly stronger, the recommendation that it should

- *not ignore the client's wishes* (ad)

or that it should

- *respond to client direction — after due thought* (ad)

Views, wishes or direction? Should the agency accept these varying degrees of instruction from its client? Advice given was that the agency

- *should not agree with client just because he's the client (other)*

- *should not produce what it believes the client wants to see* (ag)

Contacts within the agency

The preceding chapter on the advertiser stressed the need for the advertising manager to make contacts within the agency. The mirror image of this is of course for staff within the agency to make contact with the advertising manager: one quotation is sufficient to illustrate this point. This comes from the agency that felt it should

- *encourage service departments' contact with client* (ag)

Internal agency administration

The need for good administration within the agency was raised with the following rule to be followed in order to produce the best media plan

- *greater liaison between account and media people internally* (ad)

This may seem obvious, but one media planner plaintively pointed out how easily internal liaison can break down. The mistake here was

- *account executives by-passing the media department because they have an urgent meeting with client* (ag)

No doubt there are numerous media planners who will recognise the reality of this situation!

Preparation of proposals

The detailed work of preparing an effective campaign will be discussed in Part 3, but two quotations set this task in the context of the client/agency relationship. These come from client respondents who suggested the relationship they would prefer, when they stated that their agency should

● *feed the client with ideas, not vice-versa* (ad)

● *work in unison with the advertiser on marketing problems and lead in one primary way — the development of increased creativity in advertising* (ad)

Presentation to client

Assume for the moment that the agency has prepared campaign proposals on behalf of its client — what is the next stage? One practitioner urged the agency to

● *present creative and media proposals together to the client* (ag)

The first part of the chapter explained the reasoning behind this proposal, and the quotation clearly endorses the need for this approach.

Justification of recommendation

The next stage is to ensure that the client fully understands the thinking behind the agency's campaign proposals. One respondent suggested that the agency should

● *explain precisely how the schedule has been arrived at, to the client* (ag)

Whilst the need for the agency to justify its proposals was generally accepted, there were warnings about how to set about this task. One respondent advised that the agency should not

● *try to blind client with nonsense for the sake of it* (ad)

Defence of proposals

Many respondents stressed the need for agency staff to defend their proposals, should the need arise. Their advice was for the agency to

● *stick to their professional guns if they think the client is wrong (it can happen)* (ad)

161

- *be prepared to approach the client company at all levels to ensure the implementation of the scheme it believes to be in the brand's interest* (ag)

- *if the agency is entirely satisfied that its recommendations are valid, it should certainly try to resist undue client interference* (m-o)

Taking defence too far

While it was generally accepted that the agency should defend its proposals, some respondents warned against taking this to extremes. Their advice was that the agency should not

- *be adamant that their media proposals are 'spot on'* (ad)

- *be too dogmatic in its media recommendations* (ad)

Client's questioning

A variation on the theme of not defending proposals too strongly is found in the viewpoint of those who commented on the agency's attitude to questions. Their advice was that the agency

- *should not expect the client to agree its plans without question* (ad)

Client's suggestions

Moving even further away from the adamant defence approach, there is advice relating to the agency's attitude when its client suggests changes. It was suggested that the agency should not

- *refuse to consider changes suggested by client* (ad)

- *object to client demanding changes providing adequate reason is given which agency can argue on, if necessary* (ag)

- *object to client demands for changes, but should ensure client is aware of all implications* (ag)

A media-owner had very down-to-earth views in advising the agency to

- *encourage the client to question every aspect of the media plan, and not object to the client demanding changes if these are in fact successful. If, over a period, clients demand changes which are clearly counter-productive, then the agency-client relationship has become sterile and consideration should be given to breaking it up* (m-o)

Other respondents with equally down-to-earth attitudes pointed out that the agency

- *should realise it is the client who pays the bill, and therefore be prepared to accept changes* (ad)

- *it is the client's money — he has the final vote* (ag)

Client rejection

The quotation that exemplifies the attitude furthest removed from the 'defend at all costs' approach came from the agency man who felt that his firm

- *should not adopt an obstructional attitude if, after due debate, client rejects its proposals in favour of some alternative approach* (ag)

The agency's general attitude

Some respondents appear to have encountered agencies that adopt a very high-handed attitude. Their warning to the agency was that it should NOT

- *behave as if it were on Mount Olympus* (ad)

- *pretend they have found the philosopher's stone* (ad)

- *treat the client as an idiot (other)*

Needless to say, there are no quotations from agency personnel in defence of such an attitude! To the contrary two of them warned that agency men should not

- *dictate to client* (ag)

- *believe they know more than anybody else* (ag)

Working changes

Very different to changes suggested by the client are those made necessary by changed circumstances. Such possibilities were clearly in the mind of a respondent who advised the agency to

● *recommend changes to agreed plan if, for example, circumstances change* (ad)

It is perhaps surprising that this was raised more frequently as a negative matter, by practitioners commenting on practices to avoid, who advised that the agency

● *should not ignore changes relevant to (a) strategy, (b) changed conditions* (ag)

● *should not ignore changes in the market place* (ad)

Most quotations on this theme came from media-owners, who presumably encounter this problem from the receiving end. Their view was that the agency

● *should not object to changes if due to changes in market, but generally should stick to plan* (m-o)

Objections to changes

Not all changes should be accepted without question, however. Respondents from all sides of the business advised that the agency should not

● *object to client demanding changes provided they are well-reasoned — but clients do not want or need 'yes' agencies* (ad)

● *try to alter a long-standing programme unless there is a very good reason* (ag)

● *allow the client to change his plans without arguing* (m-o)

Agency authority

Although advertisers look to the agency for expert advice and do not want 'yes men', a number found it necessary to point out the need for the agency to follow orders when necessary. This was raised as a negative matter by respondents commenting on practices to avoid, who urged the agency not to

● *allow deviation from agreed plans without client authority* (ad)

- *strike up financial commitments with the media-owner without consulting the client, e.g. deals* (ad)

Other advertising managers went even further, reverting to the point at which they first agreed the campaign proposals. They stated that the agency

- *should not make out a firm order to media other than on basis of a signed order by the advertiser* (ad)

Agency freedom of action

The quotations just featured might seem a straight-jacket giving the agency little or no freedom of movement. The need for the agency to act on its client's behalf — perhaps very swiftly — was however recognised by many practitioners who suggested that the agency should

- *be encouraged to negotiate best possible 'deals' with media-owners, and be given sufficient flexibility to achieve these deals* (ad)
- *preserve its flexibility to react quickly to opportunities* (ag)
- *ensure their relations with client are such that changes can be made by either party within reasonable limits* (m-o)

Special offers

The quotations on flexibility related to special opportunities and offers, etc., and it is not surprising that this topic came up in its own right. Advice given was for the agency to

- *always be on the lookout for any particularly favourable buy, for its client* (ad)
- *investigate every piece of media information and offer that they and the client gets* (ad)

As you would expect, most comments of this nature came from advertisers, but naturally media-owners too want their offers to receive consideration. One advised that the agency should

- *forward every offer or rate deal for client's opinion* (m-o)

Another media-owner had a warning on this score, however: his advice was that the agency

- *should not assume every cut rate is a bargain* (m-o)

Agency performance

This matter was raised under several different headings — timing, initial targets, monitoring and subsequent evaluation.

Timing　　The matter of time to do the job crops up throughout this book, so only a few quotations are necessary to illustrate its importance within the agency context. These come from respondents who urged the agency to

- *work far enough ahead to be able to demand the best ad positions* (ad)
- *make media reservations as early as client's instructions allow* (m-o)

Initial targets　　The matter of initial targets was raised as a negative rather than a positive one. Two quotations from wary advertisers suggest that the agency should not

- *set low yardstick* (ad)
- *set its media targets (TV) too low in order to make its buying performance look good* (ad)

Monitoring and re-appraisal　　Other respondents commented on what the agency should be doing, whilst the campaign it recommended is running. Advice given was that the agency should

- *monitor performance very closely* (ad)
- *periodically review the schedule to ensure that all the reasons why they chose it still hold good* (ad)

Various media-owners apparently felt that they — as well as the advertisers — might well benefit if agencies undertook such periodic reviews. Their suggestions were that the agency should not

- *regard the client's media plan as sacrosanct, and incapable of adaptation once it has begun to operate* (m-o)
- *be afraid to change their schedule if a medium can prove they help to make a better one* (m-o)

Subsequent evaluation　　Many respondents — mostly the advertisers themselves — considered the agency has a responsibility in evaluating results. Advice given was for the agency to

- *always be honest about recent media performance — was it good/bad?* (ad)

Others were more specific in stipulating the *action* they expected; sometimes this related to past performance, ensuring that clients received value for money, whilst in other cases the proposed action related to possible improvements for the future. Looking first at value for money spent, advice was that the agency must

- *press the media-owner on behalf of the client for rebate, etc., whenever there is a shortfall on colour reproduction, print run, viewing figures, etc.* (ad)

- *not wait for client to complain before dealing with media errors* (ad)

The other aspect of evaluation related to possible improvements for the future, and agencies were urged to

- *report performance quickly with indicated action for the future* (ad)

Both aspects of evaluation — value for money in the past and possible improvements for the future — are discussed in more detail in Part 3. They are mentioned here in passing, however, in view of the agency's involvement.

Agency profitability

This is without doubt a controversial matter and, to put it bluntly, there are those who feel that some agencies place their own profitability before that of their client's. This was sometimes approached with the relatively mild advice that the agency

- *should put the client's results before its own* (m-o)

More usually this matter was raised, with varying degrees of vehemence, from the negative standpoint of agency profitability militating against effective use of media. One advertiser, commenting on factors which militate in this way, gave an extremely terse answer when he cited

- *agency greed* (ad)

More usually, however, comments came from media-owners, of which the following is an example:

- *media plans can be based on the 'easy way out' and take more consideration of the fastest way to earn commission than attempting to achieve the optimum* (m-o)

167

Some media-owners were even more outspoken when they cited

- *over-emphasis on agency profitability* (m-o)

- *not an error but deliberate policy to concentrate on the most profitable media, e.g. television, national press, national magazines* (m-o)

Other media-owners touched on agency profitability in another way, when commenting on value for money and what services the agency should provide in return for its commission. They urged that the agency

- *should not expect full commission for less than full agency service to both client and media-owner* (m-o)

- *should not plan to minimise its own cost at the expense of giving value to the client* (m-o)

It would be unfair to leave this controversial topic without letting the agencies, which received such a hammering, have the last word. This quotation comes from the agency man who advised that

- *you should make sure your method of remuneration allows you to give unbiased recommendations* (ag)

Who needs an agency?

The quotations selected to end this chapter reflect directly opposing views on the client's need for an agency — and come from the very sources you would expect.

A client view   One advertiser felt that

- *agencies are all too often not aware of the facts of business life. They need to become more aware of business in the round — then they might better relate to client's needs and the pressures of media-owners* (ad)

A media view   A media-owner, on the other hand, pointed out that

- *the advertiser should in his own interests develop a good relationship with media. In the trio of advertiser/agency/media the only disposable factor is 'agent'* (m-o)

The agency view   Two quotations from agencies illustrate their role as regards media planning and creative content

- *media-owners do not come into planning: their only function is to supply information. Advertisers come into it only in so far as they must be able to supply full information on their market and the financial restrictions to be imposed in getting it: the budget. That is, media-owners and advertisers don't plan: they supply information to the agency* (ag)

The importance of the agency's creative contribution is illustrated by the view of the (disposable?) agent who pointed out that

- *the agency should be the point or channel of contact between advertiser and media-owner. By-passing the agency excludes the vital creative element* (ag)

All four statements are true, needless to say. The one to which *you* give greatest emphasis depends of course on your own personal circumstances.

8

SPECIALIST SERVICES AND INFORMATION SOURCES

This chapter necessarily overlaps with earlier material: the chapter on media research and services pointed out the possibility of special computer runs based on available data, and the media-owner chapter touched on the many additional services provided in addition to delivery of your advertising message. Similarly, the advertising agency chapter mentioned specialist agencies; no doubt, some readers may feel that the 'buying shops' or media independents, the companies that undertake responsibility for buying media on behalf of advertisers (independently of the agency providing the creative work) should be covered in this chapter rather than the agency one — or even merit a chapter to themselves.

The purpose of this chapter is to draw attention to the fact that it is not only advertisers, agencies and media-owners who can con-tribute to your effective use of media: there are other specialist services which can assist in improving your advertising effectiveness.

Some — but by no means all — of these services are outlined below. While many special needs have existed for years and are covered by the services of long-established companies, the swiftly-changing nature of the business world means that new needs are constantly arising. More often than not, new organisations are set up to cater for these new needs. The fact that some organisations described below were established in the relatively brief period between my starting and finishing this manuscript is in itself evidence of the swiftness of change, and of the impossibility of trying to cover all such services within this chapter.

Before touching on individual specialist services, two general points must be made, relating to desk and field research. This book stresses the need to base media planning on *information*, and you can obtain a great deal of valuable data by checking through existing sources of information. The invaluable contribution which 'desk research' can make will be discussed in Part 3 but, if desk research cannot provide the answers to all your questions (or if you suspect some available information is out-of-date) then field research may be essential. Any book on media must necessarily cover research, and there is thus an in-built tendency for it to become a book on research as such. But a line must be drawn somewhere, so comment is restricted to the fact that there are two possibilities open to you — one is to commission your own survey and the other is to 'buy in' to one of the services already undertaking on-going research and providing information on a regular basis. These two categories may, of course, overlap. An extremely useful guide to the many services available in both categories is the booklet, *Organisations providing market research services in Great Britain*, published by the Market Research Society of 15 Belgrave Square, London SW1X 8PF.

It is recommended that initially you should read through this material swiftly, noting those services and sources which are of interest, and then return to this chapter (and that on media research and services) for more detailed study later.

ACE (Advertising Campaign Effectiveness)
(c/o IPC Magazines, King's Reach Tower, Stamford Street, London SE1 9LS)

ACE, a syndicated study run by IPC Magazines, provides a specialist research facility to assess the impact of advertising campaigns, particularly in women's magazines and on television. During waves of interviews spread over the year, information is collected on magazine reading and television viewing, together with a variety of market measures such as purchasing, awareness and attitudes. ACE then provides comparisons between sub-groups matched by media use, i.e. respondents to the *post* campaign study are grouped according to their level of probable exposure to your advertising (none, light, medium and heavy) and differences in market measures noted between those groups and matched groups taken from the pre-campaign study. The research contractor for ACE is Communication Research Ltd.

As well as ACE, IPC Magazines have facilities for *Evaluative Assessment Checks* which focus on the communication between a magazine advertisement and the reader. Discussion of such aspects of research into creative effectiveness, however, is beyond the immediate scope of this book.

AGB (Audits of Great Britain Ltd)
(Audit House, Eastcote, Ruislip, Middlesex HA4 9LT)

Founded in 1962, AGB Research is the central organisation for a group of companies providing continuous audit, panel, syndicated and omnibus research services. Certain of these companies have already been mentioned in other contexts: RSGB (Research Surveys of Great Britain — *see separate entry*) has the JICRAR contract for measuring radio audiences and TARD (Television Audience Research Division) has the JICTAR contract for television audience research.

Other companies in the AGB group offer different services, with standard reports and special analyses which provide demographic and other information to assist you in better 'aiming' your advertising and in evaluating its results. As always, there is no clear dividing line between marketing and media research, and space does not alas permit any fuller discussion of these information sources other than the brief descriptions which follow.

Television Consumer Audit (TCA)   This is sponsored by six major ITV programme companies — ATV Network, Granada Television, London Weekend Television, Southern Television, Thames Television and Trident Management — and is based on a panel of households who regularly record purchase data on a wide range of items. The physical 'pantry check' research technique reduces to a minimum reliance on the panel housewife's memory. The panel is representative of Great Britain and in addition covers Northern Ireland, with regional samples large enough to permit separate reporting on nine separate ITV regions. Product fields currently measured include canned goods, frozen and ready-packed foods, beverages, pet foods, household and toiletry items, commodity products, and meat and poultry.

Subscribers to the TCA service receive standard four-weekly reports on their selected product fields: these include the following information.
1   Total consumer expenditure and volume for individual brands and sizes.
2   Product penetration.
3   Manufacturers' special offers.
4   Average prices paid for all products and brands.
5   Analysis of consumer purchases by intensity of ITV viewing.
All data relating to each household's weekly purchasing is retained by TCA and can be provided in various forms according to the particular marketing situation to be analysed.

AGB Datafast   This is a flexible service which provides TCA clients with standard or special analysis reports within days of their being commissioned. The service will be extended to embrace the TCPI and PPI services (see below) and will also give clients opportunity to have direct access to AGB data from their own desk-top terminal.

Toiletries and Cosmetics Purchasing Index (TCP1)   This provides a continuous measurement of consumer purchases of toiletries, cosmetics and fragrances.

Personal Purchasing Index (PPI)   This provides a continuous measurement of other personal purchases such as male and female clothing, drinks and snacks, films and film processing, greetings cards, etc.

Home Audit   This provides a continuous measurement of ownership and acquisition of household products: purchases are recorded for a wide range of consumer durables, including cookers and refrigerators, dish-washers and washing machines, vacuum cleaners and carpet sweepers, home heating and insulation, leisure durables and kitchen equipment, beds and bedroom furniture, and bathroom and garden equipment.

Index   This relatively new panel (it was tested in 1977 and came into operation in 1978) monitors financial transactions and all significant discretionary expenditure (of £3 or more).

Other services   These include a *Prices Audit — Grocers* (which measures prices and distribution in retail grocery chains), *Prices Audit — Electrical Appliances* (which monitors prices and distribution of electrical appliances in major retail groups), *Retail Services* (which provides a measurement of retailer performance in a number of important product groups — groceries, toiletries, cosmetics and consumer durables) and *Tempo Computer Services* *(see separate entry)*.

Agridata Ltd.
(1 & 2 Berners Street, London W1P 3AG)

This specialist agricultural market research agency is owned jointly by the Taylor Nelson Group Ltd and Market Investigations (Pharmaceutical and Agricultural) Ltd. The company publishes a series of surveys of which that most relevant to this book is the annual National Farm Readership Survey. This covers readership of all the main agricultural journals, and the technique used for measuring readership follows the same principles as the JICNARS survey. There are nine different enterprise categories according to size and type of farm, and for each publication farmers are classified as average or regular readers. Total readership is also provided. Special analyses are also available on request.

AMSAC — *see next entry*

Attwood Statistics Ltd
(Northbridge Road, Berkhampstead, Herts HP4 1EH)

The Attwood Consumer Panels   Attwood Statistics was the first market research agency to operate a Household Consumer Panel in Great Britain, having started its operations in 1948. Attwood's Consumer Panel Data is based on information obtained regularly from randomly selected household panels, representative of the population at large. To measure purchasing characteristics regionally as well as nationally, Attwood divides Great Britain into fifteen control areas. Within each control area, private households are represented in proportion to their numbers in the population. Demographic controls such as socio-economic groupings, age of housewife, size of household and presence of children are applied to achieve a balanced sample in each area.

Each week every Attwood Panel housewife completes a detailed pre-coded diary listing her purchases of a wide range of product fields. At any one time the housewife diary may contain some fifty different product fields: obviously, not all product categories are purchased by every household every week. Through this diary the housewife provides information for each purchase occasion for each product field, enabling a wide range of marketing analyses to be provided, which can assist you both in 'aiming' your advertising and in assessing its results.

Subscribers to the Attwood Consumer Panel have a wide choice regarding how they wish to receive their market reports, which are tailored to specific requirements. Most choose to receive reports every four weeks: typical data cover the total market, the performance of selected brands, and the effects of price cuts, promotions, etc. The reports show market and brand penetration, brand shares based on quantity, and/or expenditure, nationally and by areas. Much of this is provided in running record form.

You also have the facility to purchase quarterly, half-yearly and annual reports, which provide the basis for deeper analysis of activities which affect market situations. The characteristics of the purchases can be examined in detail together with frequency of purchase, brand loyalty, duplication between brands and outlets plus many other special analyses.

Many subscribers receive their information in the form of computer tapes, from which they then program their own analyses.

Attwoods also use their panels for the administration of simple *ad hoc* questionnaires which, in the main, relate to product category items already subscribed to by the client.

AMSAC   In addition to their Household Panel, Attwoods also operate an Individuals Panel, based on the co-operation of individuals in the main panel homes. This service, named the Attwood Multi-Segmented Analysis of Consumers (AMSAC), is designed to measure those product categories where the purchase decision is likely to be made by a member of the household other than or in addition to the housewife. Subscribers may purchase those segments of this panel applicable to their market: this could be male or female buyers, particular age groups, or owners of particular types of equipment. Again, Attwood subscribers have flexibility in the way and frequency with which they receive their market data. As in the case of the Household Panel, AMSAC also provides a basis for *ad hoc* questionnaires.

Auditplan
(Park House, 22 Park Street, Croydon, Surrey CR9 1TS)

The Auditplan Division of Marplan Ltd was set up in 1962 to offer facilities in the specialist field of retail audits, distribution checks and other forms of retailer research. The division aims particularly to satisfy the needs of clients who require tailor-made projects, where the facilities available from regular syndicated panels are unsuitable.

Auditplan's national audit panels offer three specialities:
1   Audits specially designed to provide information analysed by client's own sales areas or by other regional divisions of special significance.
2   Auditing facilities within special kinds of outlet which cater specially for particular markets.
3   Audit calls at times and frequencies to suit a particular client's needs, such as at crucial times during the launch period of a new product.

Auditplan also provides facilities for setting up panels in test towns or test areas. As with national panels, particular kinds of outlet can be covered and special time-periods are available.

For clients not requiring full retail audit data, Auditplan undertakes distribution checks on a national and local level, either on an *ad hoc* basis or through its Datafast Distribution Checking Service.

This latter Datafast service offers a national panel each week, with smaller panel sizes available either nationally or by television region, covering grocers, confectioners/tobacconists/newsagents, chemists, department and variety stores, off-licences, freezer centres, and hardware/DIY outlets.

Auditplan also undertakes in-store testing to measure such variables as changes in packaging or size, and the effect of special promotions. Other additional facilities are also available, including *ad hoc* questionnaire surveys with retailers.

Baby Market Readership Research — *see RSGB*

BMRB (British Market Research Bureau Ltd)
(53 The Mall, Ealing, London W5 3TE)

This company offers a wide range of services including consumer, advertising, industrial and international research, as well as media. Its main media research service is TGI: the Target Group Index described in Part 1.

Business surveys

There are a number of surveys relevant to business and financial markets. These include the following.

Businessman Readership Survey

The 1979 survey was prepared by Research Services Ltd for the Business Media Research Committee, and continues a series of three earlier studies of businessmen's readership habits, all carried out by RSL. The research was underwritten by *The Daily Telegraph,* the *Financial Times* and *Times* Newspapers, acting jointly as the New Business Research Consortium (NBRC). These three publishers together with *The Observer,* the *Guardian* and *The Economist* comprise the primary sponsors. There are a number of secondary media sponsors.

The definition of a businessman remains unchanged from the

earlier surveys:

> 'A man or woman whose occupation implies the exercise of significant managerial, executive, technical or advisory functions and who works in an organisation eligible on grounds of size.'

Standard data in the report covers readership by age, by social grade, by highest educational qualification and by survey region. Other main sections of the survey are devoted to Income, Status, Occupation, Industry, Responsibility, Financial Investments, Travel, Car Ownership/Hire Car Usage/Credit Cards Held, ITV Viewing, Duplication Tables, Cumulative Readership and Source of Copy.

The survey is being updated and the new edition could be available by the time or soon after this book is published.

European Businessman Readership Survey

Published in 1978, this was produced by Research Services Ltd for the *Financial Times, Berlingske Tidende, Handelsblatt, Le Figaro, Les Echos,* and *Vision* and is a report of a survey of senior businessmen in large and medium-size European companies. The countries covered are Austria, Belgium/Luxembourg, Denmark, Finland, France, Germany, Italy, Netherlands, Norway, Spain, Sweden, Switzerland and the United Kingdom.

The purpose of the survey is to investigate the reading behaviour of senior executives, and to provide a profile of executives in terms of their age, salary, and frequency of air travel. The main tables of the report are devoted to Country of Residence, Industry, Responsibility, and Air Travel and Company Size. *Financial Times* supplementary analysis covers Essential Business Reading, Cumulative Coverages, Schedule Analysis Guide, Cost Ranking, and Guide to Publications.

The survey is being updated and the new edition could be available by the time or soon after this book is published.

European Institutional Investors Research

This survey was prepared for the *Financial Times,* and conducted by Research Services Ltd. The report presents the findings of a readership survey carried out among European institutional investors managing portfolios of US shares. Published in 1978, the survey updates the information obtained in earlier surveys of the readership habits and preferences of this international group of investors.

Questions in the survey covered average issue readership,

frequency of reading of publications, and which were considered 'essential business reading'. Respondents were also asked to classify themselves in terms of the interests in which their companies were primarily engaged. The tables included in the report show results for Austria, Belgium/Netherlands, France, Germany, Italy, Scandinavia, Switzerland and the United Kingdom.

This survey is also being updated, and the new edition could be available by the time or soon after this book is published.

International Financial Managers in Europe

This 1979 readership survey, undertaken by Research Services Ltd, is sponsored by the International Financial Media Research Committee — *The Economist, Euromoney* and the *Financial Times.* It was designed as a modification of the earlier *Readership Survey of Financial Managers in the World's Largest Companies.*

The survey had as its sampling frame 'Europe's 5000 largest companies' — those with a minimum turnover of US $100 million. The companies surveyed were those in 14 European countries which were involved in at least some export activity: these countries were (in descending order as a percentage of the total) Germany, Great Britain, France, Sweden, other Scandinavian countries, Netherlands, Switzerland, Italy, Belgium, Spain/Portugal, and Austria.

The tables cover Average Issue Readership; Essential Business Reading; Rank Order, Percentage of Export Business and Company Ownership; and Area of Responsibility and Job Title.

Pan European Survey

Conducted by Research Services Ltd in 1978, this is a Marketing and Readership Study of Executives and Professionals in Europe. Its sponsors are *The Economist, International Herald Tribune, Newsweek International, Scientific American* and *Time.*

The purpose of the survey is 'to provide marketers of goods and suppliers of services to one of the most affluent and influential sectors of the European population with accurate and up-to-date information on the readership of national and international publications. The survey is also a valuable source of data on the ownership and use of many products and services, and on the occupational and demographic characteristics of those men of high status who form their chief target market.'

The survey was the first in-home personal interview media survey, and pioneered a special sampling technique designed to yield comparable data despite the lack of comparability in the statistical source information available from the ten countries covered: Belgium, Denmark, France, West Germany, Great Britain, Italy, the Netherlands, Spain, Sweden and Switzerland.

A new enlarged survey is to go into the field at about the time this book is published.

Children — *see Carrick James Research*

Communication Research Ltd
(12 Bedford Square, London WC1B 3JA)

This independent research company specialises — as you would expect from its name — in communication research, and operates in a wide range of media. Certain of its activities have already been described — its Chairman published a monograph on qualitative aspects of readership data for the National Readership Surveys, and it currently operates the ACE surveys (see earlier entry) for IPC Magazines.

Most of the company's media research involves assessing the effect of advertising in different media (as opposed to head-counting readers). Some examples of its work have been described in a paper entitled 'Measuring Effects of Advertising Campaigns' presented at a recent annual conference of the Market Research Society.

The company also works on the effect of media context on communication. A paper on 'Experimental Intermedia Studies' was presented at an earlier MRS Conference, and a precise study in this area was undertaken for IPC Magazines.

Communication Research has also undertaken a considerable body of editorial research but, as this was privately commissioned, no details can be made available.

Com-share Ltd
(32-34 Great Peter Street, London SW1)

This company is authorised to provide a post survey information service for the National Readership Survey.

Farming — *see Agridata Ltd*

Gallup — *See Social Surveys (Gallup Poll) Ltd*

GSI (UK) Ltd
(83 Clerkenwell Road, London EC1)

This company is authorised to provide a post survey information service for the National Readership Survey.

HRS (Holborn Research Services)
(80 Fetter Lane, London EC4)

HRS is a registered business name of Mirror Group Newspapers. This company offers a post survey analysis on the Target Group Index and has also been authorised to provide a post survey information service for the National Readership Survey.

All the data in the National Businessman's survey can be analysed, as can the European Businessman's Survey and the Pan European Survey.

The media scheduling facilities available through the HRS Media Services Department include cross-tabulation, evaluation, and cost ranking. Access is available either through the HRS office or clients' own teletype terminals.

Home Audit — *see AGB*

IMS (Interactive Market Systems) UK Ltd
(62 Shaftesbury Avenue, London W1V 7DE)

This company offers a post survey analysis on the Target Group Index and is also authorised to provide a post survey information service for the National Readership Survey. Other surveys for which IMS provides similar services include the Businessman Readership Survey, the European Businessman Readership Survey, and the Pan European Survey. All kinds of analysis are available, including cross-analysis, schedule analysis and evaluation, cost ranking, and schedule building and optimisation. Analysis is available via IMS or via clients' own terminals.

Index — *see AGB*

Carrick James Market Research
(62 Oxford Street, London W1)

This company provides a range of research services, of which the one most relevant to this book is its syndicated media research into the children's and teenagers' markets. This covers television viewing, cinema-going, listening to radio, and readership of relevant special interest publications. The agency also specialises in research into cinema audiences.

JICMARS (Joint Industry Committee for Medical Advertising Readership Surveys)

This is a readership survey of about 1200 GPs per annum, undertaken by RSGB — Research Surveys of Great Britain. It is a continuous survey, reporting three times a year. It is unusual in that incorporated in it are measures designed to test the relative accuracy of the normal 'readership' questions. As well as readership data it also gives breakdowns for list size (number of patients), 'innovators' (usage of new or relatively new products), and exposure to other media including direct mail, pharmaceutical sponsored meetings, and pharmaceutical representatives seen.

In addition to the basic survey tables, special analyses and schedule analysis services are also available.

Media Audits Ltd
(Planet House, 12 Devereux Court, Strand, London WC2R 3JJ)

This company provides consultancy services in the measurement and use of advertising media. Media Audits neither buys nor sells media and is thus objective in measurement and interpretation. The company works for advertisers, agencies and media-owners, and is particularly involved in assessment and control procedures for major advertisers using television: it does this through its Cost/Rating Index service which monitors value obtained and identifies where action is necessary.

Media Audits' system of measurement is continuous, operating over the full 12 months of the year, and covers the complete ITV network.

The advertiser supplies Media Audits with spot-by-spot schedules, with actual ratings. Actual costs are used as opposed to rate card costs and as JICTAR subscribers, Media Audits is able to validate all rating information supplied to them. Data from the schedules are then pooled into indices, by target group — the main ones relate to the adult, housewife and male target audience groups. The Cost/Rating Index is then calculated by JICTAR period, by station. Numbers of spots, expenditure, ratings, and audience thousands are totalled and costs per thousand and rating averages are computed.

These norms then form the bases for comparison of individual campaigns.

Media Audits offers a tailored interpretation of buying results, relating each advertiser's buying achievements to the CRI base and highlighting areas of particular interest in the context of campaign objectives, e.g. the advertiser's 'par' position *versus* the CRI, cost ranges (relative position of the advertiser's campaign results within the range experienced for that period), performance trends (achievements on specific stations over a period of time, showing cost per thousand indexed against CRI and average rating performance) and the rating spread (which examines different aspects of the schedule such as duration, weight per area and spread over time). Media Audits' reports can cover either an entire campaign or alternatively a four-week JICTAR period.

Medical Advertising Readership Surveys — *see JICMARS*

A.C. Nielsen Co.
(Nielsen House, Headington, Oxford OX3 9RX)

A member of the world-wide Nielsen Research Organisation, this company provides a range of services but is perhaps best known for its shop audits, the Nielsen Retail Index Services. From the original Grocery and Chemist indexes introduced when the UK Company was started in 1939, operations have been extended to Confectioners, Off-Licences and Cash and Carry Wholesalers.

Through a system of sample selection, data collection, processing and interpretation, Nielsen clients receive full information about each of the main variable elements that contribute to a brand's success, or failure in the market — product/packaging, retail price, availability, store and consumer promotions, and advertising/ merchandising. The data also isolate other important factors such as regional and outlet type variations, and the seasonality of sales.

NOP Market Research Ltd.
(Tower House, Southampton Street, London WC2E 7HN)

This company undertakes all types of survey research. One of its media research activities, monitoring poster sites for the Poster Audit Bureau (see separate entry) has already been described in Part 1, but NOP also undertakes research into other media.

Press   Over the years NOP has conducted a large number of press studies of all types including readership, advertising, editorial and circulation research for national dailies and Sundays, provincial dailies, evenings and weeklies, and a wide range of magazines and trade publications.

Radio   NOP was one of the pioneer companies in radio research in Britain, and has worked for a number of local radio stations. The NOP Young Report of 1978 was a national survey of young people aged 15-21. The survey covered social attitudes, media exposure and purchasing habits, and included information on Radio Luxembourg, BBC and the 19 individual ILR stations.

Television   Many *ad hoc* studies have been undertaken and NOP currently carries out regular research for advertisers commissioned by Southern Television, with a special sample in this area.

(See also RAL.)

Parker Research Ltd
(22 Red Lion Street, London WC1R 4PX)

This organisation, an associate company of the Roles and Parker advertising agency, specialises in research into industrial markets and has undertaken a number of *ad hoc* media readership surveys, mainly for publishers of industrial and technical journals.

PPI (Personal Purchasing Index) — *see AGB*

Prices Audit — Electrical Appliances — *see AGB*

Prices Audit — Grocers — *see AGB*

Pritchard Brown & Taylor Ltd
(87 Charlotte Street, London W1)

This company offers post survey analysis on the Target Group Index for general survey analysis.

RAL (Retail Audits Ltd)
(390-400 High Road, Wembley, Middlesex HA9 6TB)

This organisation is a member of the NOP Group of Companies, and specialises in market research in retail trade outlets. Its main areas of activity are as follows:

National Audit Panels   RAL operates a wide range of national retail auditing panels. In most cases these are run on a regular bi-monthly basis. Report contents are designed to the requirements of individual subscribers, but can include brand shares, consumer sales, retailer purchases, stock levels — stock cover, prices, average sales per shop handling, out of stock, and various analyses of distribution of shops (stocking, purchasing, handling and selling).

Retail Distribution Checks   Regular surveys are carried out where clients may nominate products on which they seek data on retail distribution. Typical data collected for each itemised product can include in-stock distribution, temporary out of stock, prices, facings, presence and sitings of special displays, and frequency of sales representative calling.

Test marketing   New product launches can be monitored within test areas. The facility to carry out test work is available in most shop types and can be in nominated ITV areas or test towns.

Outlets covered   RAL offer either continuous auditing or distribution checks in a wide range of outlets, including grocers, chemists, cash and carry, confectioners/newsagents/tobaconnists, hardware, ironmongers, DIY, paint and wallpaper specialists, garages, filling stations, motor accessory shops, tyre and battery specialists, toy shops, department stores, stationers, garden centres, cornsmen/seedsmen/petshops, sports shops, variety chain stores, pubs, off-licences, and other licensed outlets.

Trade interviewing   RAL have set up a specialist trade interviewing company which is primarily concerned with the qualitative aspects of trade research. *(See separate entry for Trade Studies Ltd.)*

Research Services Ltd
(Station House, Harrow Road, Stonebridge Park, Wembley, Middlesex HA9 6DE)

Founded in 1946, RSL offers a full range of research facilities in consumer, industrial, social and media research. Certain of its activities have already been described. It undertook the Business Readership Surveys *(see separate entry)* and also the JICNARS National Readership Surveys *(see separate entry)* for which it is authorised to provide a post survey information service.

Retail Services *— see AGB above*

RSGB (Research Surveys of Great Britain Ltd)
(Crown House, London Road, Morden, Surrey SM4 5DT)

This company is part of the AGB group and some of its activities — the JICRAR Radio Audience Research and the JICMARS Medical Advertising Readership Surveys — have already been described.

In addition, RSGB conducts its own syndicated study on readership in the Baby Market, i.e. mothers with babies 0-2 years old. This covers baby annuals, monthly and bi-monthly magazines, weekly magazines and other baby publications and analyses readership under the following headings: average issue readership, total readership, frequency of reading, reading more than once, frequent readers, receipt of copy, specific issue receipt of copy, and publications found most useful. Analysis is by age of baby, social class, incidence of birth, and age of mother, and there is also data regarding exposure to other media.

RSGB also conducts many surveys for the editorial guidance of media-owners. Since these are not published, however, it is not possible to give any specific details of their results.

RSGB also conducts various continuous omnibus services.

RSL *— see Research Services Ltd*

Gordon Simmons Research Ltd
(80 St Martin's Lane, London WC2N 4AA and Ruxley Towers, Ruxley Ridge, Claygate, Esher, Surrey KT10 0UG)

This is an independent company offering a wide range of consumer and trade research services.

In the media research field it has undertaken specially commissioned *ad hoc* surveys into purchasing and readership of newspapers and magazines, as well as into reader attitudes.

Social Surveys (Gallup Poll) Ltd
(202 Finchley Road, London NW3 6BL)

One of the services provided by this organisation relates to the reading and noting of advertisements. This investigates the readership of individual advertisements, as distinct from general readership of the publication in which they appear.

The noting and reading technique was devised by Dr. George Gallup in America in the late 1920s, and was started in the United Kingdom by this company as a continuous technique in 1947, checking advertisements in the national, local and specialised press. The technique works on the basis that people are able to recall in a newspaper or magazine the items they have looked at and read the previous day, or the previous week. Respondents are taken through the publication and asked to indicate on the publication itself exactly what they recall reading and looking at. This information is collected on all parts of the publication including the advertisements. Thus attention paid to advertisements is measured in the context of their normal publication reading.

Information regarding advertisements is analysed and stored for comparative purposes so that the relative attention paid to specific size advertisements, or to types of advertisement, is available. The data can also be used to see the relative merits of such things as spot colour in local publications, or double-page spreads in the specialist publications. It must be remembered, however, that the data provided is an average figure and around the average there will be a wide dispersion of individual advertisement scores. The company has found that the major factor affecting the attention paid to the advertisement is the advertisement itself, and any information used in terms of media buying must be looked at with that knowledge in mind.

Other research undertaken by this company has already been mentioned, e.g. the Gallup Viewing and Listnership Survey of 1978, commissioned by Radio Luxembourg, and the Report on a Survey of Advertising Agencies Usership of Advertising and Marketing Publications of 1978. *(See separate entry for BRAD in Chapter 2.)*

Stats (MR) Ltd
(Gloucester House, Smallbrook, Queensway, Birmingham B5 4HP)

This is an independent British company incorporated in 1963, specialising in a series of retail research services. The range currently offered includes:

Continuous audits in off licences, free trade on licences, grocers, chemists, confectioners/tobacconists/newsagents, hardware outlets, garden centres and department stores.

Continuous distribution checks in on and off licences, licensed grocers/specialist off licences, grocers, chemists including Boots, Woolworths, department stores, hardware outlets, confectioners/tobacconists/newsagents and cash and carry wholesalers.

The Stats MR service provides both standard analyses and a range of special and tailor-made analyses. The company also undertakes *ad hoc* and specialist audits and distribution checks.

To facilitate use of this data, Stats MR has developed DART — its Direct Access Research Technique. This provides clients with immediate direct access to data and also provides an opportunity to cross-tabulate basic table data and undertake special analyses. This is done by accessing the Stats MR computer by standard GPO telephone line. A wide range of analyses has been programmed, including all the optional ones available on the audit and distribution checks, and additions to this range are made as occasion demands. DART can also be adapted to include information from other sources such as company sales figures, data from consumer panels and advertising expenditure, etc. For clients without terminal facilities, the service can be handled entirely by Stats MR.

TABS [Television Advertising Bureau (Surveys) Ltd]
(12/13 Greek Street, London W1V 5LE)

TABS is an independent market research company which began operation in 1976, and provides a quantitative continuous monitor of television advertising affectiveness. The various TABS 'scores' emanate from a representative panel of people who watch TV in their normal home environment.

Rather than focus on head-counting like some other surveys, TABS concentrates on 'mind-measuring', i.e. what *influence* the advertising has on those people seeing it. TABS panellists watch whatever they wish, but whenever they see a commercial they are called upon to provide information about their reactions to it, which proves *en passant* that they have seen it.

Using a special questionnaire, respondents record their reactions by putting pencil marks on scaled 'shapes': these can easily be filled in during the 2-3 seconds of 'freeze' frame between commercials (and have the advantage that they can be processed by an Optical Mark Reader, sensitive to the graphite pencil marks). These marks are then converted into various scores for the different attributes of each TV

187

commercial's effectiveness. Respondents' reactions are thus obtained as realistically as possible, in the natural viewing situation. In addition to these checks made during actual transmissions, supplementary questions are asked on a weekly basis, to establish consumer attitudes to the products advertised.

Much of the information provided has creative implications that cannot alas be discussed here, but the TABS service has considerable media planning relevance too, since it measures the number of people who have *seen* commercials, rather than simply opportunities to see. It also monitors 'decay' *after* advertising campaigns have ended, i.e. the rate at which their continuing impact is diminishing.

TABS compiles regular monthly reports on more than fifty different product groups, but special analyses are also available. As a result of accumulated experience of using the TABS scores, new special analysis applications are steadily being developed. This is especially the case with the application of TABS data to media scheduling improvements and optimisation. A great deal of work has been done on resolving the 'drip versus burst' question (see Part 3) and, experimentally, in identifying the 'best' time to advertise and reach and influence a specific target group.

TABS has published a detailed analysis entitled *Cost Per Thousand Adults. or Cost Per Thousand Empty Armchairs?*, showing FARs (adult full attention ratings), in which TABS attempt to provide some indication of the extent to which people actually watch commercial breaks. Based on detailed analysis of their own data for a four-week period in the London area, the report shows what people actually saw, break by break. The aim is to provide guidance for TV planning and buying on such topics as peak-time *versus* off-peak, weekdays *versus* weekend, the influence of social habits and the time of day when attention levels are highest.

Taylor, Nelson & Associates Ltd
(457 Kingston Road, Ewell, Epsom, Surrey KT19 0DH)

This company offers a range of services — *ad hoc* surveys in consumer, financial and industrial research, as well as syndicated studies: a social trend monitor, a family food panel and a business opinion survey. Two facilities in particular are of relevance to product promotion and campaign evaluation — these are the Monitoring Tests Markets and Model Test Market services.

The Monitoring Test Market system provides regular indications of brand awareness, advertising exposure, product trial (penetration), repeat purchase and buyer profiles, together with build up of brand sales, repeat purchase, brand switching, brand share predictions and effects of promotional activity. There are also opportunities for follow-up interviews with (heavy) buyers, brand image measurements, and for special experiments within the test market.

The Model Test Market facility is of particular value should you wish to evaluate a product promotion or campaign in one area in comparison with a 'standard' approach in another area, to assess the effects of advertising. Each model test market is tailored to fit the specific new product, so that you control the type and quality of advertising you want, as well as below-the-line activity and other variables. Throughout the test the following tables are provided:

1   Volume brand share for the test brand, competitive brands and private labels within that product field.
2   Brand share of consumer expenditure, as above.
3   Cumulative penetration giving penetration build-up.
4   Cumulative penetration by depth of trial for test brand.
5   Level of repeat purchase of test brand and two others every four weeks i.e. percentage of triers who repeat buy.

These tables can be analysed by up to ten sub-groups, e.g. four age, four social class and two usage groups. Other analyses of basic diary data and further in-depth 'diagnostic' analyses among panel members are also available.

Teenagers — *see Carrick James Research and NOP Market Research*

Television Advertising Bureau (Surveys) Ltd — *see TABS*

Television Companies Research and Marketing Facilities

The ITCA booklet *ITV Facts and Figures* (see Chapter 2) gives information about the research and marketing facilities available: a chart shows which programme companies provide any or all of the following:

1   TCA (Television Consumer Audit — *see separate entry for AGB above).*
2   Consumer research.
3   Retail audits.
4   Distribution checks.
5   Sales teams (own or contract).
6   Merchandising teams (own or contract).
7   Telephone answering service.
8   Merchandising bulletins.

TCA (Television Consumer Audit) — *see AGB*

Telmar Commumications Ltd.
(87 Jermyn Street, London SW1Y 6JD)

Telmar was formed in the United States in 1968 and commenced its UK operation in 1979. The company offers a post survey analysis on the Target Group Index, and is also authorised to provide a post survey information service for the National Readership Survey. Similar services are available for the Businessman Readership Survey, the European Businessman Readership Survey, and the Pan European Survey. The company provides computer services for media planning and evaluation, including cross-tabulation, cost ranking, schedule evaluation, schedule optimisation and evaluation of schedule performance over time. Clients can obtain analyses from Telmar or alternatively via a computer terminal installed in their own offices.

Tempo Computer Services Ltd.
(12 Sutton Row, London W1V 5FH)

Tempo is a computer service and systems company formed in 1968 which since 1977 has been part of the AGB Research Group of Companies. As well as providing clients with detailed breakdowns of data produced by AGB, Tempo also offers advertising agencies a terminal-based on-line computerised service which can manage the detailed media buying aspects of advertising campaigns, along with associated accounting and management information, thus saving much clerical time. For publishers, Tempo has developed an advertisement order processing and administration system, with facilitities for instant visual display of the advertisement booking system.

In the media research field, Tempo offers a wide variety of services including media performance evaluation, schedule optimisation, campaign planning and competitive expenditure/performance reporting.

Tempo on-line services are available through terminal facilities in clients' own offices, linked either to Tempo's computer bureau or to the clients' own in-house machine.

TCPI (Toiletries and Cosmetics Purchasing Index) — *see AGB*

Trade Studies Ltd
(York House, Empire Way, Wembley, Middlesex)

Retail Audits Ltd *(see separate entry above)* has set up a specialist trade interviewing company — Trade Studies Ltd — which is primarily concerned with the qualitative aspects of trade research.

Typical projects might include collecting the attitudes and opinions of traders towards suppliers, manufacturers, new products, existing products, selling methods, merchandising, packaging, delivery service, promotion and advertising, and shelf space allocation. The method of interviewing depends on the problems being investigated and ranges from telephone, face-to-face, to postal questionnaires.

Part 3

THE EFFECTIVE USE OF ADVERTISING MEDIA

Having considered the range of advertising media available to communicate your advertising message, and the organisations and individuals concerned, we can now examine the actual use of media — hopefully, this will be *effective* use — under the following chapter headings:

a   *Research and investigation*   Gathering the company, product and market data essential for effective planning.

b   *Problem analysis*   Deciding your campaign objective, which directly affects both media selection and the creative approach to be featured.

c   *Budgeting*   Fixing the advertising appropriation so that you spend the right amount on achieving your chosen objective.

d   *Preparation of advertising proposals*   Planning an advertising campaign, creating advertisements and selecting media, to achieve your chosen objective.

e   *The media decision process*   Ensuring that those directly concerned with media decisions are properly consulted — this affects not only planning but also approval.

f   *Approval of proposals*   Checking, prior to executing the campaign, that your proposals are likely to achieve success.

g   *Execution of these proposals*   Putting your plan into effect.

h   *Evaluation of results*   Checking that you received value for money, and seeing what lessons can be learned for the future.

These are the component tasks that overall — whether undertaken by advertiser or agency, and in which the media-owner is directly involved — make for good advertising. These tasks should be a closed loop, and evaluation of the results of this year's campaign should provide additional information on which to base next year's planning.

9
RESEARCH AND INVESTIGATION

Before you start planning to use advertising media, it is essential to have a thorough knowledge of many business aspects. You must have a full background knowledge before considering any advertising, for unless your campaign reflects these facets of your business, it cannot work to full advantage.

Your firm and its products

A full knowledge of all aspects of your firm is essential. Is it old-established so that emphasis could be placed on tradition, or is it alternatively a newly formed pioneer? Where is it based? Are you, in fact, considering a single organisation, or perhaps a range of companies? Do they operate nationally, internationally or multi-nationally? Does your firm have access to the management services and skills of a parent company? Is sufficient finance available to mount an extensive advertising campaign? Clearly all these consider-ations affect not only the size and type of your advertising campaign but also its contents, so a thorough knowledge of these different aspects is essential.

Equally important is complete knowledge of the products or services to be advertised (both individually and over the complete range), since this can affect media policy just as much as creative content. Prices, sizes, colours, flavours, packaging — all are important. What are the limits to the amount your factory can produce: there is no point in over-selling and thus boosting sales of competitors' lines. What does your product actually do? Does it have a single use, or are you considering a multiple-use product? Sales might be increased, for example, by including recipes in the advertisements, thus pointing out additional uses for your product. Is there any special guarantee, or after-sales service? Is the service element more important than the product itself, as far as users are concerned? Perhaps you are considering a service as such, and your firm is a service organisation rather than a manufacturing company.

Clearly all these different aspects have direct implications for the planning of your advertising campaign. Whether the facts are supplied to you by the production staff or, as is more likely, you try the product for yourself, you must obtain all this vital information. Furthermore, you must ensure that you are notified, well in advance, of any possible changes. Having thoroughly studied the merchandise, you can now proceed to study the potential purchasers of your goods, known in advertising terminology as the 'market'.

Your market

You must have a clear picture of the customers likely to be interested in your goods. Are they men or women? Married or single? What ages are they? What is their income? Of what 'class' are your customers — the man-in-the-street and his wife, or the 'professionals'? Who makes the actual purchase, and who influences the buying decision? The housewife may buy, but act in accordance with the wishes of her husband or children. Perhaps your potential customers are distinguished by a particular special interest, whether of race or creed, hobby or occupation. Sometimes the buyers may be other organisations rather than individuals, but it is equally important in such cases to know who makes the purchase and who influences it and what the buying process is.

Where are your customers located — are they local, in another part of the country, or spread throughout the world? Clearly this affects where you place your advertising. When do your customers buy, and how often? This information influences the timing of your campaign, and the frequency of the advertisements. Is your product bought on impulse, or only after careful consideration? How long is this consideration period? This, too, clearly affects timing, and the type of campaign to be mounted.

What use do your customers make of your product, why do they buy it and why do they select one brand in preference to others? How strong is their brand loyalty? Are some people more likely than others to adopt your new products? How many potential buyers are there? Do some buyers use the product more heavily than others? Is their number increasing or decreasing, and if so at what rate?

Part 1 outlined the socio-economic categories into which much current research groups people, and also quoted a media-owner's remark that 'If advertisers targeted their markets more exactly, i.e. not bland ABC1s, then media would make available more qualitative research to enable advertisers to understand readers/ viewers better'.

Those concerned with advertising planning have long been used to looking at demographic differences (measures such as age, income and social grade) between buyers and non-buyers. Sometimes, however, demographic measures alone fail to show real differences and, furthermore, many attitudes and interests which you might expect to relate to social grade are not, in fact, associated with grade.

Because of these weaknesses in the customary classifications, new techniques have been developed which try to distinguish buyers from non-buyers of a product by classification of personality type rather than conventional demographics. Life-style or psychographic research is a relatively new alternative approach to understanding your consumers. By gathering comprehensive information about people's attitudes, interests and activities, it produces generalised consumer profiles which are claimed to delineate 'real live people' in a superior way to the more traditional methods of classification. Protagonists assert that it has already demonstrated considerable potential in identifying new market segments and opportunities (as well as providing an extra creative input for advertising).

Anyone who has read the James Bond novels will recall how Ian Fleming's descriptions of 007's clothes, cars and drinking habits give a far more realistic impression of his life-style than simply describing him as an A-grade consumer. (Bond enthusiasts who quibble that he is only Intermediate rather than Senior managerial, administrative or professional will not argue over his distinctive life-style!). This is an extreme example, but a more down-to-earth and practical approach has been developed which classifies people according to brief 'pen-portraits' which describe their background, attitudes and habits — rather than grouping them in social grades according to the head of household's occupation.

Another approach to classifying your buyers and potential buyers is to think of their *media* habits and attitudes. Many firms already categorise their markets in terms of heavy, medium, light and non-users, and the same thinking can be applied to their 'use' of media — are they heavy, medium, light or non-users of television, radio, newspapers, magazines or other media? It is always salutory to remember that the easiest way to define a fashion-conscious woman is to point her out as 'one who reads fashion magazines'. Later, when selecting media to reach your chosen market, you should always bear in mind that advertising communication is a two-way process — how do your consumers use the media you are using to reach them?

Knowledge of all these market factors is vital if your advertising campaign is to be effective. Considerable time and money can usefully be spent on research before planning begins, for unless you know your potential market you cannot select media to reach these people, nor create advertisements that will appeal to them. In addition you must bear in mind that your market is not static, but constantly changing as old customers leave and new ones come along. The replacement customers may perhaps be different and motivated by other desires, so that mere repetition of previously successful advertising may not show the same results. Market knowledge must be kept up-to-date, and your advertising policy adjusted accordingly. Study of market trends is, in fact, a never-ending task.

With knowledge of products and market, you must now make a third study — of how your company plans to sell these products to that market: in short, its marketing policy.

Your marketing policy

Advertising policy is affected by, and should reflect your company's marketing policy. The concept of marketing was outlined earlier, and your advertising campaign should bear direct relation to a number of marketing factors. Is the purpose of your advertising to launch a new product, a reminder campaign for an existing one, or an attempt to halt a decline in the market? If, on the other hand, your marketing decision is to increase sales, how is this to be achieved? Is the drive to be in a particular area? Is distribution of your product completely even across the entire country or is it regionally biased, or perhaps even limited to certain areas? Many companies divide their selling territory into areas, and the total marketing operation thus comprises a number of individual sales drives. A 'rolling' product launch may be phased over a period of time, successively covering one area after another until national (or sometimes international) distribution is achieved. This will clearly affect media planning, since it calls for heavy initial advertising in appropriate areas during the launch periods, followed by a reminder campaign during the months that follow. Even where distribution is nation-wide, your marketing decision may be to increase sales by pin-pointing a particular segment of the market (as distinct from a geographical area) for special attention, rather than attack on all fronts. Clearly, such marketing decisions directly affect media selection, and for effective use of advertising media, you must appreciate the policy behind the choice made.

What is the structure of your sales force? How many salesmen does your company employ and how long does it take them to complete their round of calls? Do they call on all retailers, or rely on wholesalers to reach the smaller outlets? How dominant a role do the multiple shops and chains play? Is your product available freely or only in selected outlets? The need to feature names and addresses of local agents may have a marked influence on media selection. Are trade discounts competitive, or has your firm an advantage or disadvantage over rival producers? Promotional policies differ and manufacturers may adopt either a 'push' or a 'pull' approach — with the latter you give minimal discounts and use massive public advertising to pull your merchandise through the retail outlets. The retailer gets only a small amount per unit, but prospects of large sales stimulated by public advertising make him realise it will be to his advantage to stock your merchandise, so that he is ready to meet the public demand stimulated by your advertising. With a 'push' campaign, on the other hand, little is spent on public advertising, but attractive trade discounts used to persuade the retailer to promote your goods, in view of the large sum he gets for every unit sold. In practice, naturally, it is rarely a question of operating at either extreme end of this push-pull scale but at some intermediate point, but clearly such factors determine whether or not to use the trade press and the timing of the support campaign.

With a thorough knowledge of firm and products, market and marketing policy, you must next study previous advertising.

Previous advertising

You must check carefully what advertising has appeared in the past and with what results, and see what lessons can be learned to increase the effectiveness of future campaigns. All too often money is wasted through failure to keep adequate records. Careful checking of results can lead to increased efficiency, bringing better results for the same expenditure, or achieving the same results for less outlay. Either way, the benefit to your company is obvious and previous advertising must, therefore, never be overlooked. Which advertising media proved effective in the past? What creative approaches appealed to prospective customers? What did these call for in terms of advertisement size, position, use of colour, and timing and duration of the campaign? Before planning future advertising you should check what you can learn from the past and, as has already been made clear, evaluation of the results of this year's campaign should provide the basis of next year's planning. This preliminary stage of research and investigations is thus directly linked with the final planning stage of evaluation of results, to which a later chapter is devoted.

Competition

In investigating competition, you make not one study but at least four, since you must consider the competition faced from each of your rivals under the same four headings — firm and products, market, marketing policy and previous advertising.

What are the strengths and organisational weaknesses of rival companies? What products do your competitors make and how do they compare with your own? What are the strong and weak points of each? Who are your competitors' customers and how do they differ from those of your own company? And, most important, why do they purchase rival brands in preference to your own? Are your sales ahead or behind those of your competitors in the 'brand-share' table? Are you, or is one of your competitors, the brand leader and, if so, why? This may be due to differences in products or perhaps because of marketing policy, the third aspect of competitors' activity which you must study.

The marketing policy of competitive firms must be studied, item for item, against the points previously considered when investigating your own company's policy. Equal attention must be paid to the advertising campaigns of rival firms — which media do they use and what sizes and positions? How frequently do they advertise? What sales points are stressed in their advertisements and how are they illustrated?

Field Marshall Montgomery had a photograph of Rommel in his caravan HQ in the North African desert. He knew that only by getting inside the mind of his opponent could he expect to out-think and beat him. In planning your advertising, it is vital that you have a similarly thorough knowledge of the competition you face from others. A clear understanding of the indirect competition which you and rival brands face from other product groups can be equally important.

Constraints

Advertising practice is not a free-for-all with no holds barred. There are a number of legal contraints and voluntary codes that limit your actions. In some cases the constraint is fundamental and dictates media policy, e.g. you cannot advertise cigarettes on television or radio. Clearly your researches must make you fully aware of what you are (and are not) allowed to do and say — how else can you prepare an advertising campaign that satisfies these requirements? Detailed discussion of these legal and voluntary controls is beyond the scope of this book, and for the most part, they have creative rather than media implications. But, as one television contractor pointed out:

- *On television, pay respect to copy regulations. Failure to do so can inhibit media buying* (m-o)

Your use of other media can be similarly affected.

Media

As you would expect, your investigations should include gaining a first-rate knowledge of advertising media, the need for which was made clear in Part 1.

The importance of research

Without research into all seven points discussed above, it is impossible for you to plan effectively. Before thinking about future advertising, therefore, your first task is to make a full investigation of all these matters. Then, and only then, can you give thought to planning future advertising.

Research is vital for accurate media selection. Media planning can be likened to aiming a gun: you cannot hit a target unless you know what and where the target is, and it is research that frequently provides this information. Research also helps in timing your campaign, by indicating when your product is purchased and how frequently, and whether it is an impulse purchase or one that needs serious reflection, the latter calling for your advertising message to be delivered well in advance with subsequent reminders.

Research can equally be helpful to creative staff. Your product may have dozens of sales points, any one of which could be featured in your advertising, and it is of major importance to select the particular benefit that will attract attention and lead readers to study your advertisement more closely. Featuring the correct sales point attracts attention and, equally, featuring the wrong 'copy platform' loses attention — and sales. Should the creative work be based on something of lesser importance, the potential customer may not bother to read the advertisement and will thus miss the sales point which *is* of major interest — and would have clinched the sale had he known of it.

Research can thus make a significant contribution to media planning and creative work by ensuring that it is soundly based. Its purpose, however, is only to set the framework for media and creative work: it will not prepare a media schedule nor the creative

201

content of your advertisements. Research does not dispense with the need for good media planners or creative staff, but does provide an efficient tool to make their work more effective.

Market research has been defined as 'the systematic study of product (and services) — existing or potential — in relation to their markets'. You could obtain information by going out to interview potential customers personally, and the chapter on specialist services listed some of the organisations that could undertake this work on your behalf.

Field research is, however, both costly and time-consuming, and the necessary information may already have been collected by some other organisation. Research does not necessarily imply spending large sums of money calling in a professional market research company to undertake scientifically planned investigations — although naturally the information that results from such action can be invaluable. Research also includes your own reading, and the number of information sources you can consult is extremely large: there are numerous government surveys and reports, the many data sources detailed in the chapters on media research and on specialist sources, and there are the innumerable research documents published by media-owners, advertisers and agencies. If to this list is added information available from analysis of your own internal records, the research undertaken by trade, professional and technical associations and institutions, and the reports and publications available from other sources, e.g. the BLA Management Services Group, Dun & Bradstreet, the Economist Intelligence Unit, John Hogston Associates, MINTEL, Retail Business, Staniland Hall Associates and others, then the wealth of information that is available, provided you know where to look, will be apparent — as will the invaluable contribution of desk research. Good desk research could make field research unnecessary by locating the information required, perhaps a bit here and a bit there, in the many different published sources, and so not only save the expenditure of several thousand pounds on a field survey, but save vital time as well. Any book on media must necessarily cover desk research and — as when field research was discussed in an earlier chapter — there is thus an in-built tendency for it to become a book on research as such. But a line must be drawn somewhere and so, having drawn attention to its role in providing information on which to base your planning, discussion of desk research will end here, other than mentioning some reference books which might assist you in locating valuable information sources. You should be sure that you consult the latest editions of the following:

1   *European Directory of Market Research Surveys,* edited by Thomas Landau and published by Gower Press.

2   *Government Statistics* — a brief guide to sources published by the Central Statistical Office.
3   *International Directory of Published Market Research,* compiled by the British Overseas Trade Board for HM Government in association with Arlington Management Publications.
4   *Review of Consumer Research Sources for Products and Media,* published by the Institute of Practitioners in Advertising.
5   *Sources of UK Marketing Information,* compiled by Elizabeth Tupper and Gordon Wills, published by Ernest Benn.

Research and investigation in practice

The need to build your advertising plan on a sound base is so fundamental that only a few quotations are necessary to illustrate the importance of research.

Research in general

Earlier chapters featured quotations such as

● *comprehensive use of up-to-date research* (m-o)

and equally, if not more, important

● *understanding significance of research* (m-o)

This latter quotation draws attention to the fact that research is only a tool, and does not do the job for you. One practitioner urged that

● *the advertiser should question research — own, agency and media* (m-o)

Another cited, as a common mistake militating against effective use of media

● *over-dependence on research and statistics* (ad)

while another pointed out the need to

● *mix accurate market profile and deep study of media research with human judgment* (ag)

Product knowledge

Clearly, if you are to produce an advertising campaign that will persuade people to buy your product, you must know *all* about that product. The quotations selected have been chosen to illustrate how this knowledge directly affects both media choice and the creative content of your campaign:

- *specify what the product offers the buyer and what you want him to do* (ad)

- *a precise understanding of what is to be communicated and how* (ag)

- *think product not medium* (m-o)

Market knowledge

As you would expect, there were innumerable quotations on the lines of

- *be absolutely sure about what comprises your target audience* (ad)

More interesting were the variations on this theme. Some pointed out that markets were segmented:

- *define target audience(s) with importance weighting* (ad)

Others stressed geographical differences:

- *geographical segmentation of market* (ad)

- *brand managers must learn to contact the sales managers and check up on the sales of their product by small area — not merely look at the national figures month by month and think national for advertising purposes* (m-o)

Others commented on knowledge of consumers as such:

- *audience criteria (large/small, users/non-users, sophistication)* (ad)

- *precise definition of the target market in terms of socio-economic group and life-style* (m-o)

What is surprising, in view of the vital importance of market knowledge, is the fact that it arose just as frequently as a negative matter. Here are a few examples:

- *insufficient audience demographics/poor market segmentation* (ad)

- *inability of the advertiser (or unwillingness because of cost) to define markets and their relative importance accurately* (ag) and, linking back to the first point, of product knowledge:

- *not relating the product definitively enough with its probable market* (m-o)

Many of these quotations hint at the need for better market definitions, but others were specific in stressing the need for a re-examination of market research or its methodology. What they wanted was

- *more research on the advertising to buying process* (other)

- *more research on social class grading* (other)

The final quotation gives another warning, in pointing out that

- *target markets are often too broad. The potential customer is too often considered as a fixed target. He/she is frequently a moving target. His/her psychology and attitudes to products and services should be identified whenever possible. They* can *affect media planning* (ag)

Marketing knowledge

Quite apart from the obvious need for

- *in-depth knowledge of advertiser's marketing objectives* (m-o)

many quotations linked the need for marketing knowledge with the two points just discussed — knowledge of product and market. They pointed out the need to

- *know your products and markets — and objectives/timing* (ad)

and the need for

- *full marketing back-up — regularity of purchase/regularity of sales and distribution, etc.* (ag)

- *marketing objectives — geography/demography/product consumption profiles* (m-o)

The need for marketing knowledge was thus fully appreciated throughout all sections of the industry.

Previous advertising

Analysis of results will be discussed in detail in a later chapter and, until then, a single quotation must suffice to illustrate the importance of your advertising to date

- *be guided by previous response where applicable* (ad)

Competition

Only a few quotations are necessary to illustrate the importance of knowing what your competition is doing. These come from practitioners who urged that you should

- *ensure the media team is aware of competitive media exposure* (ad)
- *know your product, competitors and the market* (ag)
- *be aware of competitors' activity before preparing campaign plan* (m-o)

Constraints

The earlier text featured a quotation illustrating how lack of knowledge of copy regulations can inhibit media buying, and this matter is covered in some detail in a later chapter.

The next step

With your investigations complete, you now have a firm base on which to undertake your next task. This is problem analysis, described in the next chapter.

10

PROBLEM ANALYSIS

With a thorough knowledge of your firm and its products, its market and marketing policy, your previous advertising, the competition you face, and the various constraints imposed, you can now commence more positive action — problem analysis and determination of your specific advertising objective.

Advertising is a means of achieving a purpose. Your firm may have more than one reason for advertising, and thus two or more concurrent advertising campaigns. The underlying purpose of these campaigns may also change from time to time, with circumstances.

There is a remarkably wide range of reasons for advertising — one well-known analysis* contains a checklist of 52 advertising tasks! Even the more fundamental reasons are, surprisingly enough, a blind spot to many advertising people, who are so engrossed in the detail of their work that they overlook the need to define clearly the basic purpose of their advertising. Many times, when you enquire about the objective of a proposed advertising campaign, you receive a surprised look and the answer 'Why, it's to increase sales, of course' — as though you had asked a foolish question. But how are these increased sales to be achieved? 'Increased sales' is not a business objective but only an optimistic hope for the future. If these increased sales are, in fact, to be realised, then there must be a definite objective for, as you will see later, this will affect the type of advertising campaign, the media used and its creative content.

A useful exercise is to take a random selection of advertisements and try to 'read back' from the creative content just what was the *specific* objective. Very few participants in this exercise will achieve a 100 per cent strike rate, which surely proves two points:

1   Many advertising people have a blind spot when it comes to analysing advertising effectiveness.

2   Many advertisements are not effective, simply because those responsible for the campaign failed to establish a clear objective.

* *Defining Advertising Goals for Measured Advertising Results* by R. Colley (see Chapter 16).

This may be a 'Heads I win, tails you lose' argument, but why else should we not be able to achieve a 100 per cent success rate in analysis?

In no way should you underestimate the importance of creativity in advertising, but creativity is functional only when it contributes to achieving your campaign objective. Specification of a clear objective assists creative people by setting the parameters within which they should work: it gives a strong indication of the creative approach necessary, quite apart from being essential for good media planning. This book concentrates on direct media aspects, but these cannot be treated separately from creative considerations.

Analysis of specific objectives

Analysis of advertising campaigns in a wide range of media revealed a large number of different specific objectives: these are discussed below, but not necessarily in any order of importance. The list is not exclusive, nor should the objectives be considered as separate 'water-tight' compartments. You may wish to achieve two or more purposes simultaneously — or perhaps your company has an objective not included in the list (I readily admit my own blind spot). The main point is the essential need to set out clearly, before starting to plan your campaign, *precisely* what you hope to achieve. Planning and creativity will then follow that much more easily. Possible campaign objectives might include the following.

Reminding existing users

You must constantly remind users of your wares. Why 'must'? Well, human memory is short, and frequent reminders are necessary. Moreover, there are innumerable distracting factors which soon make memory fade. In some cases, it may be the advertising of rival firms. There is also the competition for attention faced from makers of totally different products: television sets face indirect competition from washing machines, holidays abroad, or new furniture. Taking a still wider view of the many factors competing for public attention, there are thousands of non-selling influences at work to make people forget your products — the latest news at home and abroad, the activities of family and friends, new events at work and the latest films and television programmes. The manufacturer who expects to be permanently remembered amid this host of competing calls on public attention is more than optimistic. An apocryphal story tells how Wrigley, the chewing gum magnate, was once asked during a train journey why he spent so much money on advertising. Surely, his questioner asked, everybody knew Wrigley's chewing gum and everybody chewed Wrigley's chewing gum? Why the need for such heavy advertising? Wrigley supposedly replied that he would answer if the questioner told him how fast the train was going — and promptly denied he was changing the subject. When told that the train's speed was about 70 miles an hour, Wrigley immediately asked 'Why bother keeping the engine on the front?' Reminder advertising maintains momentum in the same way and, if this is your objective, there are clear implications as to choice of media and creative content. Furthermore, constant reminders through advertising can enhance your firm's reputation and standing, and play their part in cementing customer loyalty. Reminder advertising is, however, quite distinct from the need to re-assure previous purchasers — another specific purpose discussed below.

Re-assuring previous purchasers

The need to re-assure previous purchasers is a task quite different from that of simply reminding existing users. For many products, particularly where major expenditure is involved, current owners are key figures in the decision process of potential purchasers. If you reflect on any major purchase you have made, you will realise that in almost every case you sought the advice of somebody who had already bought the product. *Their* view was far more influential than any salesman, and much current advertising therefore takes account of the theory of 'cognative dissonance'. This theory is based on the idea that if a person knows various things that are not psychologically consistent with each other he will, in a variety of ways, try to make them more consistent in order to reduce this dissonance. To illustrate how advertising planning should allow for this, take the case of someone who so dislikes waking up in ice-cold rooms that he installs central heating. After some months, the unpleasantness of cold mornings will fade from his memory, and all he remembers is the previously non-existent heating bills. Ask such a person for his views on central heating and you will hear how expensive it is to run and not a word about the benefits. As such negative reactions would put off prospective purchasers, much advertising recognises this and aims at re-assuring previous purchasers just as much as attracting new ones. If your product comes into this category, the need to 'keep customers sold' has clear implications for both media choice and creative content.

Countering the natural decline in the market

Reminder advertising can be most effective in maintaining sales, but you must face up to the fact that your existing customers, through no fault of yours, are steadily decreasing in number. The manufacturer who claims there is no need to advertise because he has all the business he needs ignores the fact that people leave the area or the country, change their circumstances or just stop using his product. The quality of your product may remain as high as ever, but sales will steadily decline through the natural diminution of the existing market. As Lord Keynes once pointed out, in the long term we're all dead! New customers must be attracted to counter this decline, and advertising is one of the means available to achieve this end.

Informing the constant flow of potential customers

The population is ceaselessly changing, not only in size but also in composition. As they grow older, people change from schoolchild to teenager, to young married to parent, and perhaps to grandparent. As they move from one consumer group to another, so their needs change; they become potential customers for goods which previously were of no interest to them. Similarly, in the technical field, firms change in size and in the scope of their operations, and need to purchase new plant, equipment or facilities. They become new prospects, and advertising can convert them into customers. Many firms mistakenly assume that, just because they have been advertising for years, people must know about the merchandise they have to offer. This ignores the fact that many prospective customers entered the market for the first time *today*, and earlier advertising therefore had only a limited effect. Research has proved that people look at advertisements for products which interest them, and ignore others. Yesterday these potential purchasers were not in the market, so were unlikely to respond to advertisements for the merchandise in question.

The constantly changing market

The fact that the market is ceaselessly changing is a blind spot for many advertisers. Markets steadily decline through natural causes, there are always potential new customers in need of information and, in the meantime, you need to remind and perhaps reassure existing customers. If you consider your own journey through life, the practical implications of this obvious statement become apparent. In your infancy you were, through your parents, in the market for nappies and talcum powder. As you left this market, the manufacturers of these products needed new customers to replace the sales lost when you no longer needed their merchandise. Your life can, in fact, be described in terms of products which you use for the first time, others about which you need reminding, and those which you eventually no longer need. Such a list would include school clothing, bicycles, razor blades and cosmetics, engagement and wedding rings, homes and furniture, baby clothes and prams, and so on through to false teeth and hair pieces. We all finish up in what has been given the macabre title of the coffin and cremation market! At every stage of our lives we represent, simultaneously, lost customers for one producer and prospective buyers for another. Advertising planning, if it is to be effective, must take account of these never-ending changes in the market.

Information about new developments

Present customers may know of your goods, but do they know of any improvements made, or of new lines added to your range? Firms devote a great deal of time, money and effort to improving their products, but this is of little purpose if customers are left in the dark about them. They must be informed about new or improved products, new packs, or the delivery of eagerly awaited goods. Prices and products are constantly changing, and it is a great mistake for any manufacturer to believe that, just because *he* knows about these things, his customers are equally well-informed. Potential customers will not become purchasers unless they know of the new developments, and advertising helps to keep them informed. Furthermore, the changes in your product line may open up new market segments, for whom your earlier products were not of interest. Again, there are clear media and creative implications.

Stabilised production

For a number of manufacturers, their advertising objective is not to increase sales but to stabilise production. If demand for your product is unsteady, your factory has to work at full capacity — perhaps even overtime — while sales are high, but when demand falls off machinery lies idle. A sales graph with great peaks and troughs makes for uneconomic production. Advertising can help to even out the graph in two different ways.

One solution to problems arising from uneven production is to plan your advertising to fill the troughs. There is a net increase in sales but you stimulate the market only at specified times of the year. The other way of levelling out your sales graph is by shifting sales from peaks to troughs: in this latter case there is no increase in sales but, by using advertising to persuade consumers to make their purchases in slack rather than peak periods, expenses are reduced with obvious increase in profit.

Advertising can facilitate making the most efficient use of your plant, and such considerations directly affect the timing of your campaign and its creative content.

Fighting declining sales

The purpose of your campaign may be not to increase or stabilise sales, but to hold off a decline. This overall category, in fact, masks various types of decline, for which different advertising approaches are necessary. One advertising campaign may have as its purpose countering the natural decline in the market, mentioned above. Another purpose might be to sustain an existing brand against competition. Other purposes might be to slow down a permanent trend, or to reverse a temporary decline.

Where the market for your product is steadily diminishing, it is unwise to expect advertising to work miracles and reverse the permanent trend: it may, however, be able to make some contribution by slowing the rate of decline, thus giving you time to seek new opportunities in other directions. Where advertising can make a far more positive contribution is in countering temporary falls in sales. The Chancellor's budget, for example, may introduce tax changes in relation to specific groups of products, or impose hire-purchase and credit restrictions which inhibit sales.

Increased advertising is one method you can adopt to avert a slump, but the underlying causes call for different types of advertising campaign.

Overcoming resistance

Many companies seem to assume a 'neutral' public, awaiting only a suitable advertising message to stimulate them into buying the product. But people are wary of buying unfamiliar products, and retailers equally shy of stocking lines unknown to their customers. More than this, people may even be hostile: consider, for example, the reluctance of many drivers and passengers to use seat belts and how the 'clunk click' campaign set about solving this problem. If your product encounters such resistance, advertising can do much to overcome this sales barrier by building up a favourable image in the public mind.

'Prestige' advertising

The popular 'title' for this type of advertising covers allied uses — you will come across references to mood-selling, image-building, corporate or institutional advertising. Certainly some organisations may need to concentrate on their image rather than their products but, alas, in many cases this approach is misused, or even taken as an easy way out! Many cynical creative men have remarked that, when all else fails, you can always rely on the old stand-by of an aerial view of the factory and a picture of the Chairman to keep everybody happy! But for this type of advertising to be effective, you must ask very fundamental questions. What opinion do people hold now? If your image is bad, is this, in fact, well deserved? If it *is*, then no amount of so-called prestige advertising can rectify matters: the true solution is to put things right and only then set about advertising. For this type of advertising to be effective, you must know who constitutes your market, what these people think now, and precisely what you want them to think in the future. Unless you have the answer to these questions you can neither choose media nor decide upon creative content.

Whilst in the general area of consumer opinions, you should also consider those cases where manufacturers attempt — perhaps at the same time as achieving the main aim of 'selling' their products — to change consumer attitudes. In such circumstances, it is vital to distinguish between basic beliefs and short-term behaviour. Many consumers have deeply entrenched views based on their total experience of a product — or product group — perhaps going back to their childhood days. As you would expect, it is no easy task for advertising to shift such views, which may be paralleled by market trends. Whilst advertising can be very effective in influencing short-term buying behaviour, changing long-term beliefs or market trends is a very different matter. Advertising can rarely reverse a negative trend (see 'fighting declining sales' above) but it can help encourage a positive one.

'Umbrella' campaigns

The underlying purpose of many corporate campaigns is not prestige

213

as such, but to link various separate activities. Examples are often found where organisations are active in various fields, with separate companies marketing separate products to separate markets via separate advertising and selling campaigns. Many such organisations realise that linking the self-contained business operations would benefit all the component companies. To illustrate how this applies in practice, organisations A, B, C and D might each have sales campaigns for their separate industrial markets, with appropriate advertising in the relevant professional or technical press. National or local press would normally be ruled out as too few readers come within the specified categories of buyer. But as many industrial purchasers buy not only product A but also perhaps B, C and D as well, the separate advertising campaigns in specialised press can be made more effective by an 'umbrella' campaign in more general media, on the creative theme of 'If you need advice on A, B, C or D, we are the experts'. Sales representatives from the individual companies then cross-refer enquiries, as necessary. Such an advertising objective clearly has a much more functional aim than a so-called 'prestige' campaign, and there are clear implications for both media choice and advertisement content. The same effect can apply, however, even within a single company, as is explained in the following section.

Benefit to other lines

A similar effect to an umbrella campaign may apply, on a smaller scale, within a single organisation. One obvious effect of advertising is to increase sales of the item featured, but a secondary result may be increased sales of *other* lines. A retailer, for example, is likely to find that people make more than one purchase when they call at his shop to buy an advertised product, and manufacturers benefit correspondingly when the publicity afforded to their brand name by advertising one item helps other lines in their range.

If advertising is likely to have a beneficial 'spin-off' for your other products, this added advantage must be borne in mind when planning your campaign. The chapter on the advertiser mentioned the existence of 'brand managers' and the question then arises of whether a company with this marketing structure is likely to adopt such a co-ordinated approach.

Launch a new product or service

For new products or services, reminder advertising is clearly inapplicable: here the task is one of basic education — informing potential customers of the benefits they will reap by purchasing your new product. A side effect of this may well be, in due course, a counter campaign to fight declining sales by the manufacturer whose product is no longer in favour.

Extending distribution

In some cases, your advertising may be aimed not at the public but at stockists. A manufacturer who finds his product in insufficient outlets will seek to widen his distribution and would use advertising as a tool for this purpose. Trade press advertising is obvious in this respect but public advertising is equally effective, when sales representatives take round proofs of advertisements which are to appear in the local paper, which they employ as a most persuasive argument in getting retailers to stock and display your merchandise. If extended distribution is the purpose of your campaign, it is often to your advantage to book advertisements of a larger size than is strictly necessary to convey the creative message, simply because of the impact this larger size has on retailers in getting them to anticipate a large demand.

Stimulate existing distribution

As with the previous case, advertising is used for its effect on retailers rather than the general public. The difference is that your product is widely distributed but you consider the stockists insufficiently active in promoting sales. To rectify this, you can use heavy local advertising to persuade hitherto passive retailers to give your products more window and in-store display. As before, larger sizes than are strictly necessary can be most helpful when using advertising in this way as a sales tool for representatives. In both this and the previous case you may find it advantageous to feature the names and addresses of stockists, perhaps on a co-operative basis. Such considerations clearly influence the choice of media, and the way in which you use it.

Back-up for sales representatives

As in the previous two cases, the underlying target for your advertising is not the general public — here, its aim is to stimulate your representatives. Salesmen, in the field all day and thus out of contact with your sales office, soon feel cut off and may become dispirited.

Advertising can give them a much needed psychological boost. Where representatives sell to industrial buyers rather than to retailers who then sell to the public, this back-up role can be vital. A McGraw-Hill advertisement, designed to promote advertising in its specialist publications, showed a steely-eyed industrial buyer looking at the reader and saying:

"I don't know who you are.

I don't know your company.

I don't know your company's product.

I don't know what your company stands for.

I don't know your company's customers.

I don't know your company's record.

I don't know your company's reputation.

Now—what was it you wanted to sell me?"

MORAL: Sales start **before** your salesman calls—
with business publication advertising.

McGRAW-HILL MAGAZINES
BUSINESS•PROFESSIONAL•TECHNICAL

Advertising aimed at extending or stimulating distribution can also be considered under this heading, for its indirect effect in boosting your salesmen's confidence and thus encouraging them in their efforts.

Leads for sales representatives

This use of advertising differs from the previous instances in that it is aimed at the public, but the salesman is still a key figure in that the purpose of the campaign is to provide him with sales leads on which to call. Salesmen's time is valuable and at a premium, and following up contracts who have indicated positive interest by, for example, returning a coupon is far more productive than cold canvassing.

This was the main advertising function for one client whose account I handled: the aim was a steady stream of leads to keep sales staff busy. Although planned on a long-term basis, scheduling was extremely flexible with advertising activity being stepped up when necessary or cut back when the representatives had more business than they could handle. For this client, effective advertising clearly demanded flexible media planning.

Direct selling and mail order

Much the same type of strategic planning may be necessary for those who sell direct to the public, using advertising to spread information about their wares and to solicit orders. As was the case when keeping representatives supplied with sales leads, a flexible media plan is necessary to keep demand and supply in balance.

Building up a mailing list

Some advertisers have found it profitable to vary this pattern when selling direct. The initial mailing list is built up by public advertising, and direct mail then used to obtain orders from those who have expressed interest. Mail order is the primary aim of the campaign, and general advertising is used to 'top up' the mailing list when necessary since this must necessarily suffer the natural decline inherent in every market.

Dispose of surplus supplies

Advertising is often used on a periodic rather than regular basis, and the 'sales' which feature so prominently on the retail scene reflect this. Sales advertising often serves two quite distinct purposes — one is to boost sales at an otherwise slack period (as described above) while the other purpose is to clear shelves of last year's stock to make way for new merchandise. The retailer makes the old stock more attractive by cutting prices, and makes this reduction known through his Sale advertising.

Dispose of by-products

In other cases, the purpose may be to dispose of by-products rather than to clear dead stocks. In manufacturing its main product, your company may produce a by-product which it wishes to sell at a profit.

This exercise differs from the main selling operation in that sales volume is dictated by the main product, demand for which determines production levels, which in turn controls the amount of by-product produced. The aim of the by-product advertising campaign is thus to sell just so much and no more, since there is little purpose in stimulating a massive demand for this secondary product when supplies could not be increased without creating an unsaleable surplus of the main product. Any promotional plan thus has a 'cut-off' point dictated by the main sales programme, which your media scheduling must clearly take into account.

Utilising other marketing strengths

There are other circumstances in which advertising planning is determined by your company's overall marketing programme, rather than by demand for the single product for which you are preparing a campaign. This can occur when manufacturers review their product range and make a work study of sales force effectiveness. A producer may find, for example, that his representatives are not working to full capacity: this is no reflection on his salesmen and their efforts, but simply recognises that the present product range does not keep them fully occupied. There is thus spare sales force capacity, and the question then is: 'What additional product, which would be of interest to current buyers, could your salesmen carry and sell effectively?' If a further item is added to round out your company's product line, this is another case where promotional planning will be determined by factors outside the usual considerations, depending on the main marketing programme.

Advertising as an aid to buying

Advertising has been defined as 'making known in order to sell' but on many occasions your aim may be the very opposite — not to sell, but to buy. Many business offers are put out to tender, the contract being advertised and the order going to the firm submitting the best bid. Similarly, 'Situations Vacant' advertisements are the recognised way of locating suitable applicants to fill staff vacancies. At the start of this chapter mention was made that the various reasons for advertising should not be considered as water-tight compartments, and that two or more purposes may be applicable at any one time: 'Situations Vacant' is an example of where this

applies. Many firms realise that, whilst a small classified advertisement might be sufficient to convey the bare facts of a post, they
face competition for the best applicants who are more likely to
respond to an advertisement which conveys that they would be
working for the leading company in the field. Employers realise
also that not only potential applicants see these advertisements
but also many others, including the public at large, suppliers, shareholders and customers. 'Situations Vacant' advertisements are
therefore correctly treated as more than the filling of posts,
although this task in itself calls for specialist skills.

Arbitrary reasons for advertising

This section should not be here but, alas, it would be unrealistic
not to recognise the sad fact that, whilst there are many sound
reasons why advertising can be the most effective way of helping
you achieve your purpose, there are also a number of other 'reasons'
for advertising which are less rational. To give one example, it is
not unknown for a producer to advertise out of personal pride:
it gives him satisfaction to see his name in print or some other
advertising medium, and to feel that his friends and acquaintances
think of him as an important man.

Media selection can also be influenced by arbitrary factors —
the advertiser's motivating force may perhaps be tradition: his
firm has always used the medium in question. Alternatively, he
may feel 'forced in' because he does not wish to be the odd man
out. Or again, he may feel he has a 'duty' to support the relevant
trade magazine or exhibition. Sometimes this latter aim is not as
irrational as it appears: some firms realise they *need* the publication or exhibition, and equally appreciate that the media-owner's
sales revenue from copies or admission is insufficient to make the
venture commercially viable. Since the manufacturers have a clear
need for this particular means of communication they support it,
and advertising thus has in it an element of subsidy. In other cases,
by booking space in special programmes, firms use advertising as
an indirect means of making donations to charity.

Increased sales

This reason for advertising has deliberately been left until last: not
because it is unimportant — far from it — but because it demands
greater attention and more detailed analysis than the other reasons
so far discussed.

The so-called aim of 'increased sales' is perhaps the most frequent blind spot in the whole advertising and marketing process. It is a great weakness that many firms, both large and small, regard 'increased sales' as a sufficiently clear objective on which to base an advertising campaign. But 'increased sales' is *not* a specific objective — it is only a wish for the future. What percentage increase are you aiming for? Where are these increased sales to come from? How are they to be achieved? The lucidity of the answers to these questions will influence the effectiveness of your advertising campaign, and directly affect not only media choice but also the way in which the selected media are used in terms of size, position and frequency. Equally fundamental is the influence of these answers on the advertising content, in terms of creative approach.

Too many people overlook the basic fact that there are three fundamentally different ways of increasing sales, each calling for a totally different type of advertising campaign. A first essential is to stop thinking in terms of increased sales, and to think instead of increased *purchases* — or, more specifically, possible purchasers and their buying patterns. Viewed in purchasing terms, there are three ways in which you can increase sales:

1   Increased purchases by existing users   Such a campaign will convert light into medium users or medium into heavy, and your aim is to extend the range of uses they make of your product, or increase their frequency of use. This will increase the value of the market, but not its size in terms of people.

2   Purchases by new users   With such a campaign, your aim is to educate non-users (who have not used your own product nor that of any rivals) to the benefits of your product, thus converting them to its use. Advertising of this type will increase the size of the market in terms of people, as well as its value. But see note below.

3   Purchases by competitors' customers   Your campaign aim here is to persuade buyers (existing or potential) of rival products to switch brands. This will not increase the 'size of the cake' — only the way it is divided.

In considering sales to 'new users' — and indeed *all* purchasers — you must be careful to distinguish between long-term basic beliefs and short-term current needs. Advertising can be most effective in influencing short-term buying behaviour but, as earlier paragraphs made clear, changing beliefs is a very different matter. A simple example is wedding dresses which, at first sight would appear to be 'purchases by new users'. In the strict sense this is of course true, but you would be very unwise to plan your advertising appeal on this basis — there is no need to 'educate non-users to the benefits of your product, thus converting them to its use': women *know* the use of a wedding dress! Equally, no woman is going to rush out and buy one because of new styles, low prices or easy credit terms: the purchase of a wedding dress depends directly on her long-term views on marriage, on accepting a proposal, and on her deeply entrenched views about white weddings. In this sense, the sale of a wedding dress is a brand-switch operation: the woman's decision is made, and your objective is to persuade her to buy a wedding dress from your company. The same reasoning applies to another example, this time for the (mostly) male market — a new exhaust system for your car. This time there are few (if any) 'basic beliefs' but in no way will you spend money on a new one until circumstances make it essential: the decision to replace your exhaust system is made for you, and your task — aided by suitable advertisements — is to decide where to go to get it. In this case you will actually seek out information, so this is another example of how people *use* advertisements that are being used to reach them. Both examples illustrate the need to consider the long-term and short-term effects of your advertising, as well as consumers' entrenched beliefs and short-term needs — your immediate campaign aim might be to attract possible customers who are in the market for product *now* but, at the same time, your advertising will also be seen by others who — although they have no need of your product at present — may want it in future and, when the time comes, may recall your company name in this respect.

Wedding dresses and exhaust systems are extreme examples and, in most cases, 'sales to new users' means just what it says, and your task is to explain to non-users the benefits they will get from your product. If your analysis is correct, they should be grateful for the information and buy the product, to your mutual benefit.

The need to analyse possible sales in terms of potential purchases is only another variation of the theme stressed by so many practitioners:

● *the need to establish a* true *campaign objective* (ad)

If the increased sales/increased purchases analysis is reduced to the most fundamental level, it will be apparent that media policy and basic creative content can then be entered on a chart as shown overleaf.

A campaign designed to meet one of these objectives is unlikely to be as successful in achieving the other two, since they call for different advertising in terms of both media and creative content.

From the creative standpoint, a campaign aimed at existing users,

Type of sales increase	Media policy	Creative content
Existing users	Maintain insertions in current media	Suggest new uses for your product, or reasons for using it more frequently.
New users	Consider new media	Explain the basic benefits of your product, to people unaware of them
Brand-switch	Consider your competitors' patterns	Comparison advertising, pointing out the advantages of your product over rival brands

suggesting further uses for your product, may not be understood by new users who are unaware of your product's basic function, let alone additional uses. A campaign designed to explain your product's basic benefits to potential purchasers may bore existing users, who are already well aware of its function. Neither will it be effective in influencing the brand loyalty of buyers of rival products. Equally, a campaign prepared to persuade buyers of rival products to switch brands, by stressing the advantages of your product over others, is likely to be less successful in educating new users to the product group's basic benefits.

Much the same can be said of media policy: to increase sales to your existing customers you would clearly wish to continue your present media pattern, whilst to reach new prospective buyers you may have to use new media. Playing 'follow my leader' rarely results in effective advertising but, if you seek brand-switch sales, clearly you will wish to influence your competitors' customers and would *deliberately* aim at the same market — and are thus likely to use the same media. This is a very different matter to blindly following your rival's lead, for lack of anything better to do.

Advertising should thus be seen in context as part of your total marketing operation. It is not a separate activity but must be based directly on marketing objectives, which should be clear and detailed. Sales force activity must equally be aimed at achieving the identical marketing objective: advertising and selling should be complementary.

Thus different types of sales increase call for different types of media schedule as well as different creative content. Like most fundamental truths this is all very obvious — once it has been pointed out. But for too many organisations it appears to be a blind spot. I have, of course, over-simplified for ease of illustration and the three types of increase are not self-exclusive. Furthermore, there certainly *are* advertisements which achieve sales in two or even three of the possible ways simultaneously. Much successful advertising recognises the three distinct ways of increasing sales and accordingly the campaign is not a single entity but comprises three separate but inter-related components, each aimed at one distinct target group. These three components are not only successful in their own right but, because they are clearly linked, each component re-inforces the effectiveness of the other two. Advertising planning such as this can be achieved only by design, never by accident.

Summary

The essential message of this chapter is the need to define clearly, before starting to plan your advertising, precisely what the under-lying objective of the campaign is to be. It is more than obvious to state that you cannot hit a target unless you know what that target is — why should it be less obvious that it is impossible to prepare advertising proposals to achieve an objective unless you know precisely what this objective is. A great deal of current advertising is, alas, ineffective simply because this fundamental truth has been ignored. Analyse your marketing objectives properly and your advertising effectiveness must increase.

Advertising as a means of communication

This book is aimed primarily at advertising people — whether with advertisers, agencies or media-owners — and there is thus no need to 'defend' advertising against some of the more foolish criticisms. Nevertheless, it is worth reminding ourselves, while examining the reasons for advertising, of the benefits it offers in comparison with other means of communication.

Any businessman, reading through the list of reasons for advertising just discussed, might justifiably comment that these are *business objectives* and not reasons for advertising. He could well add that his best advertisements were satisfied customers and ask why should he waste good money on advertising to achieve these business objectives, when word-of-mouth recommendation was spreading news of his products to potential purchasers. Most certainly any manufacturer will benefit from new purchasers learning from old about the benefits of his product and should do all he can to encourage this:

much public relations activity has this very aim. Nevertheless, the use of advertising to communicate messages brings certain specific benefits which make more than worthwhile the expenditure involved:

Speed　　Advertising communicates rapidly: many manufacturers launching new products need a return on their investment as swiftly as possible and rely on advertising to help them achieve this, rather than the gradual build-up in sales which word-of-mouth may bring.

Timing　　Personal recommendations, valuable though they are, may be spread over time in a haphazard way. Advertising, on the other hand, can be used as a precision instrument, stimulating your market when necessary. This may be a matter of seasons, promoting winter goods in the winter and summer goods in the summer, or alternatively may be a matter of days, giving customers a timely boost on a given day of the week.

Frequency　　Many manufacturers, particularly those whose goods are purchased on a repeat basis, cannot rely on recommendation. Their products are bought on a weekly or monthly basis and they need to stimulate the market at appropriate intervals: advertising can do just this, simply by booking appropriate appearances as part of your campaign plan.

Selectivity　　Personal recommendations spread indiscriminately, and you cannot rely on them to achieve full coverage of your particular target market: word often spreads to people with no interest in your product. Advertising, however, can be selective, and aimed at just the people most likely to buy your product. This may be a matter of media selection, choosing those media with good coverage of your target market, and here a fine degree of selectivity is possible, bearing in mind the wide range of media available to you. Alternatively, audience selection may be achieved by advertisement positioning just as much as media choice: as was made clear earlier, an advertisement on the gardening page of a newspaper will select gardeners out of the total readership, and the same is true of other positions which prove equally effective in selecting suitable readers for other manufacturers. Naturally, many advertisers use both methods of audience selection, booking specific positions in selected media.

Accuracy　　Word-of-mouth recommendation is unreliable in that information about your product's benefits is frequently distorted. Your product may have, say, half-a-dozen sales points, all of which you wish to communicate to potential purchasers. No doubt you can rely on your company's salesmen to convey these correctly, but beyond this point your control ends. Those who have made the purchase may, in spreading the word to their friends, perhaps forget one or two of these key points — or even invent others which are not, in fact, true. Either way, you are likely to lose sales. With press advertising, you decide precisely which words you wish to use and you equally control how they are to be conveyed. Furthermore, you receive proofs which you correct for accuracy. With other media you have equal control of advertisement content and there is no possibility of your message being distorted.

Economy   Advertising media costs-per-thousand spread over a very wide range but, whatever the figure, cost per contact is low in comparison with personal selling. Your company's salesmen play a vital role and it could be argued that the best way to spread news about your products would be to employ more salesmen. Clearly, however, this would be most uneconomic: salesmen's time can be measured in pounds (if not tens of pounds) per call, whereas advertising contacts are usually measured in pennies per thousand. Not only is advertising a more economic way of spreading messages then using your sales force, it can also be most effective in making your salesmen more productive — paving the way before they make their calls, or even providing them with direct leads to follow up.

Communications media

Compared with word-of-mouth recommendation, advertising thus has the advantages of speed, timing, frequency, selectivity, accuracy and economy and — to some extent — *all* media offer these advantages in varying degrees. Your success in selecting which to use, and the effectiveness of your advertising campaign, will depend directly on your skill in matching what the different media have to offer with the specific communication needs of your particular campaign objective. This, in turn, depends upon correct problem analysis, which is thus a first essential for effective use of advertising.

Problem analysis in practice

Various practitioners, commenting on mistakes militating against effective use of media, cited

- *poor problem analysis* (ag)
- *confused objectives* (other)

Earlier chapters stressed the importance of a proper brief and of research and investigations. An ideal brief will reflect your analysis of your company's marketing problem, in the light of your research and investigations. As one practitioner pointed out

● *the media plan should form an integral part of the campaign strategy, and the campaign strategy be an intergral part of the product marketing plan* (m-o)

Earlier paragraphs likened advertising to a gun, and pointed out that you could not hit a target unless you knew what and where the target was. Similarly, you cannot hope to mount an advertising campaign that will achieve a given objective unless you

● *give a true campaign objective* (ad)

Bearing in mind the wide range of possible objectives discussed above, this is perhaps easier said than done. It is certainly worth remembering that

● *the quality of the marketing brief decides the quality of the media plan* (m-o)

One respondent urged that

● *the planner should receive a written campaign brief including details of budget, advertising objectives and precise target audience required* (ad)

Other practitioners sought discussion rather than a written brief, pointing out that

● *adequate briefing and direct discussion of intentions is absolutely vital as different advertising aims result in different types of campaign (or should do)* (ag)

As far as I am concerned, there is no question of 'should do' — different advertising aims *must* result in different types of campaign, if these campaigns are to be effective.

One of the possible reasons for advertising discussed earlier is vividly illustrated by the following quotation, which shows in actual practice how different aims can result in different types of campaign. This came from the respondent who pointed out that

● *there are many reasons for advertising other than the apparent ones. Many small-budget advertisers need to make their customers feel they're doing more advertising than they really are. Such a campaign might make a media-buyer wince, but if it does the trick and makes a £50-thousand spend look like a £150-thousand, then it's 'effective'!* (ad)

Others looked at

● *clear identification of relevant objectives* (ad)

in even more detail. The following quotation refers to industrial markets, but the advice given is surely equally applicable to consumer products. The respondent pointed out

● *re industrial markets, the most important rule in producing the best media plan is to identify clearly what part the process of advertising plays within the total marketing communication business. Few companies make any formal assessment of the importance of advertising at each stage of the selling process — as compared with the importance of personal selling or the role of sales promotion.*

    How important is advertising to the stages of: making contact/ arousing interest/creating a preference/soliciting enquiries/ closing the sale/keeping customers sold? If this question can be quantified, then this will determine the strategy of the media plan (other)

One practitioner pointed out that your problem analysis may, in fact, lead to a re-definition of the problem you are trying to solve. Two points already made are the need for early briefing, and the fact that advertising planning should be a 'closed loop' with current plans being based on past results and future planning based on current results. One respondent linked these two points in advocating, as a basic rule for effective advertising

● *an adequate briefing — delivered in time to allow media considerations to influence marketing and creative consideration if necessary* (ag)

The most suitable final quotation I could find to link this chapter with the next ones on budgeting and preparation of proposals came from the respondent who recommended, as the procedure to follow for the best media plan

● *first to establish the marketing plan for the products or services to be promoted (the objectives) followed by the Budget, selling approach (the right message), competition, audience, timing, positioning, coverage, frequency, duration and response expected* (ad)

Having decided what you hope to achieve, you can now proceed to the next step — deciding how much you should spend on achieving this objective.

11

BUDGETING

The first essential for effective use of advertising media was gathering information on which to base your planning. Next came problem analysis and determining your specific advertising objective. With these two tasks completed, you can now tackle your third problem — deciding how much to spend on achieving your chosen objective. It is appreciated that not all readers will be directly involved — they may be on the receiving end, and have to work to a budget set by someone else. Nevertheless, it is helpful for them to appreciate the ways by which the advertising appropriation can be decided. Furthermore, if their advice is sought on whether a proposed sum is suitable, or if any agency or media-owner hopes to persuade an advertiser to spend more, then this knowledge is even more important.

Advertising is a cost, but it is usually incurred in increasing sales, from which come profits. If sales are increased by the advertising campaign, then profits are increased, and the extra profits can more than pay for the advertising. Increased sales can also lower costs, and thus enhance the margin of profit. Production in large quantities spreads overhead costs over more units of output and brings other economies of scale (such as better terms for purchasing raw materials in bulk) which lower the cost per unit produced, and thus make possible lower prices.

Increased sales, as we have seen, is by no means the only possible reason for advertising — stabilised sales make for more economic production and thus lower costs, higher profits and/or lower prices. Advertising can make a positive contribution to profitability in many ways, depending on your particular business objectives. The number of firms which imagine that advertising adds to the cost of goods, and that therefore they risk being undersold by competitors who do not advertise, are few: most firms realise that advertising is a cost, but a cost which brings savings in its wake. The problem lies not in deciding whether or not to spend money on advertising, but in deciding *how much* to spend. This, strangely enough, is another blind spot for too many organisations.

It is important to consider the advertising budget in context, as part of your total complex business operation. There are, in fact, several stages to the financial planning involved. First and foremost is the marketing plan — that you manufacture a product (or provide a service) with your product policy, advertising, distribution and selling effort all geared to achieving sales in a chosen market.

An overall allocation of funds is then made: so much for plant and equipment; so much for raw materials and labour; so much for selling effort; so much for advertising support, and so on. In this way a total budget is drawn up, showing the various financial commitments involved. It soon becomes apparent that fixing the advertising budget is a *management* decision, and part of a process of balancing expenditures when different activities compete for funds.

It is, therefore, desirable to approach this exercise from the viewpoint of ROI — Return On Investment — rather than spending money. For management to approve an advertising budget, you will need to convince your directors that advertising, rather than any other use of funds, will be the most productive form of expenditure, and make a positive contribution to profitability. Should your board view advertising as spending without results, you are unlikely to have any budget approved.

The amount to be spent on advertising is known as the 'appropriation' and appropriation policy is usually initiated by the advertising manager and then confirmed by the board, some three months or so before the start of the marketing year.

The term appropriation can be defined as 'the total amount to be spent on advertising during a given period'. Like all definitions it sounds simple, but two points merit special comment — for very practical reasons.

One point relates to 'a given period'. If you have an advertising budget of £X,000, you can have no idea whether this is a sufficient sum, or too much or too little money, unless you know the period of time for which this amount must provide advertising support. Most appropriations are for twelve-month periods, either the calendar year starting on 1 January or the financial year commencing on 5 April. Some appropriations are longer term whilst others are for shorter periods, say four months, with three appropriations per year, but the annual appropriation is more usual. Often, accounting practice makes this inflexible, so that towards the end of the period you are not permitted to 'borrow' from your next year's budget: equally, accounting practice forbids your carrying over any unspent funds. You must, therefore, be clear as to the time period to be covered by the money available, otherwise you cannot budget to cover it effectively. This, surprisingly enough, is less of a problem than the second point regarding the definition, namely the meaning of the word 'advertising'.

In its broadest sense, advertising includes anything featuring your company name or symbol, but more usually it is restricted to the conventional forms of advertising: press, posters, cinema and television and radio commercials and so on. Firms take differing views of what they include under the heading of advertising. Some exclude production costs for leaflets or display material, the money for these coming out of a separate budget. Others include them, together with such items as postage on sales letters, all of which come out of the advertising appropriation. In some firms the salaries of advertising personnel are set against the advertising appropriation, whilst in others they are considered as general staff costs. Public relations activity may have a separate budget or come out of an overall promotion budget, and the same applies to merchandising and sales promotion. In short, there is no hard and fast rule as to what comes out of the budget and what does not, and practice varies from firm to firm. However, the point is a basic one — if you are responsible for the appropriation you must have a clear idea of what it does and does not cover. It would not do for you to plan carefully how to spend your appropriation and then, towards the end of the period, get an unexpected invoice for something you did not consider as advertising, but which the accountants do.

There are many sad stories to illustrate the practical need for this clear understanding. The newly appointed advertising manager of a company was told, three-quarters of the way through the year, that he had over-spent by several thousand pounds. Even after repeated checks he still considered himself well within budget, and the difference of opinion arose because he considered sales literature as coming under the sales manager's budget, whereas the accounting staff considered it an advertising charge. As a result, the advertising manager was obliged to cancel some insertions, in order to make up the amount of money in dispute, so upsetting his carefully planned schedule. This deprived his company of valuable advertising support at a time when it was greatly needed, which resulted in lost sales which, in turn, meant loss of profits. A clear understanding of what his appropriation covered would have prevented this.

This is an extreme case, but even minor items can pose a major problem since many activities do not fit neatly into one category or another and soon add up to a considerable total expense. Is the new shop front or the new sign outside your factory an advertising expense, or should they come out of general building costs? What about the charges involved in special painting of delivery vans? Is the cost of 'Situations Vacant' advertisements to be charged against your advertising budget? There is a tendency for other departments to pass unwanted bills (and who wants bills anyway?) to the advertising manager, and if these are paid for out of the so-called advertising appropriation there is less money available for genuine media expenditure. It is therefor directly in your own interest that you are absolutely clear on this point.

The need for a proper budget

With the period of the appropriation and what it is to cover clearly defined, you can then make plans, and so fixing the budget is clearly a vital step. On what basis can you avoid spending too much or too little on advertising? Before reviewing the various methods, consider three alternatives.

1   No budget   It is vital that your advertising is carefully planned. Sometimes you may encounter a manufacturer who suddenly feels 'It's time we had an advertisement' or, occasionally, you may come up against one who advertised simply because a media representative asked for an order! Such an off-hand attitude is unlikely to bring results. If the manufacturer does not plan his advertising, the chances are that a bit of money will be spent in one medium and a bit more in another, some this month and some the next. Before long, someone will get round to adding up how much has been spent on advertising: he will usually be horrified at how expenditure has mounted up, and decide that advertising is a waste of money, And, face facts, advertising in this way *is* a waste of money. To be effective, your advertising must be planned, and planned well in advance. Your plan should be flexible rather than rigid to allow for the opportunities — and setbacks — of business, but a plan there must be. Advertising is not a separate activity unconnected with your company's other activities: advertising, sales and display effort must all be co-ordinated. When this is the case, retailers' windows, counters and shelves feature the merchandise you are advertising, and selling activity ties in with your advertising and display effort. With effective planning, sales staff have advance information about the merchandise advertised, and have been coached to draw attention to these goods. In this way your prospective customer's interest is awakened by advertisements, displays give effective reminders, and the sale is completed by counter staff. When sales staff are ignorant of the advertising, sales are lost and bad impressions created. Think of the occasions on which you asked a shop salesman for an item currently advertised, only to find he knew nothing about it: your impression — correctly

— is that the shop is slack and inefficient which, of course, it is. This is more than likely the result of unplanned and uncontrolled advertising expenditure.

2   The arbitrary 'guesstimate'   Picking a figure out of the air, by hunch or whim, rarely leads to successful advertising. This method is adopted by fewer and fewer advertisers, and most give careful thought to the amount they spend. But beware of those who disguise this approach to budgeting by claiming that 'My twenty years' experience tells me that we should spend £X,000'. Has this individual really had 20 years' experience — or only one year's experience twenty times? Certainly, as will be seen later, true experience can make a most valuable contribution, but all too often the term is used to defend what is, in truth, only a guess. The 'method' still exists, however, and so it must be mentioned — if only to point out that it has little in its favour.

3   'Chairman's Rules'   This 'method' is encountered in companies where the advertising manager has no say in deciding the appropriation, but a figure is dictated to him by his Board. In many cases, the company *does* know what it is doing, but in some instances there is no real basis for the Board decision. A figure is decided, but those concerned have little idea of whether they are budgeting too much or too little. The 'method' nevertheless exists and so must be mentioned if only to stress that — like the 'arbitrary guesstimate' — it has no sound basis.

The two last methods, however, are not entirely without merit. Both methods set a sum for advertising, and this in itself means that someone is *forced* to undertake at least basic planning. Somebody will have to ask fundamental questions such as 'There are twelve months of trading, so how shall I spread my spending over the year?' and 'There are *x* products needing advertising support: how much shall I allocate to each?' From the planning point of view, he will be forced to apportion his money between media, and decide which to use and so, in that these two methods are likely to result in some fundamental planning, they are not without merit — but, either could result in too much or too little being spent on advertising.

Most readers will know the saying attributed to Lord Leverhume — 'Half the money I spend on advertising is wasted — the trouble is, I don't know which half'. Whenever I hear this story, I always recall my visit to the merchandising vice-president of a gigantic one-stop shopping centre in Midwest America. In reply to my question as to how many people worked in the centre, his laconic reply was 'About half of them'.

Your aim must be to ensure that *all* your advertising money is working for you and, if the 'no budget/arbitrary guesstimate/ chairman's rules' methods have so little in their favour, what alternatives are open to you?

There is no single best way to decide on how much to spend. A great deal depends on circumstances: for established products, fixing the appropriation may be an annual ritual, while with the launch of a new product it may be regarded as a capital investment. Many methods are in use, each with its advantages and drawbacks, and all are used with varying degrees of success according to the circumstances in which the company operates.

Budgeting methods

Though there are many different methods, they can be considered under seven main groupings. Each of these categories has numerous variations — in some cases the necessary arithmetic can be done on the back of an envelope whereas in other instances the same method is applied in a more complex manner using a computer to undertake complicated mathematical calculations: it is, nevertheless, the same basic method. The fundamental choices open to you are outlined below, together with their advantages and drawbacks.

1 Percentage of last year's sales

Many advertisers take a set percentage — say half per cent or five per cent — of the previous year's turnover as the basis for their appropriation. If you use this method it has the advantage of safety, as you are spending money in accordance with established sales. There are, however, two drawbacks to this method. First, there is the problem of deciding what percentage it should be — half, one, two or five or more per cent? When you consider that some industrial advertisers spend less than a quarter of one per cent of sales on advertising, while for the launch of a new consumer product advertising could account for up to a quarter of the selling price, this gives you a more than wide range from which to choose! Some categories of firm have an advantage in that statistics are published showing the average for their particular trade or industry. But this advantage is not as helpful as it seems, since an average is only an *average*. Remember that half the people in the UK are below average height (the other half are above average height: that's why there is an average!). If there is an average percentage, that is because many firms are, quite rightly, spending more than the average and others, equally correctly, are spending less than the average. The first drawback to this method is determining what percentage *you* should spend.

The second basic weakness of the method is that it looks to the past rather than the future. A bad year means lower turnover and so even less on advertising — in a never-ending downward spiral. The answer to lower turnover might be for you to spend *more* on advertising rather than less, to counteract the decline, in the belief that advertising causes sales. Even if sales do not drop the method still has weaknesses: if your market is, in fact, growing by 25 per cent a year, then a sales increase of only 5 per cent means that you are losing out by some 20 per cent each year. Furthermore, it is a chicken and egg situation — did sales rise because you spent more on advertising, or did you spend more on advertising because sales had risen? In spite of its weaknesses, this method is, nevertheless, used by a large number of organisations. Others prefer to look to the future and use expected sales as their criterion.

2   Percentage of anticipated sales

This method can lead to a realistic appropriation if, for example, your aim is for a marked increase in sales. It suffers, however, from one of the same drawbacks as the previous method, that of deciding just what the percentage should be. A second drawback is that future sales cannot be precisely estimated: the sales have yet to be made and over-estimation could lead to over-spending on advertising. Examination of the 'expected sales' decision-process will reveal three broad categories:

(a) The one-man decision   In many small firms all management decisions are taken by a single individual. Since he is responsible for all aspects of his firm's activities, he usually has his finger on the pulse of the market, and takes a realistic approach.

(b) The sales versus advertising split   With some larger firms, responsibilty for the two functions is divided, the sales manager being responsible for the buying/selling operation, and the advertising manager for the advertising: this can lead to considerable problems in practice. Most sales managers have a strong optimistic streak — the nature of their job calls for it! Consequently, they frequently over-estimate unintentionally. Problems begin when expected sales are not achieved, since the advertising manager will blame the sales manager and *vice versa*. The advertising manager will point out that advertising cannot work miracles, and he is not to blame if the sales manager chooses poor merchandise. The sales manager, in his turn,

will ask how on earth can he be expected to sell merchandise with such pitiful advertising support? When the unsold stocks come to management attention the old game of 'pass the buck' commences and, in 'pecking order', sales usually ranks above advertising. The managing director will reprimand the sales manager, who vents his wrath on the advertising manager, who promptly takes it out on the agency, and blame eventually passes to the media representative, whose medium has 'proved' itself ineffective! This is a game in which nobody wins but unfortunately is played all too often, as most media representatives will confirm.

(c) The marketing approach   Here the decision is again taken by a single individual, but this is a very different matter to the one-man approach described above, since the marketing director has reporting to him executives responsible for sales, for advertising, and for market research. The sales *versus* advertising problem just described has led manufacturers to devote considerable time and effort to sales forecasting, in order to better decide the appropriation, as well as the more obvious benefit of fixing production levels with greater accuracy.

3   The unit percentage method

This approach uses detailed cost analysis as the basis for deciding the amount to spend, thus overcoming the problem common to the last two methods, of arriving at a suitable percentage figure. A costing study is made of the product: so much for raw materials, so much for direct production costs, so much for overheads, so much for packaging and so on. These figures may total, say, 35p, and if you wish to sell to the retailer for 40p this leaves a 5p margin. Of this, you can decide to keep 4p as profit and spend 1p per unit on advertising, keep 3p and spend 2p, keep 2p profit and spend 3p per unit and so on. This costing exercise can be extended to include distribution charges through to your final selling price to the public rather than stop at the factory gate but, in essence, the advertising appropriation is fixed as a residuum with profit: the difference between the selling price and all charges is a fixed amount which you spend on advertising or retain as profit. If you use this method, you are unlikely to overspend since, with a 5p margin you would never dream of spending 6p per unit on advertising. By the two previous methods, however, you could unintentionally overspend, as we have seen.

Even this method, scientific as it may appear, is not without its drawbacks. It is strictly inward-looking, since it is based on the factory floor and takes little account of the outside market. Even within the factory there is the danger that the amount per unit may not be revised as conditions alter, raw materials change in price or wage rates increase. Furthermore, overheads vary with output: the more units there are produced, the more widely costs are spread and the smaller the charges that must be borne by each unit.

Finally there is the fundamental point that all these figures are costed with a certain level of sales in mind, whereas it is possible that you may not achieve these sales. However, providing you estimate sales accurately and revise costings whenever necessary (so that the unit percentage is not passed down over the years without alteration) this method can provide a useful guide to what you can afford.

4 Competitive parity

Another way to fix your appropriation is to look at what competitors are spending and to decide your own expenditure accordingly. This method can be useful when entering a new market, for in such circumstances competitors' spending provides a useful indication of the amount of money you need to inform the market.

The weakness of the method is that although your competitors are similar they are not *identical* but vary in product, market and marketing policy and their problems are therefore different. Moreover, there is the difficulty of finding out just what competitors *are* spending. Press advertising expenditure can be calculated to a reasonable degree of accuracy and without too much trouble, simply by checking competitors' advertisements against publishers' rate cards. For the more important advertisers the task is even simpler in that you can look up their expenditure in the standard reference publications in Part 1; these also contain television billings. For other media, however, such as posters, direct mail or display material, it is far more difficult to estimate the scale of competitors' activities. And, even if this information is available, who is to say that the rival companies were correct in the first place? One advertising manager remarked, with some justification, that basing expenditure on that of your competitors is like cheating in an examination by copying your neighbours — you can't see all that clearly, and you don't know that they're right anyway! A further drawback to this method is that a new entrant to the market must have some effect on competitors' sales, with the result that they may spend more on advertising, so forcing the new manufacturer to increase his appropriation. This method, then, gives a useful opening indication, but should not be allowed to lead to an advertising 'war' wasteful to all parties.

5   Advertising share

A variation which overlaps several methods already discussed is the 'Advertising Share' approach which looks not only at your advertising expenditure in relation to your competitors, but also at your relative sales. Earlier chapters indicated sources you can consult for this information, and in both cases the figures are examined in terms of 'share'. The question then is 'Are the sales for your product the same share of the market as your advertising share?'

Analysis of this kind may result in interesting information such as an average advertising-sales ratio for the product group and whether you are 'working harder' (in terms of advertising expenditure) than your competitors and — much more important — what result is this having on sales? Observation of what happens in the market place may reveal, for example, that firms which increase their share of advertising also increase their share of the market. (Or, of course, *vice versa.)*

This study of advertising and market share may be extended over time by what has been called the 'dynamic difference' approach which looks at

Sales share in one year less sales share in the previous year

as against

Advertising share in one year less advertising share in the previous year.

The overall weaknesses of this method are those already outlined under the 'competitive parity' method and, furthermore, it does not *prove* that increased expenditure results in increased sales. Even if a sales rise is associated with increased advertising, the question then arises of *how big an increase?* One firm, for example, might increase its share of advertising, but at a *lower rate* than its main competitor who might have stepped up his advertising expenditure for some very good marketing reason which has no immediate connection with advertising.

6   The marginal method

The methods so far discussed all have one thing in common: they ask the same question, namely 'How much shall we spend?'. The marginal method poses a very different question, and asks 'How much *extra* shall we spend?'. Attention is shifted from deciding a total amount to deciding 'layer by layer', and each additional expenditure must justify itself. The claim that 'Advertising will increase sales' is frequently made: the manufacturer using the marginal method asks *how much* it will increase sales. The method is an extension of the unit percentage method, and is based on a careful assessment of the results of each *additional* amount spent on advertising. If, for example, a manufacturer makes a profit of £10 per unit sold, then an advertisement costing £1000 must sell at least 100 additional units if it is to pay for itself. 'Increased sales' of a further 50 units would be of little appeal to this advertiser, since this would involve a *loss* of £500. If you can relate sales to advertising in this way, the marginal method can prove extremely helpful. But do bear in mind just *what* you are evaluating, since the advertisement's content clearly influences its effectiveness. Your money has, in fact, bought you the most useless thing in the world — a blank space! There is no point in blaming a medium for proving ineffective in bringing increased sales, when the fault lies really in the use you have made of the space purchased. Some advertisers, in the fortunate position of having a direct response they can measure, extend the marginal method to measure creative aspects as well as media, checking creative idea A against creative idea B, headline C against headline D, illustration E *versus* illustration F and so on. Returning to the media aspects, however, the marginal method can be applied more specifically. Colour costs more than black and white and special positions cost more than run of paper insertions — are they worth it in terms of increased returns? Economists talk about the 'Law of Diminishing Returns' and supporters of the marginal method check this out in practice — large advertisements cost more than small ones and weekly insertions are some four times as expensive as a monthly appearance, so is it worth it? The fundamental question asked by those applying this method — who are in the fortunate position of being able to evaluate the answer — is 'If it costs x per cent extra, do returns increase by more than x per cent?' A later chapter covers evaluation of results in more detail but it should already be apparent that this method is ideal for those who can make their advertising 'sit up and beg' when it comes to measuring response. Many advertisers, however, are unable to establish so direct a connection and must therefore look to other methods of fixing their appropriation.

7 The target sum method

This means of determining your appropriation is on an entirely different basis from all the methods so far considered. Instead of asking 'How much (or how much extra) shall we spend?' the target sum method asks 'What will it cost?'.

The method works back from media-owners' rate cards. If you decide that to achieve a given level of sales you need, say, half-pages every week in a selected list of publications, your appropriation can thus be calculated by multiplying the cost of these advertisements by the number of insertions. Thus a schedule of weekly advertisements costing in total £10,000 for each appearance in a selected list of publications gives you an appropriation of 52 x £10,000 or £520,000, plus production costs. In practice, of course, the schedule would be more complex and the arithmetic more involved.

The method is realistic in taking into account the cost of advertising — ignored by all the previous methods. A weakness common to the other methods so far considered is that if media rates increase by, say 10 per cent, the outcome is that you are forced to book 10 per cent less space or time, since no allowance is made for actual media costs.

The problem with the target sum method lies in deciding the variables — who is to say that half-pages are the correct size, that weekly appearances are necessary and which media should be included? The danger obviously lies in being greedy: what most advertisers would really like is full pages in colour every day in every publication, posters on every hoarding, a heavy television and radio campaign, leaflets distributed door to door, and so on! In such circumstances, *all* your company's money would go on advertising. However, if you take a realistic view of what weight of advertising is really needed to inform your potential customers, this is a sound method of fixing your appropriation.

8 The composite method

This chapter began by stating that there were seven main groups of methods for fixing your advertising budget, so you may well be surprised at arriving at number eight! The eighth 'method' is, however, simply to use two or more of the previous methods together and strike a figure somewhere between those produced by the several calculations — which in any event are unlikely to be vastly different. When reviewing the various methods of fixing the budget against your own particular situation, some will immediately appear more relevant, and others less practical. By making the necessary calculations for the selected methods, you arrive at a range of figures giving your minimum and maximum expenditure levels. To 'pick a figure' somewhere in the middle of this range may sound haphazard, but consider what you have in fact achieved. Rather than any arbitrary guesstimate you have determined that, under no circumstances, should you spend less than a certain sum. Equally, you have scientifically and logically calculated a maximum figure. Your range of uncertainty has thus been narrowed down in a most practical manner, and it is at this point that experience becomes truly valuable.

This chapter warned earlier against those who made claims that 'My experience tells me we should spend £X,000' but there is a vast difference between vague guesses and the practical application of true experience. And it is experience in assessing the overall marketing situation which will tell you where, within the prescribed range, you should fix your own particular appropriation. For example, an advertising manager might consider that, with a depressed economy and consumers having little disposable cash, the signs indicate that a high budget is necessary. On the other hand might be the facts that his company's merchandise has a distinct product and price advantage, and that his main competitor's sales force and distribution are currently weak. Taking into account the strengths and weaknesses of the situation, he might decide to fix his appropriation at the lower end of the scale rather than the higher level which at first appeared necessary. Your own experience can be invaluable in reaching a decision relevant to your own particular situation, and certainly the results of your previous year's advertising should be considered also. Advertising policy thus becomes a 'circular' procedure, the results of one year's appropriation serving as a basis for establishing the subsequent year's expenditure which, in its turn, will also have to be revised to meet the needs of the following year.

Various methods of fixing the appropriation, all with numerous variations, are thus currently in use, each with its individual adherents. The descriptions given perhaps over-simplify some variations, which can be based on complex econometric approaches and mathematical models, but these are nevertheless the main methods open to you, and from which you can choose. Indeed, any of these methods is preferable to the 'bit-here-and-a-bit-there' approach, in that it will lead to planning and thus to more effective advertising.

Further points

Before leaving the matter of your appropriation, various additional points must be made. One is that a company, rather than have a single figure, may have several appropriations, one for each of its products or divisions. It may even have an additional appropriation to promote an 'umbrella' campaign for the group as a whole, rather than for any individual line.

Furthermore, the appropriation may be divided into two — for 'above the line' expenditure by the agency and a 'below the line' budget retained by the advertiser. Also, part of the budget — described as a 'Contingency Reserve' — may be set aside to cater for unexpected opportunities or setbacks. These sub-divisions within the overall appropriation are discussed elsewhere.

You may also encounter division of the budget for yet another reason: to set aside funds for manufacturer/stockist co-operative advertising. Many firms find it productive to share with retailers the cost of advertisements in local media, announcing that they stock the merchandise featured in the campaign. When retailers consider their advertising budgets, they should clearly take into account this possible source of additional funds. Some advertisers also set aside funds as a contribution to a co-operative advertising campaign mounted on an industry-wide basis, to increase demand for their product group as a whole.

Finally, mention must be made of long-term budgeting. The various methods described all imply an *annual* appropriation, but the custom of yearly decisions is largely an artificial one arising from accounting practice, and many companies now take a longer-term view. When launching a new product, they accept that it will be impossible to realise a profit within a calendar year. It is un-realistic to expect a new venture to show a profit situation within a day, a week or a month — why should you expect to move into a profit situation within a year? It is long-term prospects which are important, since your company plans to be in business long term. Accordingly, the marketing plan covers four or more years, for example, depending on the estimated time needed to capture the market. The first year of operation may involve a considerable loss, in the second year the company breaks even, the third year shows a sufficient profit to offset the first years' loss and a true profit is not made until the fourth year. The first-year loss is a calculated situation, and that year's appropriation is regarded as an investment to be recouped by subsequent sales. Some conventional accountants resist the concept of advertising as investment, since they see no tangible assets they could sell off in the same way that they can dispose of production plant. But since machinery is pur-chased not to sell but to produce, surely advertising should be treated in the same way? Accountants are more than accustomed to the concept of 'depreciation', spreading capital expenditure over a number of years, so it is surprising that many find it difficult to adopt this approach with advertising.

Long-term budgeting calls for a 'pay-out' schedule. In simplest possible terms, the company calculates two cash flows — the rate at which money is being spent, and the rate at which it is coming in. As we all know from personal experience, we soon run into difficulties if cash goes out faster than it comes in, and the same applies to companies. They must therefore work out how much capital is needed to keep things going until a profit situation is reached: it would be more than unfortunate to run out of capital on the very eve of showing the first true profit. So this is where the accountants should come into their own — a marketing-orientated accountant can make a most valuable contribution.

Equally, any advertising and marketing man will find a knowledge of financial skills and terminology a most useful asset — even if only in arguments with the more conventional accountants whose instinctive reaction in times of recession is to cut the advertising budget. Most advertising and marketing people have this argument more than once during their careers!

At the start of the chapter, mention was made that fixing the appropriation is a management decision, and it is to this point we must return before concluding. The appropriation is decided at director level, and advertising and marketing staff must learn to live with this figure. There is always a temptation to ask for more money to take advantage of some special offer. This temptation should be avoided, for the appropriation was decided after very careful thought. Even if you do decide to ask for more money, there may be no Board meeting for some weeks and, in any event, is the Board likely to view this special offer — a very minor event in the total company operation — with the same enthusiasm as you do? Covering such events is the function of the contingency reserve described later: this is a very difficult matter to a *major* overall review of company policy. Should the economic situation, for example, change to such an extent that your company's marketing plans are no longer valid, the board would swiftly meet to deal with the new situation as a matter of urgency, and would review all aspects of business activity — production levels, prices and, of course, advertising. Such a major review is a very different matter from coping with the temporary and minor setbacks which are an unfortunate but avoidable feature of business life.

Budgeting in practice

The importance of the advertising appropriation in relation to the media plan was raised by many respondents, in various ways. The points raised most frequently will be considered under the following headings: Profitability, Definition, Budget size, Budget methods, Flexibility.

Profitability

The importance of approaching your budget as an *investment* (rather than spending money) was raised by various respondents who suggested that a basic rule to be followed for the effective use of media was

● *profit for the advertiser (the advertiser is seeking sales and profit — not an elegant media plan nor, necessarily, the cheapest cost)* (m-o)

Others advised that the advertising manager

● *should appreciate his agency is his investment adviser (ag)*

The briefest advice was for you to

● *assume its your own money* (ag)

Definition

The need to spell out precisely what your budget covers — or does not cover — was widely appreciated. As one practitioner pointed out

● *the advertiser should not be ambiguous about budget availability, e.g. do budgets provided include or exclude cost of production?* (ad)

Agency men and media-owners equally appreciated the need for a firm decision on this point. The following was given as a basic rule for effective advertising

● *definition of budget parameters, i.e. ballpark* (ag)

and a media-owner pointed out the need to

● *find out the* real *appropriation, i.e. how much allowed for production, contingency reserves, etc.* (m-o)

Budget size

The advice that the advertiser should

● *make sure there are sufficient funds available* (ad)

was raised more often in reverse, when respondents cited as common errors to avoid:

- *most commonly inadequate appropriation* (ag)

- *budgets incompatible with advertising/creative strategies* (ag)

The question then arises — on what basis should you decide your appropriation?

Budget methods

This chapter described more ways of arriving at a budget decision than were, in fact, suggested by respondents but, as this matter was not specifically raised in the form circulated, this is perhaps not surprising. In the event, most comments came from media-owners and related to the target sum method.

The previous section warned against the dangers of having too low a budget and one media-owner pointed out how this might arise: a common error, in his experience was

- *Under-budgeting, e.g. not allowing for rate increases* (m-o)

The target sum method is the only one specifically based on media costs and, if this is employed, rate increases are covered automatically. Other comments which suggested the same method advised that you should

- *align the budget to the media best suited to the product and its potential market* (m-o)

Worded even more strongly was the viewpoint of the respondent who cited as a basic error

- *budget obsession — plans are worked back from the budget not built up on logical grounds* (m-o)

Flexibility

An earlier quotation referred to contingency reserves, and other respondents linked the point of clear budget definition with the need for flexibility, in advising that you must

- *establish budget/production parameters and flexibility* (m-o)

Being flexible is one thing, but various respondents warned against the extreme of chopping and changing the budget. Advice given was that you

- *should not use the media budget as a profit balancer* (ag)

and that you

- *should make clear whatever constraints exist, e.g. the need to reduce budgeted expenditure if sales shortfall arises* (ad)

- *should not use advertising money to make up for falling profits* (m-o)

The final comment on appropriations is brief and comes from the practitioner who advised, as a basic rule for effective advertising

- *keeping within the budget* (ad)

The next step

Now that your budget is known, your next task is preparation of campaign proposals to achieve your advertising objective.

12

PREPARATION OF ADVERTISING PROPOSALS

Advertising planning is only part of overall marketing, and for effective use of media you must think in terms of your marketing objective — that you manufacture a product (or provide a service), with product policy and advertising and distribution and selling effort all geared to achieving sales in a chosen segment of the market. To talk of campaign planning is misleading, however, since this implies a *single* campaign, whereas effective planning is more complex. Quite apart from the need to 'aim' your product correctly, including its branding and packaging, your promotional activities must also seek to achieve the same marketing objective and here it is usually more correct to talk of *campaigns* in the plural.

Before the public can buy your product it must be in the shops; before your product can be in the shops your salesmen must put it there; and before they can do so they must be fully briefed. Any successful campaign, therefore, has at least three components — a campaign to the public, a second to the trade, and a third aimed at your own sales force. Each of these groups could be the target of three types of promotional activity: advertising, merchandising and sales promotion, and public relations. This book is concerned with the advertising media alone, but you must consider this in context, if you are to plan effectively. Media planning, although vital, is only one part of your overall promotional campaign, and must interlock with the others.

The media brief

If you ask any media man to tell you, in confidence, what causes him the most problems, the majority will say it is a request for media proposals unaccompanied by adequate information. Many will complain of clients — or even agency executives — who rush in to demand 'a £150,000 schedule for new product X'. Such individuals fail to appreciate that a full briefing is essential for the effective use of advertising media. The adequacy of this briefing directly affects the effectiveness of the media planning. If an inadequate briefing is given, there is no firm basis on which to evaluate the advantages of the different media, or on which to construct an effective schedule. The earlier chapters on research and investigations and on problem analysis detailed much of the information you need if you are to prepare the most effective media plan. Part of your media brief has yet to come, however — the creative aspects.

Creative/media interaction

The two aspects of preparation of proposals — choosing the media and preparing the advertisements — are complementary activities and, whilst this book is concerned primarily with media, you are directly affected by creative considerations. If your schedule provides for half-page advertisements in certain publications, this implies a creative decision that the insertions are to be of half-page size in press media and, at the same time, it is equally a media decision — to book half-page advertisements in selected publications on certain dates at a cost of £X. Creative and media decisions are therefore usually taken simultaneously, but the dominant aspect may be either media or creative. For example, media selection may be determined by the creative need to show your product in colour or to employ a medium which demonstrates its use. Alternatively, creative needs may take second place to the market requirement of informing a clearly defined target group, which one medium covers more effectively than others.

The attention factor

Media decisions overlap with creative considerations in another way, when attracting potential purchasers' attention to your advertising message. It is insufficient simply to place it before them by choosing a suitable advertising medium: you must also decide how to attract their attention. The first essential for effective advertising is attention for, without this, your advertisement cannot communicate. There are various devices for attracting attention: some of them concern creative work alone, but others have media implications.

Size

A large advertisement in itself attracts attention (and is more

247

impressive to those who see it, as well as giving greater scope for creativity and the inclusion of more information). The creative/ media decision to use advertisement size as the attention device has clear scheduling implications. You should always bear in mind, however, that sheer size is no substitute for creativity and may be extremely wasteful — full pages in broadsheet newspapers may be *too* big to be read comfortably, except at arm's length.

Position

A press advertisement on the front page, or facing or next to editorial matter, or in a solus position without competition from other advertisers, is likely to be seen by more people than one appearing alongside others within the body of the publication. Again, the decision to use position as an attention device directly affects your media plan.

Colour

Colour is often used as an attraction device. Printing in a second colour can attract (and highlight parts of the advertisement) while full-colour advertisements also permit you to show your product in its natural colours which, with some merchandise, is a vital factor in influencing consumers' buying decisions. The creative need for colour to attract attention clearly influences media planning.

Illustration

A product well-illustrated is often more than half sold, and advertisements featuring illustrations usually have greater impact than those without. 'Action' pictures, showing your product in use with people enjoying its benefits, have strong attention value. Whilst these are mainly creative considerations, it is obvious that the quality of reproduction required directly affects media selection.

Movement

Movement, as in a moving window display or a unit which lights up from time to time, attracts attention through contrast with the static background.

Demonstrating your product in use can also attract attention through movement, and not all media permit this. Once again, creative requirements have strong media implications.

Sound

The human voice can quickly attract attention and also convey a message. Music and other sound effects can similarly attract attention as well as influence the mood of the listeners, who become more receptive to your advertising message. The need for sound to fulfil these functions again influences media selection.

Headlines (and body copy)

Writing headlines which serve as an attention device is the copywriter's speciality, as is producing interesting and compelling text for the body of the advertisement. There is a simple formula which provides a helpful checklist in preparing (and evaluating) advertisements. It is expressed mainly in terms of press advertising, but the points made apply to most advertisements, subject only to adaptation for the medium in question. There is an easy way of remembering the formula — the initial letters of the four checkpoints form the title of an opera: AIDA. These creative checkpoints — all of which have media implications — are:

    Attention
    Interest
    Desire
    Action

AIDA is not the only model of how advertising works — another suggests an Awareness/Comprehension/Conviction/Action process, while the ATR model is an analysis based on Awareness, Trial and Reinforcement. Detailed examination of these models is outside the immediate scope of this book, but the purpose of mentioning them is to point out their relevance to media planning. Taking the AIDA model as an example, the first and last checkpoints have immediate media implications. The use of media planning (rather than creative devices) to attract attention has clear scheduling implications, and the same is true of many 'Action devices'. If your advertising objective is consumer *action* (rather than, for example, reminder advertising or image-building) this has direct media implications, since this may demand selection of a medium which facilitates action by your potential consumers. Examples such as coupons in press advertisements, reply cards in magazines or direct mail shots, or reply services on television and radio, all clearly illustrate how the final action checkpoint has media implications which are just as direct as the opening attention factor. Even the other two checkpoints — interest and desire — cannot be considered as having creative implications only, and thus not influencing media selection: never forget that the mood of your potential purchasers, when your advertsing message is received, is an important criterion for media comparison.

Effective media planning and creation of persuasive and attention-getting advertisements are thus complementary activities and both are essential for effective advertising. Clearly there is little point in placing your advertising message before those who are not potential buyers, nor in buying media if your advertisements fail to capture attention or feature the wrong sales points or are not sufficiently persuasive. It is, therefore, essential that both media and creative staff agree that the market could best be reached by advertisements of a certain size, in an agreed broad group of media. The media staff must feel that this broad plan gives them sufficient scope for effective scheduling, and the creative staff must similarly consider that the plan permits them to express the selling message persuasively. Creative and media departments then work independently, the creative staff preparing their copy and design proposals, and the media planners calculating the scheduling possibilities within the broad media groups agreed. The next step for the media staff is to plan in detail how to spend the appropriation so as to get maximum effect for every penny spent.

Media weighting

Your media problem is not simply to decide whether or not Medium A is to appear on your schedule. The problem underlying all media planning is how your appropriation should be spread across the year, how it should be divided between the different sales areas and what weight of advertising should be directed to different sections of the market. This is sometimes decided on what is described as the 'case rate' method, by which expenditure is in direct proportion to sales. Thus, if Sales Area A accounts for 30 per cent of total purchases, it would seem logical to devote 30 per cent of your budget to media that will stimulate that area. The spread of expenditure across the year may be decided in the same way, according to each month's sales figures: months when the market is ripe in terms of actual purchases will thus receive heavier advertising than the months in which sales figures indicate that the market is not in a buying mood.

One respondent, who clearly believes in the case-rate method, gave the following as one of the most important rules to be followed in order to produce the best media plan:

- 1 *Define the market* to which it is known *the product will appeal.*
  2 *Decide the potential of each section of the market as a percentage of anticipated sales.*
  3 *Select the media and apportion the budget accordingly.* (ag)

Case-rate spending thus provides a sound basis for media scheduling: as we shall see later, however, there are often good reasons for departing from this planning base.

Media allocations

A first step in constructing the schedule most suitable for achieving your marketing objective is often to divide the overall appropriation into separate allocations for each of the different media groups on which your campaign is to be based. Amounts are allocated to individual media groups — so much for television, so much for national and local press, so much for posters, and so on. This is sometimes called the 'Media Split' stage.

Newcomers to advertising are often surprised that media planning is both precise and empirical, and that the perfect media schedule is rarely produced at the first attempt. Media planners, in fact, consider innumerable ways of spending the appropriation, assessing one schedule against others, before making final recommendations. The schedule that is finally booked may well be the end result of first calculating and then contrasting perhaps hundreds of possible alternatives.

The same practice applies when allocating between different media. Should the appropriation be divided, for example, between press and television, then possible schedules will be constructed for these two media groups and the overall costings compared: if good press coverage can be achieved without spending the provisional allocation in full but additional money is needed to obtain an adequate television schedule (or *vice versa*) then the media split will be changed and the two allocations adjusted accordingly.

Detailed planning

Within any group of media, the same contructing of alternative schedules, and consequent adjustment, is also the rule. Taking into account the duration of your campaign, the advertisement size

251

selected, the required frequency of appearance, and the list of media that initially appear most suitable (probably on a cost ranking basis, as described below), the first step is to cost a preliminary schedule. The chance of this basic arithmetic resulting in a sum that exactly balances the allocation is small, so several alternative schedules are costed out. Should the preliminary costing exceed the allocation, then expenditure must be cut back and you must evaluate the best way to do this. In the simplest possible terms, there are just four ways in which your preliminary schedule can be adjusted. These are:

1   Advertisement unit   One solution might be to reduce the size of your advertisement, or to abandon the use of colour, of special positions or of peak time. If essential creative or other considerations make this impossible, then you must consider other alternatives.

2   Frequency   Another approach would be to reduce frequency and have, for example, fortnightly instead of weekly insertions. Marketing requirements, however, may make this solution unacceptable and you must, therefore, consider other possibilities.

3   Duration   Another alternative would be to curtail your campaign and maintain it for only (for example) 11 months instead of a full year, omitting periods when the market is dead. There is, however, a fourth possibility you must also consider.

4   Media list   Another solution is to reduce the number of media included in your schedule, in order to maintain the weight of advertising in those retained.

The variables you can use for media planning permutations are thus basically four: dominance (in terms of size, position or colour), frequency of appearance, duration/continuity of campaign, and the media list. In every case, except the last, you must take into account *non-media* considerations, since the advertisement unit can be changed only after consultation with creative staff, and the frequency of appearance and length of campaign are determined by how often your buyers must be reminded, and the duration of your selling campaign. Often, these considerations lead inevitably to a re-consideration of the case-rate spending method. Case-rate spending, with expenditure proportionate to sales, can be likened to a chicken and egg situation. Should you spend 30 per cent of budget to maintain the 30 per cent of sales — or have you achieved 30 per cent of sales in that month or this area simply because you have always devoted to it 30 per cent of your advertising expenditure? This leads to a marketing-cum-media re-examination of the cause-

and-effect of the case-rate situation: from this re-examination two other strategies may arise. The two alternatives — 'Boost' or 'Abandon' — are both based on consideration of *potential* as distinct from actual sales.

1   Boost   You may decide to boost a particular month or area by devoting *more* than the case-rate amount on the assumption that, although according to past sales figures it merits only, for example, 10 per cent of expenditure, there is in fact a far greater potential which would respond to added stimulation. Hence the media/marketing decision to step up the advertising in the selected area, market segment or time of year. But with limited funds, where is the additional expenditure to come from, if not from the standard four variables already mentioned? The other alternative to case-rate spending, in fact, releases funds rather than calling for additional expenditure.

2   Abandon   Here, your assumption is that demand is relatively stable: in economic terms, it is 'inelastic'. People have perhaps got to buy a certain minimum amount of your product. After heavy Christmas spending, for example, many people have no funds to spare and keep their spending to a minimum. No amount of heavy advertising can persuade them to buy more, since they just do not have the cash to do so. Conversely, however, there is a minimum amount they must buy — and would do so even without any advertising stimulus. Hence you may take the media/marketing decision to 'abandon' a particular month or market in the belief that demand is inelastic and sales will remain at that level even when advertising is cut. This was clearly in the mind of the respondent who urged

● *If the budget is insufficient,* concentrate. *In time, regionally or by part of target audience, i.e. shorter schedule, or by some other means. Don't spread the jam too thinly.* (ad)

Other variables

The balancing of advertisement unit, frequency, duration and media list, and re-examination of these four variables against the case-rate method, by no means exhausts the media scheduling possibilities open to you. Other variations should also be considered.

Multiple-size campaigns   Many campaigns call for more than one size of advertisement so that, rather than use one uniform size throughout, you plan your media schedule using two or more sizes — and a new possibility in the media 'balancing act' is thus open to you. For example, you may open your campaign with a half-page advertisement, followed by quarter-page advertisements in each of the following three weeks, reverting to a half-page advertisement and more quarter-pages in a repeating pattern. Use of two sizes enables you to get the best of the two worlds of impact and repetition, and many campaigns are based on this principle. Sometimes a third and very dominant size, perhaps a full-page advertisement, may be used to launch your campaign, simply to impress retailers and assist your salesmen in persuading them to both stock and display your merchandise.

Drip versus burst   A variation on the boost versus abandon and multiple-size approaches is to base your planning on 'Burst' rather than 'Drip' advertising. A campaign based on the drip approach calls for steady advertising over a period, on the premise that 'constant dripping wears away a stone'. The burst approach on the other hand concentrates resources into a limited number of weeks to achieve greater impact (larger sizes, greater frequency or more extensive media list) within the period. A typical burst campaign might consist of three weeks on/two weeks off/three weeks on, in a repeating pattern. This variation of the multiple-size campaign incorporates the boost versus abandon approach to planning, the difference being that one of the multiple 'sizes' is zero, i.e. advertising is abandoned in certain weeks in order to boost the others.

Media in combination   Few campaigns are based on a single medium, but rely on various media used at the same time. Economists refer to the 'Law of Diminishing Returns' and this applies just as much to media planning as to other types of expenditure. You may feel that one medium has received a sufficient weight of advertising, and that it would not be worth while spending any more money in it. You therefore consider other media for this reason, and also because it permits you to reach the same market but by other means, for fresh impact. The chapter on budgeting outlined the marginal method of deciding your appropriation, and this approach can be applied to the use of media in combination — will the last £X,000 spent on your first medium bring as good a result as the same £X,000 spent in the alternatives?

The term 'media in combination' masks two separate considerations. One concerns the 'media split' stage, and thus refers to multimedia campaigns which cover, for example, newspapers *and* television *and* magazines. The other consideration concerns media *within* a group e.g. within press using publications A *and* B (*or* C?) With both aspects of the term, you encounter the problem of distinguishing between 'duplication' and 'net extra coverage'.

Duplication   Duplication means reaching the same market by different media. To some extent all media duplicate since people read newspapers and magazines, watch television and see posters, and advertisers contact them through all these media. Duplication, viewed from another standpoint, represents increased frequency. If monthly contact with prospective buyers is your aim, monthly insertions in two media whose coverage overlaps means that those who see both media see two advertisements each month instead of one, and therefore receive double the frequency you think necessary. Two alternatives are open to you: to maintain monthly insertions in one publication and delete the other from your schedule, or to use the two publications but only in alternate months, thus maintaining regularity but giving this part of your market a monthly stimulus through alternative means, for variety of impact.

Net extra coverage   If duplication and thus excess repetition is to be avoided, you will seek media giving you the greatest net extra coverage. Two additional publications may be under consideration, one of which has a much larger readership than the other and there-fore, on the surface, seems a better proposition. However, if most of this larger readership is already covered by media already on your schedule, this means you would contact these people with higher frequency than is necessary. If, on the other hand, the publication with the smaller readership gives little duplication, then by using this medium you will reach entirely new prospects to whom no advertising message has yet been delivered. By seeking net extra coverage, you thus increase the overall *penetration* of your campaign. The two factors of duplication and net extra coverage reflect con-trasting marketing objectives. If your marketing aim is to reach as many prospective buyers as possible (even if with only a single advertising message) then you should aim for net extra coverage and thus maximum penetration. If, however, your marketing objective is to achieve maximum repetition, duplication of coverage is preferable. In practice, however, you are unlikely to want to operate at either *extreme* end of this scale.

Cumulative coverage (or reach)   Coverage is the proportion of the target group who have at least one opportunity of seeing your advertisement. Although the number of people reading the average issue of a publication remains constant, the same people do not always read every issue of a publication. Thus additional advertise-ments in a series can add new readers, thereby increasing your cumulative audience (as well as giving those already covered an additional opportunity to see your advertisement). Cumulative cover in this sense reflects the penetration of your campaign.

Opportunities-to-see   How many advertisements will your target group see? The average frequency is often called the average 'OTS' or opportunities-to-see (or hear), and is defined as the number of exposures received by the average reader/viewer/listener. The average OTS or OTH figure must be treated with care when considering a possible schedule, for it can mask wide variations in the number of opportunities received by different members of your target group.

Frequency distribution   This will give you a more detailed breakdown in terms of opportunities-to-see across your target group in terms of coverage. Coverage is very often linked with the levels of opportunities-to-see, *viz* 2+, 3+, 4+ and so on, showing the number (or percentage) of the audience likely to have that stated number of opportunities to see your campaign.

Some uncharted territories

The fact that you can pump statistics about net extra coverage *versus* duplication through a computer to see the effect of adding publication A rather than publication B to your schedule has led many people to think the 'science' of advertising is at a very advanced state. And, taking mechanical aids into account and setting aside any research weaknesses (what *is* a reader/viewer/listener?) then our industry has made enormous strides in recent years — and is light years ahead of those countries which do not have authentic circulation figures, let alone reliable viewing, reading or listening figures.

It would be a false kindness, however, to omit mention of any weaknesses. When it comes to the basic matter of how advertising *works* and how the whole marketing communications/purchasing-decision process operates, it must be bluntly stated that there is a great deal more to know before we can claim complete mastery of advertising as a business tool. It would need another book to discuss these uncharted areas in full, so they can be touched on only briefly here. The fields in which we need more knowledge include the following:

Campaign period

This is not a matter of whether your campaign runs for 6, 8 or 12 months, but of the campaign's effects on consumers. What is the 'life' of an advertisement or of a campaign, and what would happen if you stop advertising? Chapter 10 described the natural decline built in to any market and the need to remind those remaining but, should you stop advertising, how fast would its effects 'decay' and how swiftly would your sales start to fall? How strong is brand loyalty to your products, and what part does advertising play in maintaining this loyalty? As campaign duration is a basic variable in your media-balancing act, more information is needed. Under this heading — but beyond the scope of this book — you should also consider the creative use made of the space booked. How quickly will your current campaign 'wear out', and how swiftly should you replace it with a new one? This may in turn be affected by the next factor — the frequency with which people see your advertisements.

Frequency

This is another basic variable, but little is known *in detail* about its effects. It is all very well to have rules-of-thumb about weekly reminders for weekly products and so on, and these do perhaps give a guide to the minimum frequency required. But what about *maximum* frequency? Is increased frequency necessarily beneficial? Can you always equate heavy usage of your product with heavy exposure to your advertising? And can you, in fact, dissociate this from your campaign's *creative content?* Will over-exposure perhaps be counter-productive? People have argued, for example, that some heavily repeated television commercials have an irritation factor which harms rather than helps sales. All of us have seen humorous commercials which were extremely amusing at first viewing but for which we dreaded subsequent screenings and, with some people, hard-sell commercials have the same effect. There is very little published data on this area.

Multi-media campaigns

You can compare with relative accuracy the results — in numerical terms — of adding Newspaper A rather than B to your schedule, or Magazine C instead of D. When it comes to comparing different media groups — comparing *Newspaper* A or B with *Magazine* C or D — you are on less certain ground. And when it comes to assessing these in comparison with a totally different medium — whether this be television, cinema, radio, outdoor or any other media — you are in largely uncharted territory. While *intra*-media research (comparing publication A with B) is relatively advanced, *inter*-media research is still at the experimental stage. When looked at in terms of the way advertising works and the purchasing-decision process, there is certainly no 'map' to help you find your way. There are, however, a few 'pointers'. If, as the Law of Diminishing Returns suggests, you should use more than one medium or one media group, it is best to examine the possible ways which you could use them, and then evaluate these alternatives against your advertising objective. In making such an assessment there are marketing and creative as well as media considerations. Multi-media schedules can achieve various objectives.

1   *Additional coverage*   By adding new media you can increase your cumulative cover and thus the total penetration of your campaign. A variation on the same theme is to rectify any weaknesses in the coverage of those media already on your schedule. Clearly this is a matter of marketing/media rather than creative consider-ations.

2   *Added frequency*   Through a multi-media campaign, your target market may have more opportunities to see your advertise-ments. This again has mainly marketing/media considerations, but you should consider how your customers will react to this increased frequency.

3   *Different media*   The aim here is the very opposite of (1): rather than increase penetration, you wish to reach the same people. It overlaps with (2) but, even though you may deliver the same message more often, your target audience receives it through a *new* medium for fresh impact. This is not a simple matter of added frequency and there are important creative considerations, as some media groups are more complementary than others when used in combination. The term 'synergism' (or visual transfer) is used to describe, for example, the degree to which people exposed to a given TV campaign can re-create the visual component with only the TV soundtrack to trigger their memories. TV *plus* radio is the obvious example, but the same principle of beneficial 'transfer', with one medium reinforcing the other, applies to other combinations.

4   *Strategy variations*   All three variations so far described assume your advertisements have the same creative content: the variables are *who* you reach, *how* you reach them and *how often* — not *what you say*.

Should this be so, or should you consider variations in creative strategy? The concept of 'mood' is nothing new in media evaluation, and the same is true of creating advertisements to suit the media that are to carry them. Even if reaching the same people in demo-graphic terms, many advertising practitioners put these two concepts into practice, and develop different creative approaches to suit the

258

different media. Others ask if you will, in fact, reach the same *kind* of people, even if the standard demographic characteristics are similar? Are the people you reach through one medium more (or less) likely to buy — or try — your product than the people you reach through alternative media? And should your media selection and creative content change accordingly?

Added cost

In addition to considering these possible ways of mounting a multi-media campaign, you must also bear in mind you have changed yet another variable: cost. Quite apart from the fundamental cost of buying an additional medium there is the added expense — in terms of time and effort as well as money — of preparing advertisements for the new medium.

Multi-media campaigns thus have implications far beyond media choice alone, and these fundamental questions give a new importance to problem analysis and the vital need to 'establish a *true* campaign objective' as urged by so many respondents. Before leaving these relatively uncharted areas, you should bear in mind that a great deal of exploratory work is being done — with some very interesting results. Much of this pioneer work is undertaken to gain a competitive advantage and, understandably, the results are not always published — but Part 1 listed sources of media news, and you should therefore consult these regularly to keep up-to-date with new developments.

Response functions

Balancing cover against repetition has always been a difficult planning problem, and most decisions have been taken after analysing schedules rather than applying a 'Response Factor' when preparing them. Given a fixed budget, the variable of cover as against repetition is the amount of advertising each individual receives and, when a mathematical response model is used, you must state the objectives of your campaign in numerical terms. These numbers describe the response you expect from the individuals exposed to your advertising.

A response function is a weighting system for overall schedule construction, based on your subjective judgment of how your advertising works and specifically how many exposures are necessary for your advertising to be effective. A *cumulative* response function is a set of numbers defining the relative value to the advertiser of an individual in his target group receiving one, two or more advertising

259

RESPONSE FUNCTIONS

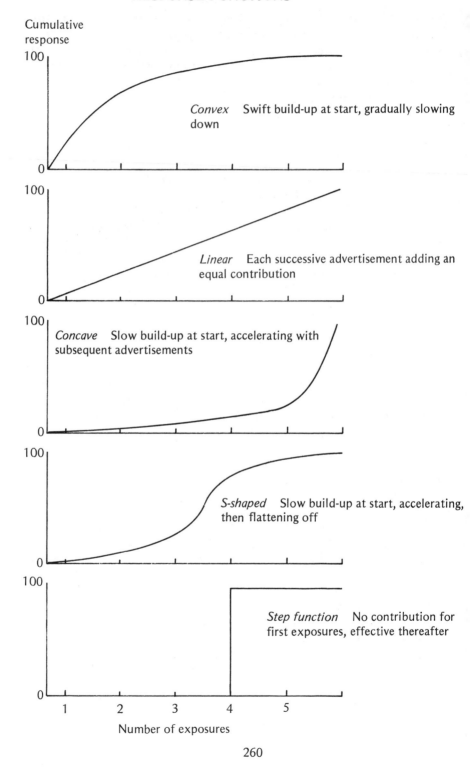

Cumulative response

100

Convex   Swift build-up at start, gradually slowing down

100

Linear   Each successive advertisement adding an equal contribution

100

Concave   Slow build-up at start, accelerating with subsequent advertisements

100

S-shaped   Slow build-up at start, accelerating, then flattening off

100

Step function   No contribution for first exposures, effective thereafter

Number of exposures

impressions, and must be distinguished from the corresponding *additional* response function — the added value given by each separate additional exposure.

Response functions are often employed when using a computer optimisation program (see below) to construct a schedule. Although expressed numerically to give the computer a weighting factor for each successive advertising exposure received by the individual, graphs are often used in formulating response functions and as a basis for discussing the type of advertising campaign best suited to achieve your chosen objective. Such discussion must necessarily be general, involving creative and marketing considerations as well as media. In that these graphs reflect the 'shape' of your campaign, five possible response functions are illustrated here, rather than in the later discussion on computers.

Resolving the inevitable conflict

In balancing all these variable factors, there is necessarily some element of conflict, and you must be aware of the danger of trying to meet *all* requirements, since it is unlikely that you can meet them all. Somebody once said that a camel looks like a horse designed by a committee. Similarly, if you try to balance the variables by merely reaching a compromise, the result is likely to be an ineffective schedule. In another sense, however, all media planning is a compromise — if you satisfy the requirement for one of the variables in the media balancing act, you are likely to fall short on the others. It is important, therefore, for you to establish whether impact is more important than repetition, and the relative priority of other factors. Trying to please everybody may lead to the appropriation being so widely dispersed that your advertising ceases to have any solid impact. One generally accepted rule is to give each medium a sufficient weight of advertising before adding others to the schedule. For this reason, the suggestion that you cut back 'just one' insertion in one medium to permit inclusion of another in your schedule, is unlikely to result in effective advertising.

The shotgun principle

One way to avoid a weak compromise is the well-established 'concentration-domination-repetition' principle advocated by many practitioners. The very opposite approach to media planning is the 'shotgun' principle often followed by advertisers whose fragmented markets cannot be defined in terms of age, sex, social grade, occupation, geographical location or any other conventional demographic criteria. How can you communicate advertising messages to clear but widely diffused markets (such as people who need glasses, have bad breath or back trouble, or suffer from haemorroids) when there may be no medium, or group of media, which gives particular coverage of these target groups? If it is impossible to achieve concentration, domination and repetition, one alternative is to pepper the market on the shotgun principle, often with a wide spread of small advertisements which, through their headlines, select potential purchasers from the total audience reached by the media in which they appear.

Scheduling stages

There are thus two distinct stages in scheduling. First, there is the arithmetical work of costing and balancing alternative schedules taking into account cost ranking and other variables discussed below. Second, and more important, is the work of evaluating these schedules to select the best. The second task involves just as much arithmetic as the first, in assessing facts about coverage and cost per thousand, quite apart from value judgments about such factors as the means of transmitting your message, and the mood of prospective purchasers when they receive it. The process of schedule construction, calculating possible alternatives and contrasting each to see which gives the best results, means a tremendous amount of work in evaluating media research data and in sheer arithmetical calculations. Many advertisers, agencies and media-owners therefore now use computers to make these calculations.

The computer in media-scheduling

Most automatic data processing experts stress that a computer is nothing more than an incredibly fast and accurate idiot, which does exactly what you tell it and nothing more. The way in which a computer is instructed is known as a 'program': note that this is spelt differently from the conventional theatre 'programme'. The names of these programs are often based on initials: thus AASAM stands for Area Allocation System for Advertising Money, SORBA stands for Systems for Optimising Regional Budget Allocations and BAR stands for Budget Allocation by Region — all three programs are variations on the case-rate spending method, which take into account a wide range of different variables. The computer experts even have a name for the program which reveals the computer's idiocy — GIGO, standing for 'Garbage In, Garbage Out' or, in more British terms — 'Ask a silly question and you get a silly answer'.

The computer is basically a calculating machine consisting of an input unit, a store or memory unit, a calculating unit, an output unit, and a control unit. The contribution the computer can make to media scheduling depends on these units and the program by which they are instructed. The computing units themselves are known as the 'hardware' and the programming side as 'software'. The two are equally important, and useless without each other. Different companies give different names to their particular software, so you may encounter more than one title for similar programs — the variations in program are significant, however, and should be checked out carefully.

Computers have influenced the effective use of advertising media in various ways, one of which is simply accounting and control. A great deal of straightforward office work has been transferred to computers. In essence this amounts only to shifting the burden of work rather than venturing into new fields, but there are further repercussions. The computer can lead to far greater efficiency in normal office routine with faster, more up-to-date and accurate paperwork. Speeded-up paperwork can lead to invoices being paid more promptly. The computer cannot extract money, but it can 'invite' people to pay earlier, simply by sending out invoices more quickly. Similarly, payments can be made by the computer which can, if necessary, even write out cheques. Many of these points apply to all those concerned with the effective use of media — advertisers, agencies, media-owners and specialist services.

Computers can, however, make a more positive contribution to effective use of media, but it is important to bear in mind that the underlying principles of media planning remain the same whether or not a computer is used: the computer merely helps you to work more efficiently. The contribution the computer can make to media planning depends on the information it is given and the calculations it is asked to make.

Input

The information supplied to a computer, as the basis for its calculations, falls into two broad categories.

1 Factual data Research statistics, such as the size and composition of the media audience and the wealth of data described in Part 1, can easily be put into the computer's memory, as can information about costs.

2   Quantified value judgments   This involves you in assigning 'weights' to various intangible factors, such as whether you think mood and the time spent reading a publication make magazine readers more 'valuable' than newspaper readers. Similarly, you might wish to assign relative media values to high quality reproduction, or to colour as against black and white, or to availability of sound and movement and so on.

If you value a magazine reader as 1½ units and a newspaper reader as only 1, because you believe that magazines are better able to communicate your advertising message, this will clearly bias the results in favour of magazines. Value judgments are not infallible simply because they are processed by a computer. Effective use of media is still based on media research data backed up by media judgment, a situation no different from that encountered in the past. The task is basically unchanged, once the veil of mystery that surrounds computers is removed.

Calculations

You can instruct the computer to perform various types of operation:

1   Cross-tabulation   The computer can cross-tabulate the data contained in any readership or market research survey, to provide additional analyses not included in the standard tables.

2   Cost ranking   Media can be ranked in cost-efficiency terms against your target market, taking the price to be paid for the space available and relating this to the readership. In this way the computer establishes an order of priority for media to appear on your schedule, expressed in terms of cost efficiency. If desired, you can include your own weights for the demographic constituents of the market and for the media themselves.

3   Schedule optimisation   Because of the speed of operation, it is possible for the computer to contrast literally thousands of possible schedules within a very brief space of time, and select the best. If maximum coverage of a selected market group at the most economic cost is your aim, you can instruct the computer to calculate the combination of media which, for a given expenditure, produces the highest total coverage at the lowest cost per thousand. Value judgments, as well as research data and costs, can also be taken into account if required.

4   Schedule evaluation   The purpose of this approach is not to say whether a schedule is the best possible, but to estimate what a schedule will achieve. You can use it, for example, to estimate what total coverage would be achieved for each market group for each month of your schedule. An evaluation program can compute the coverage, the gross opportunities-to-see, the average frequency, the schedule cost, the cost per thousand opportunities-to-see and the frequency distribution of these opportunities. Evaluation techniques tell you what you get for your money, leaving you to make your own decision.

5   *Performance evaluation*   The computer can be instructed to evaluate schedule performance over time (comparing the results of one advertising period with another) to improve advertising scheduling to suit marketing objectives.

Whichever task the computer performs, you are free from the chore of innumerable mathematical calculations, and can concentrate on your main task of planning. Consideration of alternative schedules need no longer be limited by the work involved in producing them.

An indirect advantage of using a computer is that media are no longer vaguely assessed. To use the computer, you must draw up precise criteria by which to judge media, and you no longer evaluate them by loose 'experience and judgment'. Media planning moves from vague personal preferences into the area of facts, clearly stated value judgments and specific performance criteria.

Media planning in practice

As in previous chapters, this part concentrates on those points respondents raised most frequently, which are illustrated by relevant quotations.

The importance of budgeting was covered in the last chapter, and some respondents suggested your objective in media planning must be

● *maximum benefit from the budget allowed* (ad)

The various points you should consider when planning to achieve this objective are illustrated by appropriate quotations below.

Planning

In planning a media schedule, the need for you to

● *follow a clear-cut structure* (ag)

- *give a proper rationale for each decision* (ag)

was surprisingly raised more often in reverse, by respondents commenting on practices to avoid. They cited the following as errors militating against effective use of media:

- *lack of clear thinking* (ad)

- *lack of preparation and planning* (ag)

- *lack of organised thought* (m-o)

Careful planning can, however, be taken too far in terms of following formal rules. Some respondents pointed this out when they advised that

- *you should not apply standard rules but think through each campaign afresh relating the creative approach to the advertising objectives* (m-o)

- *there are no rules. It is the belief that there are rules or pre-set formulas or steps to follow that inhibit the production of good creative advertising.* (ag)

Another practitioner was quite terse in blaming

- *over-theorisation* (ag)

At the opposite end of the scale was the warning that you

- *should not plan on over-simple criteria* (ag)

Mistakes

Despite the doubts cast by some practitioners on 'rules' to be followed, there was unanimity about certain mistakes to avoid.

One of these was the hardy perennial of timing. The importance of sufficient time to do a proper job has already been stressed, so few quotations are necessary within this chapter. These come from respondents who blamed

- *planning time scales too short* (ad)

- *inadequate time scale* (ag)

- *lack of time* (m-o)

Timing is but one of many mistakes raised, and a sad editorial observation is that, overall, more emphasis was placed on pitfalls to avoid than advice given on paths to be followed. These various warnings will be discussed in the chapter on approval of proposals which covers how you should evaluate proposals, to ensure your campaign proposals are the best possible to achieve your intended objective.

The rules

I do not agree with the practitioner quoted earlier who said 'There are no rules', but certainly accept the advice' '. . . to think through every campaign afresh . . .'. There *are* rules, but not universal laws which apply in every case. Different rules are applicable under different circumstances. The 'rules' practitioners suggested are outlined below and, as you will see, there is no unanimity about how best to plan your media schedule. The advice comes from current practitioners, and your task is to analyse your own business situation in the light of this advice, assess which 'rules' seem most applicable to your own particular marketing problem — and make up your own mind accordingly.

Matching media with market

Earlier chapters explained the importance of a clear understanding of your product/service and its potential market(s), and there was widespread agreement on the need to

- *match the media's audience with the consumer* (ad)
- *seek effective coverage of target audience* (ag)
- *match the media coverages/penetration to the marketing targets* (m-o)

These statements, while correct, are very broad and, to make this 'matching' effective, it is essential to examine the process in detail. One practitioner explained how he set about it:

- *we work very closely with our agents on the selection of media based on our advertising objectives and, obviously, on the target audience we wish to reach. There is a great deal of discussion arising from this on, say, the respective merits of outdoor advertising as opposed to press advertising and, of course, costs.* (ad)

This mention of respective merits and costs provides a basis for further analysis.

No medium is perfect

As Part 1 pointed out, there is no 'best' medium — some optimistic souls nevertheless hope for the impossible. One practitioner warned that

● *the advertiser should not expect any medium to achieve all objectives (if he has defined them) and fit all criteria, however unreasonable. This applies particularly to TV — 'Great results, but costs more than 2 X 2 inches' (m-o)*

Another media-owner suggested you should look at

● *coverage of candidate media of target market* (m-o)

and, more specifically

● *percentage of product users who are covered by the medium* (m-o)

The inference of these two quotations is that not *all* users are covered. One advertiser raised this directly when he explained

● *our agency is very specific in their approach and perhaps to this extent we are spoilt. We even go into what we call areas of weakness. How, for example, does one reach the target audience in an area where the circulation of the leading publication is low? This is not an easy question to answer, but we attempt to do so* (ad)

Creativity as well as coverage is important and, before looking at media selection in detail, it is essential to look at the controversial matter of creative influences on media planning.

The creative influence

The relative importance of creative content in influencing media selection is a topic on which there is no unanimity of view — in fact all shades of opinion are represented. At one end of the scale are those who state

● *a good creative idea should always override a theoretically correct media selection* (m-o)

● *marketing objectives and good creative ideas must always count more than media planning or buying. These functions, especially the buying, should be regarded as techinical areas which follow the previous decisions. In recent years the stress has tended to move further down the line, e.g. the supremacy of the media-buyer* (m-o)

At the other end of the scale, you have those practitioners who warned against

- *creative department in an agency may come up with an approach that requires a particular medium — which precludes using others which might be more appropriate to the advertiser's marketing plan* (ad)

- *creative decisions already made, e.g. television, radio, etc.* (ag)

- *creative requirements wagging media dog* (m-o)

A third viewpoint drew attention to another pitfall, rather than putting creative content at either end of an importance scale. This was

- *the danger of giving statistics too great a precedence over creative needs* (ag)

Many comments were in this middle ground, and can be grouped according to their particular aspect — some practitioners were interested in advertisement content, some in creative use, and others in media merits, creative liaison or in practical implications.

Creative content

Some practitioners concentrated on your advertising message, in asking

- *what image/personality are you trying to develop for the brand?* (ad)

- *be clear about how you should present your product* (ag)

- *the message — which medium can do the job?* (m-o)

Creative use

Others raised the matter of the way in which media were used, in urging

- *more creative use of media* (ad)

- *creative use of the media itself* (ag)

- *maximum use of creative capabilities of each medium in its way* (m-o)

These points call for examination of each medium's intrinsic qualities.

Media merits

Some respondents recommended that you should

- *look for the media approach which provides a dramatic lift for the creative idea* (ag)

Other points on the same theme were

- *is the editorial/audio-visual environment suitable?* (m-o) m-o)
- *the correct environment for the creative approach* (m-o)

Practical implications

The importance of the effectiveness with which your message is delivered has already been stressed, and one practitioner gave an excellent example of the practicality of this consideration

- *the creative brief is also important to media selection, not only in determining, say, the length of the television spots. If one is using colour in the press, repro quality is also an important consideration, which is sometimes not sufficiently thought about (I have known clients complain about the reproduction of their ads in certain magazines which the agency has recommended, unavailingly, chopping from the schedule for the reason!)* (ag)

Creative liaison

An equally practical approach was adopted by practitioners for whom effective use of media depended on creative/planning liaison. Their advice was that you should

- *agree creative strategy* (ad)
- *co-ordinate media inputs with creative inputs* (ad)

More often than not, this obvious need was alas expressed negatively. Viewed from this angle, however, the point comes across more realistically, as the following warning makes clear:

- *media planning carried out in isolation. This can lead to a plan which is arithmetically sound but fails to meet the real needs of the advertising campaign, e.g. it may be predicated on a time plan (TV) of 15 seconds when the proposition can only be expressed in terms of 30 seconds. It also encourages a quantitative instead of qualitative approach to media* (ad).

The qualitative viewpoint

Numerous respondents urged that you should

- *show imagination* (ad)
- *be adventurous* (ag)
- *try something different once in a while* (m-o)

Viewed in practical terms, however, the New Year Resolution 'I will be innovative' does not alas give much guidance on how to set about it. Some practitioners suggested as a start that you must

- *keep an open mind and assess all available data (from media and agency)* (ad)

- *keep an open mind across all media* (ag)

- *once product market is known, keep an open mind − permit each (reasonably) possible media full thought and throw out only when obviously 'out of court'* (m-o)

The question which this advice raises is − an open mind about *what?* Various respondents urged you consider the range of media, planning practice, and alternative courses of action.

The range of media

Various practitioners emphasised considering new media as well as those currently on your schedule. Their advice was that you should

- *be prepared to investigate and if appropriate recommend new media* (ad)

- *be willing and able to test new media* (ag)

The final quotation on this theme sets new media in context, and comes from the practitioner who felt that

- *a balance needs to be struck between the value of established media (partly due to their familiarity) and over or under valuing new media (due to lack of knowledge) − in other words, too many people have set ideas* (m-o)

Planning practice

Other respondents concentrated on the ways in which you plan media: their advice was for you to

- *be creative in media/planning/selection and innovation* (ad)

- *consistently work out new ways to use media* (ag)

- *be prepared to embrace new planning ideas* (m-o)

Alternative schedules

For some practitioners, the recommended route to effective use of media was to consider a range of alternatives, then select the best. Some were perhaps extreme in advising

- *the consideration of every possibility (not just the obvious)* (ad)

- *always consider all the alternatives* (ag)

- *examine all the options* (m-o)

If not examining *all* options, the minimum is to consider *some:* hence the advice to

- *study cost effectiveness of alternatives* (ad)

- *demand alternative concepts* (m-o)

and the statement that

- *the agency's campaign should have developed as a result (jointly with client) of having considered alternatives* (ag)

Campaign structure

In preparing alternatives, what should you aim for in terms of media scheduling? Some respondents went straight back to the starting point of your original campaign objective. Advice given drew attention to the need for you to

- *determine nature of impact needed — block-buster or drip-drip* (ad)

- *construct media strategy relative to the objective* (other)

Another respondent drew attention to the importance of

- *correct weight of advertising at the right time* (m-o)

Given the fact that there is more than one way to achieve your objective, and many practitioners suggest you consider alternatives, on what basis should you build your schedule? What should you aim for? As you would expect, cost and efficiency were well to the fore, and many practitioners recommended you should seek

- *cost-effectiveness and frequency* (ad)

- *effective coverage of target audience, frequency and cost efficiency* (ag)

- *cost-effectiveness and visibility* (ad)

Thus, as well as cost-effectiveness, it was suggested that you should also aim for coverage, frequency and visibility within chosen media. One practitioner linked all these variables when he suggested that you must

● *always remember that a media-planner's function is to reach the target audience as visibly, suitably and frequently as possible* (ag)

Concentration, domination and repetition

Any attempt to achieve all possible objectives with large sizes and high frequency over an extensive range of media could lead to your campaign becoming fragmented. Many respondents reverted to long-established planning principles when they recommended

● *concentration, domination, repetition (corny, but true)* (ad)

● *periodic concentrated bursts on TV or big spaces in press are more effective than spreading budget thinly across many media or over long time* (ad)

This advice was given more often in reverse, when the *action* you should take becomes more apparent. Advice given was to

● *never spread the bread too widely: have a short list. The main thing to be avoided is spreading the budget too thinly. A short media list is always more effective* (ag)

The ultimate warning against splitting your budget was surely given tongue-in-cheek, but I could not resist including it! This comes from the practitioner who advised

● *if there are two publications giving equally good coverage of the market and you only have enough money to go effectively into one, never split it between the two. Timid media planning is no good. Just toss a coin and if it doesn't come down first time in favour of the publication that gives the best lunch, keep tossing it until it does* (ag)

I wonder if the respondent making this comment had just enjoyed such a lunch?

Too much concentration

Some practitioners pointed out the possible dangers of carrying 'concentration, domination and repetition' too far, and advised

273

against

● *spending more than is necessary in a single medium* (m-o)

Others pointed out the need for

● *correct balance concentration* versus *continuity/multi-media* (ag)

Some recommended that

● *media work best in combination, so don't be afraid to add coverage and frequency together despite what the text books say* (ag)

and that you

● *should not reject multi-media schedules* (m-o)

Others warned against

● *the tendency to think 'one medium' only when a mix would bring better results* (m-o)

● *at media split stage, not properly considering roles which different media play in people's lives* (m-o)

The extreme view was

● *in deciding how best to talk to people the norm should be to use a range of media in as many cases as possible. That is to say, repetition employing different media channels is likely to be more efficient than repetition on the same channel, simply because this will enable the advertiser to put across his message from different angles and with different tones of voice. I do not consider that the counter-argument to this proposition, namely that advertisers need to dominate a medium, has much validity. Certainly to my knowledge there is no published evidence to support it. In contrast, the objective should be to dominate minds and our conviction is that this is best achieved by a mix of media.* (m-o)

Domination/repetition versus *multi-media*

You may support either of these standpoints — but it is worth asking if the two are entirely incompatable. Depending on the size of budget, it may be possible to achieve concentration, domination and repetition in more than one medium.

Respondents suggested various ways in which you can concentrate your campaign and not all related to the media list, so perhaps you can 'get the best of both worlds'. So, as one practitioner advised, you should

● *listen to a media proposal with an open mind* (ag)

Bargains and deals

Whichever scheduling approach you adopt, value for money should be high on your list of planning criteria. This is not without its dangers, however, and various respondents warned against

● *chasing bargains from media* (ad)

● *seeking lowest 'cost per 1000'* (ag)

● *buying a deal at the best possible rate, not necessarily in the most appropriate medium* (m-o)

The human element

Media planning principles, however statistical or scientific, are applied by *people*, whose personal needs you should take into account. Some practitioners recommended that you should

● *obtain the fullest possible brief – know the team that produced it. Become part of the team.* (m-o)

● *not fail to praise as well as criticise* (ag)

● *take great care that executives are working willingly and enthusiastically for you.* (other)

Other advice was for you to

● *take greater interest in the spending of media money* (m-o)

● *not be seen to treat advertising as an afterthought* (ag)

and finally that you must remember

● *planning is a creative function as well as a well-tried theoretical exercise based on 'known facts'* (m-o)

With your campaign proposals prepared your next step is to evaluate them as carefully as possible, to ensure to your best ability that they will achieve your chosen objective. Before doing so, however, we should examine the media decision process, which is discussed in the next chapter.

13

THE MEDIA
DECISION PROCESS

Respondents were asked who, in their opinion, were the key individuals in ensuring effective media decisions and to list and state their job functions in order of importance, e.g. advertisement manager, advertising manager, account executive, creative director, marketing director, media planner or buyer, media representative or other (to be specified).

I must admit, to my shame, my fear that results would indicate a strong sense of self-importance, with advertising managers putting advertising managers first, agency personnel voting for agency personnel, media-owners putting themselves at the head of the list, and so on. I am pleased to report that my fears were groundless.

The introduction made it clear that my researches were not intended to provide the basis for statistical tables and, in any event, response to this question was not capable of such analysis: hence this chapter will be brief.

What is clear, however, is that the media function alone was rarely cited as the key to effective media decisions: respondents recognised that overall marketing planning has direct media implications.

Many respondents declined to follow my 'please list in order' request, and preferred instead to comment. Some felt that it was not possible to generalise:

● *this is absolutely impossible to answer. Any answer must be a generalisation, and each situation in reality would have a different weighting and ranking of importances here. Companies vary enormously and so do the gamut of relationships and systems of buying between clients and agencies* (ad)

● *you cannot generalise — every client will be different* (ag)

● *this is difficult — job titles mean different functions throughout the industry* (m-o)

One quotation, by which I enjoyed being put very firmly in my place, was

- *people must avoid attempted generalisations of this kind at all costs* (m-o)

Other respondents attempted to shed light on the problem by drawing attention to different aspects of the decision process, and how the various individuals concerned were involved. Practitioners commented as follows:

- *depends on job functions:*
  1 *Brand manager – fix objectives*
  2 *Ad manager – media objectives*
  3 *Media planner/buyer* (ad)

- 1 *Account administrator or account executive – define the brief from client.*
  2 *Media manager – providing data: monitoring selection of media.*
  3 *Advertiser – be prepared to question assumptions about what media 'pull'.* (ag)

- 1 *Marketing director (client) – overall policy directions*
  2 *Media planner (agency) devising overall media plan within budget, creative restraints and market variables*
  3 *Advertising manager (client) – day-to-day control of media plan* (m-o)

Although giving different people different responsibilities, all these quotations nevertheless indicate a team approach, and other respondents made this very point, when commenting:

- *business decisions are seldom made today on a hierarchical basis – for better or worse, decisions are made by 'teams'. So there are no key individuals – or everyone is key* (ad)

- *varies enormously – everybody should be involved* (ag)

- *all are of equal importance and should be used as a think-tank* (m-o)

Others explained how this 'team' operated:

- *different decisions come about in different ways, and not always in the same order of importance, e.g.*
      between media planning   *– creative head*
                                   – account planner   *all*
                                   – media manager   *equal*
                                   – account director

within media planning   *— media manager*
                                    — account planner
                                    — account director
within media buying   *— media manager*
Media decisions and all advertising decisions within our agency are taken within an account group system — the most important influence in any one decision can be from anyone in the group. Different groups divide up their work in different ways (ag)

Two media-owners had apparently studied the team operation and the media-decision process in some detail, and observed what I can only call 'The *yes/no* syndrome'. The *yes* syndrome is illustrated by the comment that

●   *The subject is so vast, and so variable — within categories and over time — that it is impossible to set out golden rules which cover all cases, especially with the importance of personnel. In any selling operation, the salesman must locate the man who can say YES — there's only one of him, but several who can say NO, usually* (m-o)

The *no* version of the same syndrome is effectively explained by another media-owner who commented that

●   *some years ago we looked in detail at the media decision-making process and came to the conclusion that whilst many people had the ability to say NO almost nobody ever had the ability (or was allowed) to say YES. This means that often the plan which is accepted is the one nobody says NO to. According to some recent information this is how the Japanese Government was run pre-war, and as the only proposal before the Government that nobody said NO to was War, they bombed Pearl Harbour. Idiosyncratic decisions often prove more effective than democratic ones* (m-o)

Hence the advice that you

●   *should not take decision by committee* (ad)

Rather than finish on this depressing note, the chapter concludes with two quotations (the first of which puts me in my place again!) which perhaps gets as close as possible to resolving the media-decision problem:

●   *silly question this: it is the result of the agency/client team preparing, agreeing and implementing an effective market plan for the product* (ad)

●   *efficient media planning requires a clear statement of the advertising objectives, which can only be produced within the framework of a precise and well-reasoned marketing plan. A comprehensive media brief should relate to these objectives and include details of budget and precise target audience sought together with some mention of the creative approach envisaged. On this basis in most agencies efficient media planning involves the participation, at some stage, of marketing, creative and media people. All are essential to the process working with optimum efficiency* (ag)

A line must be drawn between 'consultation' *versus* 'committee' but whatever the process by which you reach media decisions the next step remains the same — ensuring that the proposed advertising campaign is a good one which, if executed, will achieve your chosen objective.

14

APPROVAL OF ADVERTISING PROPOSALS

Approval of proposals is far more complex a matter than it appears, and you will need time to review the proposals overall, to check the reasoning behind the media schedule, to study the creative proposals, and to ensure that all the component parts of the plan interlock. When your campaign is a large and complex one, this task may take some weeks, but even with a relatively simple campaign it is rarely possible to give an instant 'O.K.'. What is not always apparent is that approval of proposals has repercussions far beyond advertising alone. Before you can approve any campaign proposals, you must in fact check them from three entirely different standpoints — advertising, marketing, and general background, each of which is discussed below.

Advertising aspects

Checking campaign proposals is something that *everybody* thinks they can do — show an advertisement to a layman and he can always suggest improvements! Too many people look only at the pieces of paper in front of them and fail to 'think back' to see how these integrate with the marketing objective which underlies the whole campaign. Before looking at any media schedule or at creative proposals, you should ask three fundamental questions:

1   What is your specific advertising objective?   As was made clear earlier, it is no use hoping that an advertisement will 'increase sales'. Where are these increased sales to come from — increased purchases by existing users, conversion of new users, or brand-switch by the buyers of rival products? These and many other possible objectives were discussed in Chapter 10: your specific campaign objective affects media selection as well as creative content.

2   What fundamental appeal has been selected to appeal to your target group?   Of the many appeals you could make to potential buyers, which is the correct copy platform that will trigger them into action? Cheapness? Effectiveness? Value for money? Better performance? If you select the wrong benefit, out of the many which your product offers, clearly you will fail to achieve your objective. This question is a creative one and thus outside the scope of this book, but the answer has media implications: there is little point in constructing an effective media schedule, only to have it deliver the wrong message to your potential purchasers.

Good creative work is vital for effective advertising, but you must avoid the mistake of seeking creativity for its own sake. Your campaign must relate to your specific objective and, when approving any proposals, you should beware of advertisements which sell creative gimmicks rather than your products.

3   How effectively will this appeal be conveyed to the selected target group? This in turn breaks down into two separate checking operations — creative and media. Could the creative proposals be improved — does the illustration convey the selected appeal effectively, and is this backed up by equally persuasive copy? Will the advertisement convey your message to maximum advantage as regards printing or transmission? Equally important, and more the subject of this book, in checking your advertising proposals from the media stand-point — is the schedule as effective as possible in media selection and in the way the selected media are used — sizes, positions, frequency and dates, and duration of campaign? The chapter on preparation of proposals outlined the two-stage process — construction of various possible schedules, followed by evaluation to select the best, so there is no need to describe this process again. What *is* necessary is to set this checking operation in the context of the two preliminary questions — what is your specific objective, and what appeal did you select for your target group? Only after the answers to these two questions are clearly established is it worth checking the efficiency of the media schedule — a missile aimed with great accuracy at the wrong target does not win any battles, except by accident! Advice as to how best to set about this checking is given below in the second half of the chapter, which features practitioners' recommendations (and warnings) on this topic.

The marketing standpoint

Before planning any advertising proposals, your first step was investigations into firm and product, market and marketing policy, previous

advertising and competition. You must bear in mind that preparation of proposals took time and that things may have changed since the investigations, on which your proposals were based, took place. For example, the original plan might have been to market your product in a choice of colours, but subsequent production problems necessitate a reduction in the range. Clearly your creative proposals must be amended, for there is no point in stimulating prospective customers into demanding a colour which will not be available. Such action is likely to result in disappointed buyers and perhaps an increase in sales of competitors' products. This is only one example of changes that may have occured since your original investigations.

In addition to checking your proposals from the product/creative changes standpoint, you must also ensure that the media aspects still dovetail in with your company's marketing activities. Campaign timing is vital, for consumer advertising must not appear before your goods are in the shops, ready for people to buy. Your campaign plan must therefore allow for the delivery time needed to get goods to the shops once the order has been received, and further allowance must be made for the time needed by salesmen to get orders. To assist salesmen in their work, your consumer campaign may be supported by trade advertisements, and further help provided by heralding your salesman's call with a letter. The timing of each campaign stage must match the other marketing and promotional activities.

The timing of these many aspects of your overall marketing campaign does not depend on the advertising manager alone and, accordingly, you must check to ensure that your proposals interlock with salesforce movements and with other parts of the overall plan. Delivery dates might have changed since your first investigations — will the product in fact be in stock and on display when your advertising breaks, or has there been some unexpected hold-up? If for some good reason or other things are not proceeding according to the original plan, then clearly you must take action to remedy the breakdown in the plan or alternatively amend your proposals to take account of the changes.

Advertising proposals are designed to solve a particular problem, and the facts of this problem may have changed: you must therefore check these marketing aspects before executing your campaign proposals. Clearly, approval cannot be given overnight, for you may need to consult the sales manager, production manager, transport manager, and many others.

Background aspects

As well as checking campaign proposals from the advertising and marketing standpoints, you should also check background aspects. This is a creative/marketing matter for the most part, but it is nevertheless necessary to discuss it in some detail, and for you to remember the numerous legal and voluntary controls which affect advertising, and thus your own campaign proposals.

You should certainly obtain a copy of the *British Code of Advertising Practice*, which is under the general supervision of the Advertising Standards Authority and has the support of the major organisations representing advertisers, agencies and media-owners, whose representatives constitute the Code of Advertising Practice (CAP) Committee. The Code is published by the CAP Committee, whose address is Brook House, Torrington Place, London WC1.

As the Code itself points out, its rules are not the only ones to affect advertising. There are many provisions, both in the common law and in statutes, which can determine the form or the content of your advertisements. The code is not in competition with the law: its rules, and the machinery through which they are enforced, are designed to complement the legal controls.

An appendix to the Code covers legal restraints on advertising, and lists more than 70 statutes and statutory instruments with special relevance to advertising and related trade practices. This appendix also points out that 'In addition to statutory provisions there are certain common law rights which can also have a relevance to advertising and retail trade practices'. The appendix adds that 'The legal rules governing advertising both statutory and common law, can be extremely complicated and professional advice should be sought when in doubt'. I strongly endorse this recommendation! For those who seek preliminary reading prior to seeking such advice, Chapter 15 lists recommended books.

The *British Code of Advertising Practice* does not apply to broadcast commercials. Television and radio advertisements are subject to a separate, closely related code administered by the Independent Broadcasting Authority (IBA) of 70 Brompton Road, London SW3 1EY. The IBA works closely with the Independent Television Companies Association (ITCA) which is responsible for much pre-clearance work. ITCA is a member organisation of the CAP Committee, as is the Association of Independent Radio Contractors (AIRC).

The *IBA Code of Advertising Standards and Practice* is a comprehensive document of general rules, and three main appendices deal in more detail with advertising in relation to children, finance and medicines and treatments.

It has become almost universal practice to forward scripts of proposed TV advertisements for clearance by IBA in advance of production. The Authority's Advertising Control Division and a specialist advertising copy clearance group set up by the programme companies under the aegis of the ITCA work in close co-operation on the examination of more than 7000 new television advertisement scripts per year.

The scripts are considered in relation to the Code, with the help of independent consultants in special fields; and discussion of any seemingly doubtful points ensures that the television commercials in their final form are likely to comply with the Code.

At the end of these discussions and investigations, eight out of ten television advertisement scripts are found to meet the requirements of the Code as originally submitted. The other 20 per cent are returned for amendment to bring them into line with the accepted interpretation of the Code. In due course the specialist staff of the Authority and the programme companies join in closed-circuit viewing of finished commercials before they are accepted for broadcasting, to ensure that they conform with the agreed script and that there is nothing unacceptable about the tone and style of presentation, or other aspects of the film treatment of the subject. Between 2 and 3 per cent of finished commercials need revision before final acceptance.

Control of radio advertisements is equally thorough. All advertisements for Independent Local Radio must comply with the *IBA Code of Advertising Standards and Practice.* From the beginning of ILR in 1973 the Authority was determined to ensure that the high standards achieved in Independent Television advertising should be maintained in the new radio service. Its *Code of Advertising Standards and Practice*, originally drawn up for television, was amended to take into account the special requirements of radio. (Luxembourg, while not under the jurisdiction of the IBA, closely follows their rulings).

Special arrangements for copy clearance were also necessary, in view of the differences between the two media. Some 90 per cent of television advertising is for nationally produced and marketed products and much is planned weeks prior to transmission dates. This enables the central commercial clearing machinery to ensure that the advertising complies with the IBA Code and the rules and regulations established over the years. Much radio advertising, however, is local — in some cases the proportion is as high as 70 per cent — and the advertising of nationally marketed products often has a 'local flavour'. To enable the radio programme companies to operate efficiently, the Authority delegated responsibility to the local companies to clear the bulk of radio advertising in relation to the Code, and the Notes for Guidance issued by the Authority. Speedy clearance of radio commercials is achieved by programme company staff experienced in the field of copy control clearing local advertisements in consultation with IBA staff when necessary. There are however, certain categories of advertising which must be cleared centrally — medicinal, financial, alcohol, advertisements containing claims relating to guarantes and those needing the advice of specialist consultants. These are referred to the central copy clearance office, operated jointly by the ITCA and AIRC. In consultation with IBA staff and, when necessary, the Medical Advisory Panel, scripts are swiftly processed to enable advertisements to reach the air without delay.

Cinema commercials are checked by the Screen Advertising Association which is the trade association of cinema advertising contractors in the UK. Its role is partly one of a watchdog, acting to ensure that professional standards are met and maintained by the cinema advertising industry. It is responsible for vetting all commercials prior to screening in cinemas, in order to ensure that they do not make unfair advertising claims or offend public taste.

Pre-clearance of advertisements for these and other media implies a thorough knowledge of the Codes *prior to preparing your proposals*, quite apart from the need to check your proposals against them afterwards. The earlier chapter on research and investigations stressed, under 'Constraints', the need for you to be aware of the legal and voluntary controls which affect advertising, but these controls are not static: like your product or the marketing situation they too may have changed since your first investigations, so a rechecking, under the general heading of approval of proposals, is a necessary safety measure. Quite apart from being desirable in its own right, such double-checking can avoid the unfortunate consequences of failure to comply — 2 to 3 per cent of finished television commercials being unacceptable may seem a small proportion, but consider the position of those advertisers who find themselves deprived of advertising support through lack of any commercials to screen, quite apart from the considerable funds wasted in producing a useless commercial. Careful attention to this matter will ensure that you are not numbered among this unfortunate few.

Once you have approved your campaign proposals from these three standpoints — advertising, marketing and background — you can take immediate steps to put them into effect.

Campaign approval in practice

As customary, this part deals with those points raised most frequently by respondents, which are illustrated by relevant quotations.

The need for careful checking

It is surprising that some firms are apparently insufficiently careful in checking campaign proposals before giving their OK. One respondent commented on

- *unwillingness by advertisers (often because they are technically incapable) to spend time studying arguments for or against specific media relations and making decisions based on hunch or feelings, rather than facts* (ag)

In case this sounds like agency blaming client, the point was raised more often by advertising managers themselves. An earlier chapter quoted the client who remarked on people who 'ignore the agency's recommendations and rely on gut feelings' and another warned against

- *the temptation to follow hunches or inadequate information* (ad)

The most telling argument for careful checking came from the advertising manager who drew attention to the negative result lack of care is likely to produce. Quite apart from losing the benefits of careful evaluation, there are harmful side effects. He warned against

- *a non-numerate approach by advertisers to media proposals presented by media specialists, which results in the latter adopting a cynical 'why bother' attitude* (ad)

This leads straight back to the importance of the human element mentioned when discussing preparation of proposals, and which is equally important when it comes to their evaluation.

Criteria for approval (or rejection?)

The preparation of proposals chapter stressed the importance of careful planning, and you should look for this when evaluating the outcome of this earlier activity. You are advised to

- *ensure that proposals have been really thought out and researched/tested where possible* (ad)

The key question is, of course, by which criteria should you approve — or reject — campaign proposals? Most points raised were negative, warning against pitfalls to avoid rather than advising you on paths to follow.

Follow my leader

Many respondents warned against following competitors, when they cited the following mistakes:

- *being led by competitors* (ad)
- *duplicating competitors' media plans* (ag)
- *every other . . . is on . . ., so we must be: they can't all be wrong!!* (m-o)

These are only three of many similar quotations, from all sides of our business, so there was unanimity on this mistake to avoid.

Following precedent

Numerous practitioners pointed out the danger of a 'Play it again, Sam' approach, keeping on with the same old media schedule. Errors to avoid included:

- *lack of imagination leading to repeat performance of previous plans* (ad)
- *should not blindly continue using established media plan simply because it has always worked in the past* (m-o)

Media-owners gave an interesting range of reasons for this:

- *inertia from previous planning* (m-o)
- *resistance to change* (m-o)
- *the ease of following precedent — rather than exploring new media opportunities, or mixed media campaigns that achieve the required impact levels* (m-o)

Perhaps most telling was the final reason quoted

- *Fear. Agencies often recommend the 'tried' route. Weak agencies especially or indeed weak clients fear visible failure more than their urge to beat moderate success* (m-o)

Hence the positive advice that you

- *should question all historical solutions* (ag)
- *should not accept stereotyped media plans* (m-o)

Before breaking away from your previous advertising pattern, however, you must beware seeking change for its own sake, which is nearly always harmful. Change should be deliberate and positive, leading to a better route to your objective, arising from evaluation of results.

Personal bias

Another danger to which a large number of respondents drew attention, with varying degrees of vehemence, was that of bias — for or against certain media. At the mild end of the scale were those who commented on

● *emotional rather than qualified/quantified decisions* (ad)

● *subjective judgements on selected media* (ag)

● *subjective judgements about media by planners and/or account group or client* (m-o)

Moving along the scale of bias, other practitioners warned against

● *media planners/buyers may lose objectivity and have 'soft spots' and also prejudices* (ad)

● *client prejudices* (ag)

● *prejudice — either by planner or client* (m-o)

Although dealt with briefly here, this possibility was raised by a very large number of respondents — so be warned!

Personal preconceptions

This is really an extension of the previous warning, but merits separate attention because various respondents explained just how bias might arise — your own personal media habits might unconciously affect your views. One practitioner put this in research terms when he advised that you

● *should not indulge in the sample-of-one* (ag)

Others were more specific in commenting on

● *personal reading habits* (ad)

● *agency should not allow prejudice on the client side to invalidate specific recommendations, i.e. 'I only watch BBC2' or 'Only dirty old men read the News of the World'* (ag)

● *client's reactions to the agency recommendations should be as objective as the agency's. But . . . the old story of what the Chairman's wife reads has happened to me too!* (ag)

● *should not allow the 'Chairman's wife' syndrome to affect planning and buying decisions, i.e. my wife never watches that programme on television* (m-o)

Author's note: These were two different Chairmen: any readers whose wives happen to be married to other Chairmen might have a discreet word with them in private!

The closed mind

In some cases, bias or prejudice appears to be so strong as to be insurmountable. If not, why should it be necessary to warn against

● *agency rigidity in sticking to main media, especially TV* (ad)

● *preconceived ideas by client not allowing for fresh planning ideas* (ag)

● *closed doors to media approach through a prejudiced view of a particular medium, which might extend the knowledge of the 'media market'* (m-o)

Cost-effectiveness

One client gave the following advice:

● *determine choice of media by empirical cost/1000 data, then see if it 'looks right' using knowledge of the habits, preferences, political leanings, etc., of the target group* (ad)

A media-owner suggested that you should ask

● *is it cost-effective — bearing in mind suitable editorial/audio-visual environment?* (m-o)

While cost-effectiveness is without doubt important, more often than not it was raised as a negative matter, with warnings against

● *substituting head-counting for judgement* (ad)

● *too much concentration on 'cost per thousand' rather than an equal balance of reaching target audience as visibly, suitably and frequently as possible* (ag)

● *undue concentration on CPT* (m-o)

● *following computer data too slavishly — not applying creative flair to media buying* (ad)

These are only a few of many quotations on the same theme.

The overall campaign

A few brief quotations might help set the task of approving media proposals in its proper context as part of your overall advertising campaign, which in its turn must contribute to your company's marketing objective.

The tersest advice on the media planning aspects was the warning that you

● *should not be blinded by media science* (ad)

Equally terse on the creative side was the following advice:

● *don't be beguiled by 'showbiz' aspects of advertising* (m-o)

A few other brief quotations set these media and creative aspects into their overall context. These come from practitioners who advised that you

● *should not assume that media, marketing and creative are divorced* (ag)

● *should ensure that choice of media is compatible with budget available* (ad)

that you

● *should not regard the media plan as an esoteric exercise* (ag)

but remember that

● *it is creative exercise and not just merely arithmetic: it is part of the total plan and must be related to all aspects of it* (ad)

The dangers of delay

The hardy perennial of Time blooms again! While advertising proposals demand careful checking, numerous practitioners warned against taking too long before giving your approval. One advertising manager pointed out the need to

● *evaluate plan as soon as possible, and amend as necessary* (ad)

As you would expect, however, the matter of delay was raised more frequently by those on the receiving end of decisions (or lack of them) who cited the following mistakes as militating against effective use of media

● *late client approval* (ag)

● *decisions left too late* (m-o)

There were numerous other quotations on the same lines, but it is only fair to give the last word to the advertisers, one of whom warned against another mistake

- *being too ready to spend* (ad)

Others advised that you

- *should not be steam-rollered by the agency on choice of media* (ad)

and

- *should not proceed until the facts and figures are convincing* (ad)

Another agreed, however, that

- *indecisive management prevents good long-term media planning* (ad)

The next step

Once you are sure that the advertising proposals in their final form will make the maximum possible contribution to achieving your campaign objectives the next task is to put them into effect.

15

EXECUTION OF ADVERTISING PROPOSALS

Once you have approved your campaign proposals, the next step is to put them into effect: this is more difficult a task than would appear at first sight. Some campaigns may include hundreds or even thousands of individual advertisements in a whole range of media, and the execution of such a plan calls for meticulous attention to detail.

The task of converting a media schedule — which is nothing more than a plan on paper — into formal orders placed with media-owners is discussed below, but mention must also be made of the creative side, which also calls for considerable detail work — commissioning artwork and marking-up the copywriter's words for typesetting. Appropriate material must be sent to the selected publishers, and advertisement proofs checked. Other media call for similar work.

Accuracy is vital in its own right, but the need for accuracy is emphasised by the time limits imposed by the media-owners' 'copy dates' which allow little or no opportunity to correct errors. If a media-owner's copy date is 1 September, this means that material for the advertisement is needed by that date if it is to appear on time. Media-owners' copy dates are difficult if not impossible to postpone.

The task of executing creative proposals may, like the work of preparing them, be undertaken in a variety of ways. The advertising department may do the work itself, it may be handled by an agency, or it may be divided between the two. Some smaller advertisers may rely on the media-owner's service facilities for help in implementing the proposals as well as advice on preparing them.

Implementing your media schedule: planning versus buying

The task of converting your media plan into firm orders placed with media-owners is more than simply an administrative task, and here the difference between media planning and media buying becomes all important. For example, your approved media schedule might show a series of television commercials to be transmitted in various time segments on certain dates. When the plan was drawn up, however, it was impossible to know the viewing figures that would be achieved many months ahead. So a great deal of skill is called for in negotiating the best possible spots at times when your commercials will be seen by the largest number of people. Similar detailed negotiations will be necessary with the owners of other media.

The up-to-the-minute buying function contrasts sharply with the earlier planning stage, which produced only an outline plan to be implemented in the light of subsequent information. Media buying calls for a highly competitive cut and thrust approach which many find more exciting than the abstract planning stage which, in contrast, seems a rather boring mechanical exercise. Some practitioners argue that the personal qualities called for in planners and buyers are so very different that few individuals can do both jobs properly. The vital importance of the buying side is illustrated by the growth of the media independents, by the separation within many agency media departments of the planning and buying functions, and by the fact that advertisers have been known to move their accounts from one agency to another simply because of its better buying performance. In such cases, media considerations clearly have just as high a priority as the creative side of advertising.

Schedule improvement

Few advertising campaigns are ever executed exactly as originally planned, and you should keep your schedule under constant scrutiny and make whatever improvements are possible. A marginal improvement of, say, 10 per cent in coverage is equivalent to a 10 per cent increase in your appropriation, so you should keep your schedule under review and adjust it in the light of subsequent information.

The next chapter deals with evaluation of results as such, but it would be very wrong to consider this an exercise to be undertaken only *after* your campaign: you should monitor performance throughout and, with television advertising, schedule improvement is just as important as the original plan. Changes are less frequent with press or other media but the case for schedule improvement is just as valid. The publication of new readership data or the launch of a new publication, for example, should lead you to re-examine your current media plans.

Other changes

In addition to the normal on-going work of schedule improvement, it may be necessary for you to make other changes, to cater for the inevitable set-backs — and unexpected opportunities — which occur from time to time in normal business practice. These can be considered under two main headings — minor and major changes.

Minor changes   Although media planners always complain that the appropriation is never sufficient, you will find they rarely budget to spend *all* the money at their disposal. In preparing your own advertising campaign, you would be well advised to keep back part of your appropriation, in recognition of the fact that no amount of forward planning can predict every possible future event, and that some unforeseen eventuality is bound to occur. Rates may increase or attractive offers be made by media-owners, and a 'Contingency Reserve' allows for such events, and also for unexpected set-backs.

In a highly volatile market, it may be desirable to keep back a considerable contingency reserve, while in a stable marketing situation a nominal reserve may be quite sufficient. In fixing your contingency reserve, you are in fact attempting to predict the unpredictable: this is a most difficult decision, for if contingencies are under-estimated and call for more than the amount set aside then you must cancel some advertising to provide the necessary money, and your carefully planned schedule will be ruined. If on the other hand you over-estimate the amount, there is a temptation to fritter away this too large reserve at the end of the year, rather than leave it unspent and face criticism from your firm's financial staff when seeking budget increases in the future. The correct amount can perhaps be determined only through trial and error over the years. In some cases, however, the unexpected may occur on such a scale that your contingency reserve cannot possibly cope.

Major changes   You may bestow great care, time and effort on preparing your advertising campaign only to have your work wasted, through no fault of your own. One advertiser's national campaign was at proof stage when a new competitor unexpectedly changed the marketing situation to such an extent that the whole advertising campaign had to be scrapped. The thinking behind the proposals had been correct at the time they were put forward, but the unexpected changes meant that the campaign no longer applied to the new marketing problem. Similar situations have arisen following major economic changes or governmental action such as alterations to tax structure or credit and hire-purchase restrictions. The task then is to produce another campaign to deal effectively with the new situation, in the shortest possible time. In such circumstances, resilience and the ability to 'bounce back' when all your work is scrapped are just as important as being able to handle the new situation with a clear head and without getting flustered. Hopefully, however, there will be no major upheavals and contingency reserves will enable you to cope with such unexpected changes as do occur.

In other circumstances, however, major changes may take place that make no call on contingency reserves: to the contrary, you are forced to cut back your advertising. The outbreak of fire or an explosion or strike which stops your production line all illustrate this point, for in such unfortunate circumstances you might well call a halt to advertising aimed at stimulating a demand your company is incapable of satisfying. After an initial advertisement announcing the cause of the delay, you might cancel all advertising other than occasional reminder advertisements, until your production line is rolling again.

If all goes well, however, such problems will not arise and your task in implementing your media plan will then be mainly an administrative one.

Media administration

The agreed schedule shows an overall picture of your proposed campaign: for press media it will include name of publication, size of advertisement, whether this is run-of-paper or a special position, black and white or colour, together with the cost per advertisement, number of insertions, total cost and dates of appearance. For other media, similar details are given. A television or radio schedule, for example, shows region and contractor, length of commercial, the time segments in which the commercials are to be screened, cost per transmission, total cost and transmission dates. For other media, this information pattern is adapted to show the relevant details. The schedule, however, is nothing more than a plan on paper and must now be converted into firm bookings.

In preparing media proposals you frequently make advance contact with media-owners to check if certain sizes or positions will be available on certain dates, for it is a waste of time to prepare suggestions if these are not realisable. The agency which obtained its client's consent to book a certain schedule, for example, only to report later that few of the spaces suggested were in fact available would look more than foolish in the client's eyes. The same would be true of an advertising manager who obtained Board approval only to report later that the plan could not be put into practice. Accordingly, you may have sought the media-owner's co-operation by asking that certain spaces be reserved for a given length of time pending formal approval. In any event, no firm bookings have yet been made and you now have the considerable task of sending out confirming orders to all media included in the schedule.

You should not under-rate this routine task of converting a single document into a number of individual orders, for accuracy is vital. A media schedule may include insertions in a large number of individual media: on more complex schedules there may be dozens of different publications — national and local newspapers, consumer and trade magazines — as well as transmissions on television and radio, and bookings for cinema, posters, exhibitions or other media. All these must now be translated into individual orders for each of the media-owners concerned, who may possibly total a hundred or more. Each individual order will contain numerous items of information, and must be accurate as to name of medium, sizes and positions and dates of advertisements, as well as costs and discounts.

A simple typing mistake can cause a great deal of trouble or even jeopardise an entire campaign. If your media schedule features an advertisement to appear on, say, the 9th of the month and the order to the media-owner is incorrectly marked for the 19th, your company would rightly be more than annoyed at lack of advertising support when expected, at what would most certainly be a vital time. This simple typing error could endanger the success of the complete campaign. If the fault lay with the agency, it would find itself in an exceptionally difficult position. In such circumstances the agency might, for example, be too late to cancel the booking for the 19th but would be legally liable to pay the media-owner for it, whereas the client need not pay the agency since he had not authorised it.

Similarly, carelessness in checking could bring trouble of a different kind. If, for example, the true cost of £950 for an advertisement is, by mistake, shown on the client's schedule as £590, then £590 is the amount the client has authorised the agency to spend on his behalf — or which the Board has given the advertising manager authority to spend. Or again, orders have sometimes been sent to the wrong media-owners and advertisements included in the wrong media: this is not as unlikely as it sounds, as many publications have similar names and can easily be confused. Needless to say, no client would be under any obligation to pay his agency for such unauthorised insertions. Accuracy in paperwork and meticulous checking for possible errors is therefore essential.

Even when the individual orders have been typed, checked and posted, however, your administrative work is not at an end. It is necessary to retain and file reference copies, and also to check carefully that every order is acknowledged by the media-owner to whom it was sent. Mere posting of an order does not ensure appearance of your advertising, for there is always the possibility that the order may go astray. Such a mishap rarely occurs but when it does the consequent absence of advertising support could have very damaging effects. To facilitate the order-checking procedure, many order forms have a tear-off acknowledgement slip for media-owners to complete and return. Some media-owners use these slips, while others prefer to use their own 'Acknowledgement of Order' forms: but either way the responsibility for checking that orders have been received and acknowledged still rests with the advertiser or his agency.

Even after a schedule has been planned, booked and acknowledged, changes may become necessary, for the reasons discussed above. For example, should demand so exceed supply that further advertising would be an embarrassment, it may be desirable for you to cancel some insertions. Alternatively, it may be necessary to transfer a booking from one date to another. Often there are special forms for these purposes and, when cancellations are called for, then special 'Stop Orders' — frequently printed in red for immediate attention — might be used. Similarly, there may be 'Amendment Orders' to affect changes within a series of insertions. As before, stop or amendment orders must be meticulously checked, and care taken to see that they are duly acknowledged.

Before leaving this administrative aspect of media, it should be pointed out that a great deal of the drudgery is being taken over by the new technologies. The chapter on specialist services drew attention to the computer services available to advertiser, agency and media-owner which, in addition to their positive contribution to media planning, can also do much of the 'housekeeping' work, thus freeing staff for more constructive activities. A recent mailing by a media-owner illustrates this in practice (and also reinforces the point about accuracy — and possible errors!) The mailing reads

● *We shall be accepting bookings on the computer from* (date) *onwards. Currently we have to rely on a large number of verbal agreements and the normal practice is for agencies to send us confirmatory orders. Many of the orders arrive late, some after transmission and they contain inaccuracies which complicate our internal administrative system.*

  Therefore, as from (date) *onwards we will no longer require written confirmation of bookings placed with us. We will forward to you a printed acceptance as soon as your agreement to the negotiations is complete.*

It is understood that you may need to complete certain paperwork for your own administrative purposes, however, we will no longer require copies, although this does not prevent you from sending them if you so wish. (m-o)

The legal position

Orders sent to confirm bookings and requests for cancellation both raise the legal aspects of contracts with media-owners. This is a complex matter which is admirably dealt with in Diana Woolley's *Advertising Law Handbook*, published by Business Books on behalf of the Institute of Practitioners in Advertising, by whose permission the following paragraph is quoted:

● *. . . media-owners specify in rate cards the conditions on which they will sell space or time to agencies, and it is an advertising trade custom that such conditions will apply to all contracts for purchase of space or time, even if no reference is made to them in the media booking form, which may be an extremely simple document. So, when an agency books space or time, if it wishes to avoid any of the media-owner's conditions, it must expressly exclude them in its order and, unless its exclusion is accepted by the media-owners, the agency will be subject to all the conditions regardless.*

This is only one paragraph of an extremely valuable book, which you are urged to read in its entirety. Another strongly recommended book is Dr Richard Lawson's *Advertising Law*, published by Macdonald & Evans.

Those particularly concerned with keeping up-to-date with the latest legal position might wish to consult the new *Media Law and Practice* journal, the first issue of which was published by Frank Cass in May 1980.

Proposal execution in practice

As in previous chapters, this part features quotations from current practitioners.

Previous contacts with media

The descriptive part of this chapter explained how advance contact is often made with media-owners prior to any formal order, to check what space or time is available. The point made was that the agency which obtained its client's consent to book a certain schedule, only to report later that few of the spaces suggested were in fact available, would look more than foolish in the client's eyes. The dangers are illustrated by the following warnings:

- *the agency should not submit plans which may be unachievable after client agreement* (ag)

- *the agency should not make any assumptions regarding availability of media* (m-o)

Although the quotations refer to agencies, the point made is universal.

Implementation

Planning and buying, while separate functions, must be integrated. One practitioner warned against

- *division of planning and buying disciplines* (ag)

The planning function was covered in an earlier chapter, so quotations here are restricted to the buying aspect, where there was a range of advice. One advertiser urged his agency to

- *remember he is a* buyer *— get the best possible price consistent with the market plan* (ad)

Others cited, as rules to follow for effective use of media:

- *price and position negotiations* (ag)

- *efficient buying* (ag)

As you would expect, some media-owners had reservations. One warned against

- *over-aggressive negotiations* (m-o)

Changes

Earlier chapters warned against certain types of change: that you should not

- *change objectives in mid-stream* (ag)

- *make last-minute alterations unless absolutely necessary* (ad)

The next paragraph therefore looks at the changes that *are* essential.

Contingency reserves

The possibility of minor changes and the consequent need for contingency reserves was raised in both positive and negative forms. One advertiser urged that you should

● *tie up the complete plan – allow flexibility only within set parameters* (ad)

More frequently, however, the point was made in reverse. The briefest quote cited the following mistake to avoid:

● *inflexibility* (ag)

Another practitioner urged that you

● *should not fail to set aside a substantial tactical reserve to take advantage of short-term buying opportunities* (m-o)

Another useful suggestion, to complement this, was that you should have

● *stand-by copy for short-term buying* (ag)

The possible absence of any reserve is illustrated by the following warning:

● *should not raid advertising budgets for last-minute cash contributions, e.g. year end, union deals, etc.* (m-o)

Schedule improvement

The fact that approval of campaign proposals is not an 'over and done with' operation is illustrated by respondents who pointed out that

● *what is planned/bought must be subject to objective on-going evaluation to ensure that what happens in the market place squares with that intention* (ad)

● *every media plan can and should be improved in the light of new information* (m-o)

Administrative and production problems

Some very down-to-earth advice was that you should

● *understand the mechanics involved – this can save costly changes later* (ad)

300

The 'mechanics' can — and do — overlap with earlier matters. The administrative and production work involved in using some media is heavier than with others, and some media-owners (naturally, those directly concerned) felt that this unfairly influenced media selection. This links with other chapters, but it seems more logical to cover it here, since it largely concerns actual execution. The following comments should therefore be viewed in this light, as reflecting a practical problem (rather than as criticism of agencies). One media-owner pointed out that

● *agency staff find TV commercial production easier and less time-consuming than dealing with the regional press* (m-o)

Another explained that

● *subjectively, I believe that agencies are prone to dismiss the regional press as being too expensive, but I know that judgement is reinforced by the high production and administrative costs which have to be borne in addition to pure space costs thus undermining agency profitability* (m-o)

Perhaps the most practical suggestion came from the media-owner who observed:

● *agencies tend not to favour inclusion of provincial press in campaign planning because of the degree of difficulty in space reservation and copy provision to a large number of publishers — clients' campaigns can therefore suffer because the agent has opted for the 'one order, one copy instruction, one account' campaign method. Organisations like ENAB and WNAB should be used more by the agents as these bodies can ease the 'booking and copy' burden* (m-o)

This matter is further proof of my premise that you cannot separate media planning principles from the people applying them or the organisations in which they work.

A final quotation

The last comment in this chapter comes from the practitioner who urged that there should be

● *a clear, full brief and a continuing dialogue between strategy generation, design, media planning and the proposed media* (ad)

With your campaign now running, your next task is to evaluate its results, to see what lessons you can learn for the future.

16

EVALUATION OF RESULTS

Skill in evaluating results is an important talent for you to develop if you are to use advertising media effectively. This task should be approached from three standpoints — checking backwards, other influences and looking forward.

Checking backwards

Evaluation of results involves, first, the relatively straightforward task of ensuring that you got value for money. For every insertion booked, you should carefully check the voucher copy sent by the publisher (or obtain a voucher if the media-owner has overlooked sending one). Has your advertisement appeared as booked: in the selected position on the appropriate page on the correct date? Where no special position was booked, did the media-owner place your advertisement wisely, or does its position compare unfavourably with those of competitors? What about adjacent editorial matter? An advertiser of tinned food would rightly be annoyed if his advertisement was foolishly placed on a page featuring an article on food poisoning. If your advertisement featured a coupon, does this back upon another advertiser's coupon on the reverse side of the page? Should this occur, neither advertiser can obtain maximum results. What is the standard of printing? Has the illustration been reproduced to maximum effect? With full-colour advertisements, is your product shown with true colour values? For food or cosmetics, even a slight variation in colour can detract considerably from your advertisement's effectiveness. Has the publisher, in fact, inserted the correct advertisement? It is not unknown for a media-owner to repeat a previous advertisement instead of replacing it with a new one as instructed. There may be few occasions in the year when you need to take up any of these matters with media-owners but such mistakes do occur and you must, therefore, examine every voucher copy and carry out similar checks with other media. One respondent quoted earlier gave as advice:

● *press the media-owner for rebate, etc., whenever there is a shortfall on colour reproduction, print run, viewing figures etc.* (ad)

Allow for other influences

When keeping records, you should make a note of those events — other than advertising — which influence sales and, unless allowed for, would give you a mistaken idea of your campaign effectiveness. A heatwave, for example, will push up sales of cold drinks and ice-cream and, whilst advertising can help channel demand towards your product, it would clearly be incorrect when evaluating results to conclude that advertising *caused* increased sales.

A whole host of events can affect your results, including special incentives to sales staff, entertainment and sporting events, strikes, fuel crises and so on. A record of such influences is vital in evaluating past performance and also provides a useful guide for future planning, indicating desirable or avoiding action you should take when preparing next year's campaign. Annual events such as the Cup Final will push up sales of some products at the same time as they depress others and, if your market is affected in this way, you should clearly make allowances in your media scheduling.

Looking forward

Ensuring that you got value for money is important, but a far more significant aspect of evaluating results concerns checking effectiveness. Here your aim is different: your concern is not what happened in the past, but improvements for the future.

Did you achieve your objective? This question takes you straight back to the second basic requirement for effective use of advertising media. The first task was investigations, gathering information on which to base your advertising planning. The second task was deciding your specific objective and the point was made that planning should be a 'closed loop' with evaluation of results of this year's campaign providing additional information on which to base next year's planning.

The direct link between the evaluation of results and the determination of specific objectives is best illustrated by reference to the DAGMAR concept. These initials stand for 'Defining Advertising Goals for Measured Advertising Results', an approach that was developed by R. Colley. To put this another way, unless you know where you are going, how can you know whether or not you have got there? At its most basic, the Dagmar approach points out the vital need for a specific objective, and then asks if you achieved it. If not, why not? Failure to achieve your objective could arise from one of two reasons — either your objective was wrong (perhaps too ambitious) or alternatively your advertising campaign was at fault. This is an over simplification, as there are other alternatives — circumstances may have changed during the year, or perhaps your method of measuring is not as accurate as it should be. But, whatever the reason — wrong objective, wrong campaign, wrong evaluation or change of circumstances — the DAGMAR approach leads to a re-examination of the advertising plan and its inter-relationship with your total marketing operation. If you did not achieve your objective, it is not necessarily the advertising that is to blame — perhaps the marketing was at fault. But even if your objective was achieved, this is no cause for complacency — could your advertising have done better? Hence the need to analyse advertising results meticulously. As a first step, you must establish whether you are considering direct response or alternatively evaluting results indirectly by some form of survey of retailers or consumers.

Direct response

The positive improvements you can achieve by evaluating results are best illustrated by the example of those fortunate enough to be able to relate advertising directly to its results. Such is the case with many retailers, organisations with showrooms, or advertisers selling direct or whose advertisements feature reader request coupons. Direct response can also arise through various reply service facilities provided by media-owners.

When you invite such a direct response, you can 'key' each advertisement so that respondents indicate in which publication and on what date they saw your advertisement. Inclusion of a 'key number' such as 'SE7' would indicate that the coupon came from an advertisement in the *Sunday Express* on the 7th. The principle of keying advertisements is simple, but you must take care that your system is foolproof. Does 'DM13' indicate *Daily Mirror* or *Daily Mail*, and does '13' imply the date of insertion or the thirteenth appearance in that publication? You must ensure that your system tells you, without fail, the source of every coupon. Even if your advertisement includes no coupon, it can still be keyed by asking readers to write to a certain department or to address their reply to a certain individual, to Desk Number X or Room Y.

Increasing postal costs have resulted in people thinking more carefully before writing for leaflets, so many firms now take advantage of the FREEPOST system whereby they rather than prospective purchasers pay the postage. It also provides a further incentive in that some potential purchasers might be willing to pay postage but simply do not have a stamp handy: FREEPOST can help overcome this inertia on the part of potential buyers. Increased postal costs have also resulted in an increase in showroom enquiries rather than coupon response, and many advertisers therefore take care to include these enquiries since evaluation of postal response alone clearly gives a very incomplete picture.

The labour in checking keyed responses must not be under-estimated, and you should ensure you have the necessary staff to undertake this vital chore. Much valuable information is thrown into the wastepaper basket for lack of staff to make the necessary evaluation — yet the improvements which could be achieved would more than pay for the labour costs involved, and even make a major contribution to profits! Should your advertising feature coupons regularly, there may be thousands or even millions to handle annually, and this necessitates establishing a carefully planned sorting and checking operation. Imagine yourself responsible for an advertising campaign which includes perhaps a hundred or more advertisements every month, all featuring coupons and appearing in numerous different publications — national and local newspapers, and magazines of various types. What could you learn from a careful study of coupon returns (or some other form of direct response) and what improvements could you recommend for the future?

Numerical response   The number of coupons brought in by one medium can be compared with the response produced by others. If comparing press media, for example, publications with poor returns could then be eliminated from the schedule and the money spent to better advantage elsewhere.

Area of coverage   Where do the coupons come from? One medium may bring a good response when measured in numbers of coupons, but many may perhaps come from outside your sales area. For a local advertiser, or one with a restricted sales or service area, this factor is of major importance. Area response can be very important even for an advertiser with national distribution, and if one region responded more than others, you might decide to follow up this local interest by booking additional insertions in local papers. Alternatively, returns might be extremely poor in one area and this would lead you to investigate the cause of the low response. You might then discover your company faced severe competition from a small local company and that the competitive strategy in the area needed reconsideration. Another reason for weak response in a particular area is the fact that even so-called 'national' media vary in their intensity of coverage in different parts of the country: should this be the case, low penetration in a particular area might call for reinforcement advertising support in local media.

Type of response   Careful analysis of the type of person returning your coupons can also yield valuable information. Are the coupons mostly completed by men or by women? Where coupons appear in technical publications, one industry might show more interest than others when judged by coupon response and therefore be ripe for exploitation by a special sales drive.

Cost per reply   Numbers of coupons, completed by respondents of the right type and within your sales area, can be evaluated in terms of value for money, and cost per reply calculated. High numbers are insufficient in themselves: coupons must be returned by prospective customers and at an economic rate. Publications with uneconomic returns can then be eliminated. The chapter on budgeting mentioned the 'Marginal Method' of fixing the budget, which is based on such an immediate evaluation of results.

Conversions   Where customer response provides leads for sales force activity, you can calculate the number of enquiries which result in actual sales. One medium might have a low response rate, but if every enquiry leads to a sale it will clearly merit retention on your schedule. Conversely, if the conversion rate of another is low, you would no doubt want to cancel further insertions.

The advertisement unit: size, position and colour   Large advertisements cost more than small ones and special positions or colour also increase costs. Comparison of response rates can indicate whether the added expense was worthwhile.

Frequency   High frequency costs more than less regular appearances: evaluation of results can indicate if the additional cost was worthwhile. Does the profile of heavy and light users of your product match in with heavy or light exposure to your advertising? If not, why not?

Timing   Timing can be a matter of seasons, weeks, or days. By analysing response records you can discover the most suitable day of the week for your advertisements, or when the buying season starts.

Non-media aspects   Some response measures mentioned above clearly have *marketing* as well as media implications: they may indicate a new potential market or likely sales area, or touch on other marketing activities. Other response aspects also have implications for marketing, or for creativity.

Product offer   You may decide to vary the basic product offer featured in your advertising, and so judge the relative merits of different prices, packs or product versions.

Creative theme   The chapter on approval of proposals asked 'What fundamental appeal has been selected, to appeal to your target group?'. The results of two alternative creative themes can be contrasted and keying used to show which is the more effective.

Creative expression   The approval of proposals chapter also asked 'How effectively will this appeal be conveyed to the selected target group?'. A given creative theme can be expressed in a variety of ways whilst the fundamental appeal remains unchanged — the theme can be conveyed by different headlines, illustrations, copy and typefaces. Analysis of which version pulled best has clear implications for creative staff.

Cross comparisons   The various comparisons listed above cannot be considered in isolation, as they frequently overlap. For example, people in a particular area may be attracted by one offer rather than another *and* respond more on a particular day of the week (perhaps affected by a major employer's pay-day). These regional and other differences will then lead to appropriately differing advertising patterns.

Other types of response

The direct response achieved by coupon advertising is an extreme case, and if you have such a clear indicator to the success of your campaign you are indeed fortunate. Even where no such direct response exists, however, you must nevertheless attempt to evaluate results and to follow up leads which could improve your future advertising: this might be by sales audits or consumer surveys.

Sales audits   Many retail advertisers have direct results not in coupon form, but in sales. Manufacturers with showrooms take into account over-the-counter enquiries as well as coupon response when assessing overall results.

Other manufacturers without their own outlets attempt to evaluate results by analysing their salesmen's order books (another example of desk research) to check seasonal or geographical variations in relation to advertising effort. 'Sales in' to retailers are not always followed by 'sales out' however, so factory sales figures are an insufficient measure of success, since goods despatched from your factory might sit on retailers' shelves for months, with no sales resulting. Some companies therefore measure results by retail audits, subscribing to one of the research services which provide this data on a commercial basis. In essence, the idea is a simple one: if the stock held in a shop at the start of a month is known and deliveries made during the month are taken into account, the difference between this figure and the total remaining at the end of the month is an accurate indication of the quantity sold over the counter. If your advertising objective was to extend your present distribution or to stimulate your current outlets, a retail audit will give you the answer.

Consumer surveys   Rather than evaluate results indirectly via retail audits, you may wish to measure customer action, researching purchases rather than sales. A retail audit may reveal an increase of say 20 per cent in comparison with the last period, but it does not tell you *how* this increase was achieved. If your sales increased, you need to know in which of three ways this came about — increased purchases by existing users, conversion of new users, or buyers of rival products switching brands. If the specific purpose of your advertising campaign was to persuade existing users to use more, consumer research can give you valuable information which no form of retail audit can ever reveal. Various research organisations maintain representative panels of consumers, which can make this information available to you.

In some cases, rather than measure actions such as sales or purchases, you may wish to measure changes in, for example, consumer awareness of your product in relation to its competitors. If your specific campaign purpose is to change consumers' attitudes, you may wish to commission research to ascertain their viewpoints before and after the campaign. Even here, however, a specific purpose is essential since 'attitude' is a very broad term. What precisely do you wish to change — your brand image, the degree to which people believe your product claims, their liking for your firm, or the likelihood of them buying your product?

Test marketing   Evaluation of results may even extend to test campaigns. A national launch, however carefully planned, is an expensive and risky undertaking: marketing is increasingly competitive and great amounts of capital are involved. Many manufacturers therefore attempt to reproduce in advance, on a smaller scale, the conditions they will encounter on a national basis. By evaluating the results of the test campaign, the manufacturer can spot any weaknesses in his marketing plan, and adjust it prior to the national launch.

When planning a test campaign, your aim must be to reproduce the entire national campaign in miniature, in both selling and advertising. The advertising schedule must recreate in the local campaign the same proportionate weight of advertising to be mounted nationally. If, for example, the national TV campaign is to be launched with one 30-second peak time and two off-peak commercials each week, then this is the amount of advertising to be booked in the TV area selected for the launch. Similarly, if half-page advertisements are to appear each week in the national press, then this weight of advertising must be booked in the local press. This general principle of using the equivalent weight of advertising applies to all media, for there is no point in forcing the campaign to be a success by mounting a level of advertising which your company cannot afford on a national basis.

In planning the schedule for your test campaign, account must be taken of the comparative coverage of the national press that would be used for the main campaign and of the local press to be used in the test campaign, and allowance made for any qualitative differences, e.g. class coverage, male/female bias, printing quality, editorial environment, etc., between them, before a realistic assessment of the 'real' national equivalent of a test campaign can be made.

One prime purpose of test marketing is to reveal any possible weaknesses, and to adjust your advertising plan accordingly. In other cases, two parallel test campaigns may be run, to evaluate the effect of different product formalae or prices, to select that most acceptable to the market. Different weights of advertising expenditure, different media schedules (or alternative creative themes) can be tested in the same way.

Future action

The purpose of evaluation is *action* and this can be of two different types.

1   Follow up leads   Evaluation of results can lead to your taking action, e.g. to exploit a target group not included in your original market estimate but which, by its response, has proved its interest in your product. Evaluation of results thus leads to changes in marketing activity, rather than advertising alone. Alternatively, the target market may remain unchanged but, by evaluation of results, you improve the productivity of your advertising campaign by getting better results for the same money.

2   *Elimination of weaknesses*   The reverse side of the 'better results for the same money' coin is 'same results for less money'. Elimination of weaknesses permits you to use the 'saved' money to buy what you could not afford before — and always remember that no budget is ever sufficient to do *everything* you wanted.

In defence of unproductive advertisements

An advertisement which does not bring results is not *always* a waste of money. Depending on your viewpoint, it can also be an investment. The 'investment' comes from the fact that you found out — the hard way — that it did not work, and this prevents further waste in future. Alas, a great deal of advertising money is wasted by those who make *no* attempt to evaluate results in the mistaken belief that it is impossible to do so. In such cases, their campaigns continue repeating unproductive advertisements year after year in unproductive media: this is a very different matter to investing money to prevent future waste.

Closing the loop

Schedule improvement is as important as the original plan, and monitoring performance during your campaign is equally important as post-campaign assessment. Advertising planning must be a closed loop: this chapter completes the circle since what you learn from evaluation of results provides the basis for your future planning.

Evaluation of results in practice

As usual, this part of the chapter features comments made by practitioners.

Measurement against objectives

The fact that it is impossible to evaluate results unless you know just what you plan to achieve was endorsed by various respondents who recommended that you should

- *be clear about the type of response you require* (ad)
- *set targets and monitor results* (ad)

The base to build on

Evaluation of results concerns current analysis of previous results, just as much as checking in due course the results of the campaign you are now planning. Respondents pointed out the need for you to

- *align creative input with company's marketing objectives and defined target audience(s) and past advertising history* (ad)
- *follow guidelines provided by previous advertising in this market* (ag)

The usual matter of the time needed to do a proper job arose again and, as usual, with a negative comment warning against

- *insufficient forward planning and time for preparation, including analysing previous results and making sure that all relevant information is available* (ad)

On-going evaluation

This overlaps earlier chapters but is nevertheless included since it is impossible to separate evaluation of results from normal working relationships. Advice given was for you to

- *constantly monitor media performance* (ad)
- *check the media plan and buying performance against plan, but leave details to the agency* (ad)
- *review the agency's buying performance at least once a month formally* (ad)

Record keeping

Evaluation of results naturally implies having results to analyse — hence the recommendation that you should

- *maintain accurate and detailed response records for comparison and analysis* (ad)

In order that you can keep the necessary response records, excellent advice is that

● *before embarking on campaign, method of post evaluation should be decided* (ad)

What to evaluate?

Specific suggestions were that you should

● *attempt to evaluate the effectiveness of the different media in sales terms* (m-o)

● *measure sales responses at different advertising investments and use results* (ad)

● *response data is of overall importance for many campaigns: cost-per-sale for mail order, cost-per-reply for couponed advertisements, etc. Research findings are the next best thing to response data* (ad)

The final quotation makes a suggestion which most people in the industry would like to see implemented:

● *agents, clients and media-owners should attempt to work together to introduce an acceptable basis for monitoring/ researching advertising response* (m-o)

Earlier chapters outlined some of the specialist services and information sources available to help you evaluate results but, at the time of writing, there is no monitoring basis that is 'acceptable' in the same way as the Joint Industry Committees which collect data for the industry at large.

The next step

Return to Chapter 8 — you now have new information on which to base your future planning.

POSTSCRIPT:

media planning practice—past, present and future

The form circulated invited comments on matters other than those specifically raised and made clear that space should not be a restriction — should respondents wish to attach additional explanatory sheets, these would be most welcome.

One agency media manager took both invitations literally, and commented on a number of areas not touched on by my question-naire — major shifts in the media industry over past decades (and those likely to occur) which contribute to the effective use of media.

This book, therefore, ends with an outline of how media planning practice has changed over the years, and with a prediction for the future.

- *I see the post-war period as the 'El Vino' era of the press buyer, where the media department's role was to obtain required space in times of post-war paper restrictions. Gin and tonics helped to smooth relationships (the buyer paying) and deliver space. Later, as paper controls eased so the seller bought the drinks and the alcoholic culture of the media industry continued (it all started, I'm told, in the 1930s).*

  In the late 1950s press readership research came in, and through this period a new kind of figure — the media planner — came into existence. By the mid-1950s television arrived and though at first press buyers were turned into TV buyers over-night, the TV-buying function soon developed its own characteristics and was hived off to a separate and specialist buying department — the advent of the TV buyer and the establishment of the TV-buying ground rules.

313

By the middle 1960s there was computerisation, reading frequency and a wildly optimistic belief that the right research could solve all the classic media planning problems. In this period media departments flourished, and the majority of to-day's main media directors came from this golden era.

The balloon burst in the 1970s with the energy crisis, three-day weeks and a general swing back to buying as a media department focus. There was a disillusionment with media research and the media department's stock as a contributor to the agency's business fell. With rampant staff cuts every-where, it was the TV buyer who emerged as king of this Brass Balls Buying era — in the face of ever more complex TV rate cards and selling policies.

Young TV-buying Turks lived on expenses and drove home in agency BMWs, or so rumour had it (popular jibe: our TV buyer had to have a BMW because he couldn't spell Porsche).

Perhaps media departments did lose respect from their agency colleagues, or at least somehow became a little divorced because buying shops, run by ex-agency professional media buyers, came into existence primarily to provide a quality media service for some large do-it-yourself clients and the many more small agencies who could not afford to pay top rates for skilled media buyers. These independents flourished and there are now around 36 of them.

By the end of the 1970s the media industry began to feel that too much emphasis was being placed on buying at the expense of planning the media investment, and a sort of balance seems to be emerging between the over-intellectualist and theoretical media planning of the 1960s and the unremitting crudeness of 1970s' buying.

In the 1980s I see a new media realism, where the relative importance of media buying and planning is equalised. I consider that the key media figure of the 1970s was the media buyer-planner — an individual of mixed skills who planned and then bought mixed media on all his accounts (including TV), though few agency media departments adopted the system. My experience of operating a buyer-planner system is that media individuals rarely excel at both skills, although allowing TV buyers to plan media does generate more job satisfaction for the TV buyer (hence lower turn-over of talented buyers for the agency).

In the 1980s I see the separatism of TV buying and media planning breaking down at last — either with buyer/planner figures, or with TV buyers forming teams with media planners and sharing the media task.

In the 1980s the focus will still remain on good aggressive and creative media buying but with a front-end planned approach. The planner and buyer will share all aspects of the planning and buying task, with the former responsible for developing strategies, rationalising, documenting and appraising, and the latter for culling the best possible buying deal, so that the advertiser's money goes further, in the most effective media.
The era of new media realism is dawning (ag)

The final realistic advice for the future, and the concluding quotation of the book, was also raised under the heading of 'other matters', and comes from the agency man who advocated

● *more time spent on making what we know work — rather than continually chasing ever more abstruse and complicated formulae for confusing us all.* (ag)

Index

322